EDGE OF YOUR SEAT

Women in Peril: Lee Remick, menaced in *Experiment in Terror*.

EDGE
OF YOUR
SEAT

THE 100 GREATEST
MOVIE THRILLERS

DOUGLAS BRODE

CITADEL PRESS
Kensington Publishing Corp.
www.kensingtonbooks.com

CITADEL PRESS BOOKS are published by

Kensington Publishing Corp.
850 Third Avenue
New York, NY 10022

All Kensington titles, imprints, and distributed lines
are available at special quantity discounts for bulk
purchases for sales promotions, premiums, fund-raising,
educational, or institutional use. Special book excerpts
or customized printings can also be created to fit
specific needs. For details, write or phone the office
of the Kensington special sales manager: Kensington
Publishing Corp., 850 Third Avenue, New York, NY
10022, attn: Special Sales Department;
phone 1-800-221-2647.

First printing: October 2003

10 9 8 7 6 5 4 3 2 1

Printed in the United States of America

Library of Congress Control Number: 2003106279

ISBN 0-8065-2382-4

To my son,
Shaun Lichenstein Brode,
who never ceases to thrill me!

CONTENTS

ACKNOWLEDGMENTS

Thanks most of all to Harold "Rob" Thousand III, whose willingness to endlessly research background materials made the completion of this book possible. Also, thanks to the various movie companies that were so generous in supplying stills and permissions, as well as Jerry Ohlinger's Movie Material Store, Cinema Collectors, and Larry Edmond's Bookstore.

A NOTE ON SELECTION

Any attempt to select the one hundred greatest examples of any genre will leave even the most sympathetic reader hurrying to ask, "Why did you ever include *that*?" or, just as likely, "How could you *not* have included *this*?" Every fan of the thriller will have his or her own favorite, some of which will coincide with my own list, some that will not. Please take into account that I was well aware of what I consider "the big hitch"—the entire top fifty films in my selection could easily have been given over to Hitchcock classics. This would have been to the detriment of so many fine thrillers by other people that I finally had to limit myself to only a few by the master of suspense. Also, I wanted to include the remarkably wide world of the suspense thriller, which breaks down into many sub-genres: the psychological thriller, sci-fi thriller, erotic thriller, mystery thriller, political thriller, comedic thriller, caper thriller, romantic thriller, noir thriller, spy thriller, social-message thriller, action thriller, gothic thriller, ghost-story thriller, historical thriller, and the realistic thriller, to name just some of them. Finally, the book is being completed at the very end of 2002, and that was always in my mind. I have rated the films in terms of their abilities to thrill us still. If asked to pick the most significant film ever made, I would certainly consider naming *The Cabinet of Dr. Caligari* (1919). However, that does not happen to be the basis for this listing. Rather, it is the ability of the films to still terrify us today, whether they were made this year or the better part of a century ago.

Rod Lurie directs a tense scene from *The Contender*.

FOREWORD

About a decade ago, when I was the film critic for *Los Angeles Magazine*, Doug Brode was my mentor. It wasn't that he taught me *about* film; my education was more about how to look at movies, how to evaluate, criticize, and how to *admire*. We'd sit in bars and restaurants and talk movies—endlessly. I was stunned by his knowledge of film and his love of the art. He would talk with passion and relevance about both the masterpieces (I seem to recall one all-nighter about Kenneth Branagh's *Henry V*) and the ones he hated (note to filmmakers: this is not a place you want to be). I loved those conversations. Doug's love of the art and his sincerity of respect were probably what most encouraged me to become a filmmaker myself.

So let me tell you this, then. I envy two groups of people immensely: Doug's students and his readers. In fact, they are basically interchangeable.

When I received the galleys of this book, I was swept right back to learning from Doug, to being entertained by him. His ability to deconstruct a film is uncanny. It is impossible to discuss any movie with him and then not want to see it again. So, be prepared to see all the films mentioned in this book . . . for a second time if necessary.

All the respect that I have for Doug doesn't mean I agree with all of his choices. For example, *Psycho* belongs in the number one position if we assume its impact at the time of release. It is hard to imagine that a film so famous, so imitated, and with gimmicks so out of date (such as the killing off of the then-very-famous Janet Leigh in the first half of the film), that it seems impossible it would shock anybody today. I would instead put another Hitchcock film, the stylishly elegant and creepy *Notorious*, at the head of the class (and if not that film, then another Brode-Hitchcock entry, *Strangers on a Train*).

Let's see. Where else might we differ? In the De Palma world, I'd take *Blow Out* over *Carrie*, *Fail-Safe* over *Dr. Strangelove* (Kubrick made the better film but not the better thriller), and where, by the way, is *Chinatown* and *Dog Day Afternoon*? Of course, if I actually discussed those differences of opinion with Doug, he would have me over to his side in an hour, maybe two.

Here, however, are my ten favorite thrillers—all considered within the context of an audience seeing them today:

1. *Notorious*
2. *Strangers on a Train*
3. *Jaws*
4. *The Killing*
5. *Alien*
6. *Se7en*
7. *Rififi*
8. *Manhunter*
9. *Blood Simple*
10. *The French Connection*

That's that for what it's worth. Lists are fun, that's for sure. But when they come from Doug Brode, they are also an education.

—Rod Lurie
Pasadena, CA

THE THRILL OF IT ALL:
SUSPENSE IN THE CINEMA

"A bomb is under the table, and it explodes: That is surprise.
The bomb is under the table but it does *not* explode: *That
is suspense!*"

—Alfred Hitchcock

Thrillers," Roger Ebert lamented in 1995, "are a much-debased genre these days, depending on special effects and formula for much of their content." The Pulitzer-prize winning critic recalled "an earlier, more classic time, when acting, character, and dialogue were meant to stand on their own, and where characters continued to change and develop right up until the last frame." However correct he may have been then, it's heartening to note that since Ebert wrote those words, we've witnessed a redemption of the thriller form. Films like *Open Your Eyes* (1998), *The Sixth Sense* (1999, #24), and *The Others* (2001 #76) all contain a modicum of modern F/X. Their ability to deeply touch an audience derives from something more emotional and intellectual than even the most virtuoso pyro-technical displays can ever provide.

First, though, what is a thriller? Defining it, simply and clearly, is not an easy task. Somewhat more "doable" is explaining what it is *not*. First and foremost, the thriller is not a horror movie. A horror movie pits its hero—always an audience

The Scream of Fear: (clockwise from upper left) Vera Miles in *Psycho*, Genevieve Bujold in *Coma*, Tippi Hedren in *The Birds*, Audrey Hepburn in *Wait Until Dark*, Joan Crawford in *Sudden Fear*.

surrogate, his dangerous situation onscreen incarnating our worst nightmare-scenario made temporarily "real"—off against a highly visible creature, one that appears regularly throughout the story: Dracula (in the guise of a ghoul, beginning with F.W. Murnau's *Nosferatu*, 1922), the Frankenstein monster, the Mummy (who,

in his crumbling bandages, shuffles after victims and strangles them when they unaccountably fail to turn and run for their lives), the Werewolf (including his most famous incarnation, the Wolfman), and the Creature from the Black Lagoon. Always, the object of horror is a creature with some power we mere mortals lack, be it superhuman strength (the great ape in *King Kong*, 1933) or a vastly advanced intellect (the martians in *The War of the Worlds*, 1953).

Here, then, is a first key distinction between the horror film and the suspense-thriller. In the latter, the figure of menace—however undefeatable it may at first seem—proves to be surprisingly mortal and vulnerable. Once, that is, the protagonist—and, with him, the viewer—sets fear aside and determines to somehow win against all odds. At this point, the concept of theme comes into play, the central idea that serves as a driving force for all that occurs. This may at first seem a lofty notion for a type of popular culture more often than not designed and marketed, like Stephen King's novels, as commercial entertainment rather than high art. King is correct when, in *Danse Macabre*, he argues that "in place of the ideas that (serious-minded) novels give us, the movies often substitute large helpings of gut emotion." Yet that describes only (in Robert Warshow's words) the *immediate* experience of moviegoing. Beneath that surface, ideas do exist, lying in wait like the immense lower portions of an iceberg. Whether the filmmakers consciously intended to convey a point or not, movies—by their very identity as a part of pop culture—reflect the current zeitgeist while helping to form it, even in the case of seemingly escapist thrillers.

There are ideas in such films, as in the horror film, and we must, to understand either form, deal with the concepts they state or imply.

What examples of the two genres "say" to us have considerably less in common than we might assume. Robin Wood notes that "the true subject of the horror genre is the struggle for recognition of all that our civilization represses or oppresses." Though this interpretation is debatable, to accept Wood's theory is to perceive the traditional horror film as essentially anti-establishment. This concept, of course, is limited to the classic horror film as it existed before the birth of the slasher movie, with its teen orientation and cautionary fable warning against promiscuity—the "final girl" always a virgin (who remains alive at the film's end, after defeating whatever has threatened her and eliminated her promiscuous girl-friends). As to classic horror, however, anyone who ever felt saddened by the plight of King Kong or Frankenstein at society's hands can grasp Wood's point about horror causing us to align with the abnormal, at least while viewing.

Not so the traditional thriller, for here is a genre in which our sympathies are always with agents of the norm, be it classical or contemporary. This point holds true when the protagonists work within the official bounds of society's standards, like the good cops who populate such postwar noir thrillers as Barry Fitzgerald in Jules Dassin's *The Naked City* (1948) or Warner Anderson in Don Siegel's *The Lineup* (1958). Even when our antihero was a criminal—the case with Sterling Hayden in both *The Asphalt Jungle* (1950) and *The Killing* (1956)—the central character is the least violent (even anti-violent) member of the group, a good man turned bad not by inherent evil but by all the wrong breaks, and only wants to score one last time so that he can finally live a normal life, more often than not with a nice girl. He is us, in our nightmare-scenario vision of ourselves, driven to the very edge, trying to fight our way back.

This is the way things work within the context of the modern crime thriller, even when antiheroes step outside accepted patterns of behavior. Clint Eastwood in *Dirty Harry* and Gene Hackman in *The French Connection* (both 1971) go to exorbitant, even illegal lengths to rid the world of serial killers and drug dealers. A controversy has arisen as to this apparent acceptance of vigilante mentality, best expressed by Dana B. Polan while voicing concern for "the creation and exploita-tion of a thrill of violence to ends supportive of (absolute) authority." To a degree, this is unarguably true. Yet it exists because, as is always the case with the most popular films of any genre, they simply purvey what the audience demands.

Noel Carroll has stated that the horror film's "basic subject matter is fear." The basic subject matter of the thriller, I would argue, is *anxiety*. Fear has to do with inexplicable things, those forces we only half believe in, fantasy elements we

The Man with a Gun: Gene Hackman as Popeye Doyle in *The French Connection*.

convince ourselves do not exist, if in our secret places continue to fear they do. "There's no such thing as monsters," our mothers told us as children at bedtime, in hope of dispelling such fear. Still, we had trouble sleeping, projecting mythic and metaphysical notions (even at an age when we likely hadn't heard those terms) onto what surrounds us in the darkness of night.

In the thriller, our fears are more realistically grounded, though the elements we grow anxious about are often kept just beyond full view. Ghost stories, then, lend themselves more to the thriller than the horror genre. How different the situation is from films about the Frankenstein monster or the Creature from the Black Lagoon, though these are utterly appealing in their own right. Still, they must be considered monster movies, not suspense thrillers. In each of them, we see the "monster" clearly for the first time a third of the way through, then continue to see more of it as the story progresses. As we watch the inevitable sequels, what ini-

The "Other": Villains in thrillers can be as real as Andy Robinson in *Dirty Harry* or as otherworldly as the creeping hand in *The Fog*.

tially struck us as an icon of horror becomes ever more seen, thus, better known and, finally, less frightening than we initially imagined, owing to what Frank McConnell tagged as the monster's "absurd presence." This is particularly problematic in movies made before the birth of modern special effects, when the zipper could sometimes be glimpsed running up the back of the creature's costume.

Importantly, none of this is meant as a criticism, stated or implied, of the horror genre, but a possible explanation of our ongoing love for such films. As

The Voyeur as Hero: Catherine Deneuve in *Belle de Jour*.

Barry Keith Grant has written, horror is the genre that, when "experienced communally, has liberated monsters—brought them out of the closet, so to speak—by making them at once visible and public." Thus, Bela Lugosi as Dracula was transformed from a figure of abject terror (in Todd Browning's 1931 film) to one of gentle ridicule (in the 1948 film, *Abbott and Costello Meet Frankenstein*). And, more recently, into child-friendly images (The Count on *Sesame Street* and Count Chokula on cereal boxes).

Though it's often argued that seeing is believing, more often than not it leads to disbelieving, if only in the sense of having our worst fears dispelled. The original version of *The Blob* (1958) was, at least according to this line of arguing, a thriller, despite its grounding in science-fiction conventions, because we never once experienced a single good view of that title figure of menace. In truth, this was largely due to budget restrictions; all that the B-movie producers could afford in the way of special effects was a huge slab of a jello-like substance, which they wisely revealed only in brief subliminal shots. Nonetheless, the effect worked. Teenagers who flocked to see *The Blob* on its initial release (I speak from experience) couldn't sleep properly for weeks. Here, "the pleasure," as Dennis Giles has put it, "is *not* seeing [italics mine] the delayed, blocked, or partial vision" that allows us to glimpse something in the shadows without precisely revealing what that form (if the thing does indeed *have* a form) may be.

The 1988 remake, replete with expensive state-of-the-art effects, conversely played as a horror film, and not a particularly good one at that. Step-by-step, we saw more and more of the monster. As we did, a catharsis took place. For the horror film gradually relieves us of our fears, which is why we go to see it. What's up there on-screen, as King has noted, is never as bad as what we imagined it might look like. The thriller, however, refuses to allow us that easy an exit. So *The Blair Witch Project* (1999, #99), owing to its ambiguous ending, rates as a thriller, not a horror film.

Think back to Hitchcock's bomb under the table, and the unrelieved anxiety so essential to suspense in the cinema. If the bomb did explode, and we witnessed

The Lonely Crowd: Sterling Hayden (second from left) organizes a team of thieves in *The Asphalt Jungle*.

the results, the film would be horrific. That was the case with Hitchcock's own early English film *Sabotage* (1936), in which the bomb did indeed go off on a crowded bus. After shooting that film, Hitchcock denounced his own work, insisting it had been a grave mistake to kill all those normal, ordinary, everyday people, including a mentally deficient child. He had produced, without meaning to, an example of horror, and he would not do it again—no, for those of you who are thinking ahead, not even in *The Birds* (1963). To be fair, Hitchcock was young when he made *Sabotage*, still learning what kind of movie he most wanted to make. From that point on, he grasped his calling and self-consciously made suspense thrillers.

"What's the difference between suspense and horror?" Ty Burr asked in a recent *Entertainment Weekly* article. "One is sensing, the other is seeing; one is expectation, the other is follow-through; one leaves the bloody details to your imagination, the other shows that imagination can fall pitifully short." When we want the latter, we go to horror; when desiring (or in need of) the former, we seek out a thriller. Why? In part because the suspense thriller touches upon what Stephen King calls "phobic pressure points." The author of the most popular stories in the genre to appear in the twentieth century notes that the most successful (i.e., suspenseful) thrillers "almost always seem to play upon and express fears which exist across a wide spectrum of people." These "terminals of fear" are "so deeply buried and yet so vital that we may tap into them like artesian wells." He speaks, of course, about the subtext of films that, on a conscious level, attract audiences eager for entertainment of a most peculiar kind.

After all, these are not musicals or romances, which allow us to temporarily forget any and all of our everyday troubles, offering an escape route into an alternative world of sweetness and beauty. Nor, for that matter, are they westerns (with certain notable exceptions, like *High Noon* [1952, #13]) or the period-crime films. Both those genres present the viewer with characters caught in historical situations so much worse than our own that, by comparison, we appreciate our lots in life.

True, the thriller also allows us to temporarily escape, but in a considerably different way. This is not the musical's alternative universe of the ideal—life as we wish it could be—or the gangster saga's believable world as it once was for people who had it worse than we do. Rather, the thriller addresses ordinary, everyday reality in a unique way, presenting us with the worst-case scenario, a paradigm of possible consequences that happen to characters not unlike ourselves. In this vein, Jonathan Lemkin has argued that "*Jaws* (1975, #7) is *not* a monster movie," in any horror flick sense, in part because of the film's setting. Rather, *Jaws* "is about America—perhaps an America that does not exist and never did, but one the audience recognizes nonetheless." The America, that is, once depicted in the Andy Hardy small-town comedies of the thirties or an America which, in faux-form, can be visited at Disney theme parks. Before heading for the exciting rides spread throughout the Disney property, visitors must first pass through Main Street, U.S.A.—a romanticization of the past as we like to believe it once was.

Highly influenced by Disney as well as by Hitchcock, Steven Spielberg recreated the dimly realistic "Amity" of Peter Benchley's negligible novel, coming up with something at once symbolic and archetypal for his monumental film. As Lemkin rightly argues, *Jaws* is a thriller, not a horror movie, because it's grounded in our commonly accepted idealization of all we believe to be archetypically American.

D.W. Griffith, who arguably invented and certainly perfected pretty much everything of any importance in the movie medium, sensed the importance of symbolic archetypes early on. As legendary film historian Paul Rotha noted, "Griffith always chose his characters from the normal stream of life, and developed their fictitiously constructed lives in (the context of) a world quite normal to them." No better example exists from Griffith's pre-*Birth of a Nation* (1915) experimental period than a seminal short called *The Lonely Villa* (1909). The narrative line of this ten minute mini-masterpiece is classically simple: as a husband leaves his isolated home, heading for work in the city, a dangerous man approaches the house and menaces the wife. She sends word for help; can her spouse make it back in time? For Rotha, the results constitute one of Griffith's "well-constructed models of contrasted tension . . . with the action planned in such a manner that the dramatic tension rises to a powerful climax at the conclusion." Such effects were heightened when Griffith "improved the tension created by parallel action by addition of the close-up."

Women in the audience could associate with the victim; men, with the husband hopeful of saving her. However melodramatic the fictionalized incident may have been, it took place entirely in a world that clearly resembled our own. Ever since, this has been the case with exercises in suspense as diverse as the contemporary antiterrorist action thriller, *Die Hard* (1988, #78) or the more understated but no less involved study of female frigidity and repressed violence in a modern marriage gone wrong, *Cat People* (1942, # 70). J.P. Telotte has, in *Dreams of Darkness*, written about the unique approach that created a key distinction between the thrillers Val Lewton produced at R.K.O. during the 1940s and the more traditional horror films of Carl Laemmle at Universal a decade earlier. Beginning with *Cat People*, the Lewton films were most often rooted in the mundane, the characters walking down streets of big cities or prowling the byways of small towns not unlike those inhabited by members of the audience.

His modestly-budgeted programmers concentrated on the work lives of key characters, to a degree that few Hollywood films, whatever their genre, have done before or since. That rooting in reality is essential to the thriller in a way it never has been to the horror film. There is, in fact, a small European country called Transylvania and a man named Vlad Tseppes (the model for the best known of all vampires) once ruled there. But Bram Stoker—who cemented a vivid if utterly fanciful image of that remote land and its "count" in *Dracula* (1888)—never visited the place. This Dublin-based author, too ill to travel, created his own imagined Transylvania, a negative Ruritania fashioned from shards of reality (travel booklets, old maps) which were then combined with scary stories about hideous vampires and their lovely virginal victims that Stoker had heard.

What he (among others) created was a fairytale for adults: the gothic horror tale which, despite endless updates, remains potent still. And even when Dracula leaves that fabled land to visit a real place like London, his victims—the Harkers, the Holmwoods, the good doctors Van Helsing and Seward—are utterly unlike

The World's Greatest Detective: Basil Rathbone, Ida Lupino, and Nigel Bruce in *The Adventures of Sherlock Holmes*.

I Walk Alone: The alienated anti-hero of the social thriller, incarnated by Spencer Tracy in *Bad Day at Black Rock*.

ourselves. So the frissons—the scary and erotic pinpricks of emotion that these films inspire—are always distanced from our circle of experience. *This is happening to them*, we take refuge in thinking. For they, like F. Scott Fitzgerald's very rich, are (thankfully, in this case) different from you and me.

Not so the characters in a thriller. In the hands of a true artist like Hitchcock, the film based on suspense rather than horror does not so much transport us out of the everyday and into a nightmare realm so much as it "makes life dreamlike, its surface a thin crust over a substratum of fear, insecurity, unconscious anxiety, and guilt," according to Albert J. LaValley. Or, as Raymond Durgnat put it, the thriller allows us "a sense of having penetrated from an apparently tolerant, even permissive, world to a grimmer one." This world he speaks of does not exist as a distant alternative to our own but as a substratum of the everyday life we constantly brush up against. It is a level of existence which we nearly touch, and yet fail to recognize, perhaps in an act of either conscious or unconscious denial, until—

like the amiable if insensitive hero of Hitchcock's *North by Northwest* (1959, #8)—we are suddenly, inexorably plunged into its dark recesses.

At this point, the protagonist—and the audience—is forced to survive in an artistically created universe that has a clear connection to the ordinary world which the hero and viewer have stepped out of and will eventually return to. It is a world, in the words of J.P. Telotte, "simultaneously more real and more truly fantastic" than the fabled. "One goes to a horror film to have a nightmare," Bruce Kawin has observed. Or—more correctly—we experience a work of entertainment that partakes of the dark dreams that haunt us when we are asleep and, thus, out of control. Part of the perverse pleasure this genre offers is our knowledge that we are, actually, *in* control. When and if things become *too* terrible, we can always hop out of our cushioned seats, then bolt and run.

Conversely, one attends a thriller to confront reality at its worst possible extreme. The "others" in horror may be creatures from beyond the stars, armed with remarkable weapons of destruction. But when, on rare occasion, the science-fiction film presents itself not in the guise of horror but as a thriller—as it most clearly does in *The Thing From Another World* (1951, #30)—there are no such conventional genre elements on view. The "thing" is a living, breathing, and (once the heroes get a grip on themselves and consider their enemy closely) vulnerable figure, in this case a human vegetable. Likewise, the menaced people are as ordinary as those seated in the theatre.

In *The Thing*, producer Howard Hawks portrayed what very likely would have occurred in the real world if a flying saucer were to crash-land on earth. Whether the "others" were Nazi spies (in the forties), communist agents (in the fifties), our supposedly sane neighbors (in the sixties), drugged-out street people (in the seventies), or terrorists (in the eighties)—or, on rare occasion, vampires or space creatures—they are, if the film is a thriller, comprehensible in realistic terms. A horror movie rendering of *Dracula* has the title character—as in Francis Ford Coppola's glorious 1992 version—flying through the air or taking the shape of a wolf, bat, and, on occasion, mist. But in a thriller incarnation—most notably *Horror of Dracula* (1958, #81)—he turns out to be only a man (if a notably oversexed one) who suffers from a rare disease called porphyria. This condition, it has been argued, results from an intense craving for human blood.

Because of this grounding in everyday reality, the thriller is often subject to moral criticism that its more fantastical distant cousin, the horror movie, sometimes avoids. Taking a politically correct position toward both Hitchcock's *Psycho* (1960, #1) and John Carpenter's *Halloween* (1978, #56), Morris Dickstein complains that "the murderer is a voyeur enraged by his own excitement, and the camera appeals to our complicity by putting us repeatedly in his position, seeing what he sees, tempted to feel what he feels." Though this attitude has become generally accepted as part of a feminist bias against the thriller, nothing could be further from the truth. In the earlier film, we associate not with the shadowy killer who tears away the shower curtain, but with Janet Leigh, the flawed but worthwhile woman who is executed at precisely that moment when she has achieved a modicum of moral redemption, deciding to return the stolen money. In Carpenter's own unofficial remake of / semi-sequel to Hitchcock's greatest film, he (in obvious homage) casts Leigh's daughter, Jamie Lee Curtis, in a similar position.

The Hitchcock Blonde: Grace Kelly projected an image of an iceberg surface with a volcano about to explode beneath in *To Catch a Thief*, *Dial M for Murder*, and *Rear Window*.

Again, we identify *with* her and "Sam Loomis" (John Gavin in the earlier film, Donald Pleasence in the latter), and *against* the "boogeyman"—that shadowy thing which menaces her/us.

Thrillers are too often films which, in Tania Modleski's words, force (or at least lure) us into an acceptance of "the passive (female) object . . . with the active (usually male) subject." Though Hitchcock's woman was indeed a victim, it's only fair to recall that his movie was made before feminism forever changed the misconception that the female of the species is the weaker sex. For Carpenter and other contemporary creators of the thriller, the woman is, more often than not, deadlier than the male, as the "final girl" in today's teen-oriented works of suspense—like *Scream* (1996, #87)—makes clear. Though there are conventions to the thriller, as there are to any other genre, they are not set in cement and can change with the times. However, certain things do remain constant, one of these being, as S.S. Prawer has pointed out, "the need to test and objectify and come to grips with one's terrors in a setting of ultimate security, where one can tell oneself at any moment: 'It is only a film.' " This holds as true for a contemporary work like *Se7en* (1995, #62) as a classic from Hollywood's golden age, such as *The Spiral Staircase* (1946, #59).

Anyone who has ever been a part of an audience for any particularly effective thriller knows full well the remarkable silence that descends on people who do not know each other when they walk in, yet find themselves transformed into a momentary community of mutual fear. The phenomenon is remarkable, for, like the disparate citizens who wandered into the theatre of Athens to see Sophocles's *Oedipus the King*—arguably the first thriller ever to be performed in public—some 2,450 years ago, we begin the viewing experience as isolated individuals. Nonetheless, we leave with an unspoken sense of connection to those who have shared the terrifying and, if unlikely, all too possible experience with us.

The thriller taps into Jung's "collective unconscious" or what, in the popular idiom, Burt Hatlen has tagged "the myth pool." It is, in the end, the one type of film that—despite its offer of an avenue of escapism—must be considered extremely significant in terms of our grasp on reality. This remains true over the years because the thriller is the genre that cuts quick and deep to the very essence of what it means to be human.

100:

THE CABINET OF DR. CALIGARI (1919)

U.F.A. (Germany)

"There is something evil in our midst!"
—Francis

CAST:

Werner Krauss (*Dr. Caligari*); Lil Dagover (*Jane*); Conrad Veidt (*Cesare*); Friedrich Feher (*Francis*); Hans Heinrich von Twardowski (*Alan*); Rudolf Lettinger (*Dr. Olson*); Rudolf Klein-Rogge (*The Wrong Man*).

CREDITS:

Director, Robert Wiene; screenplay, Hans Janowitz and Carl Mayer; producers, Rudolf Meinert and Erich Pommer; cinematographer, Willy Hameister; production designers, Walter Reimann, Walter Röhrig, and Hermann Warm; creative contributors, Rochus Gliese and (uncredited) Fritz Lang; running time, 69 min.

THE PLOT:

An old man sits by a wall, concluding a bizarre story he's just related to his young companion. Francis, in turn, says he has an even stranger tale to tell. Some time ago, Francis and a friend, Alan, lived in Hostenwald; both were in love with the same girl, Jane. One day, the pals went to the fairgrounds and caught a tent show held by a darkly-clad hypnotist, Caligari. His zombie-like companion, Cesare, predicted the future of various people, cryptically pronouncing to Alan, "You die at dawn." The following morning, Alan was found dead in his apartment. When

Francis ran to the police and told them what had occurred, they assumed him to be mad, eventually arresting one of "the usual suspects" for this crime.

Francis informs Jane and her influential family and they begin spying on Caligari. Cesare the somnambulist, meanwhile, slips out into the night, assigned to murder Francis's fiancée, but is unable to kill the girl, owing to her beauty. With Jane's confirmation of Francis's worst fears, he knows that he can convince others. They surround Caligari's gypsy-like wagon, revealing that inside Cesare's cabinet, a dummy sat in Cesare's place. His ruse revealed, Caligari hurries away, pursued by Francis. Francis tracks Caligari to the grounds of an insane asylum. The doctor in charge turns out to be Caligari; his special study is mesmerism, and he became obsessed with seeing if he could make a human bend entirely to his will after encountering a somnambulist whom he transformed into Cesare. With the help of several interns, Francis unmasks Caligari who, screaming, is dragged off to a cell.

Francis concludes his story, and he and his companion decide to go inside. We then realize they are patients at the asylum. Francis, apparently arrested for killing his best friend over the girl, has repressed his own dark desires and projected them onto the innocent doctor, who only wants to help him.

THE FILM:

Nineteen-year-old Alfred Hitchcock, part of a newly formed British film company, was one of the fortunate few invited to visit Germany shortly after the end of World War I to normalize relations between the two countries by sharing secrets and skills of moviemaking. Though never involved in the production of *The Cabinet of Dr. Caligari*, Hitchcock did visit the set, later claiming to have been amazed and astounded. In interviews during his lifetime, Hitchcock often cited this movie as the inspiration for his body of work.

Most significant was the use of Expressionistic sets for the story within the story, though not the framing device, which is realistically rendered. The bookends serve as the filmmakers' way of informing their audience that the brief prologue and epilogue are set in "objective" reality, the story itself entirely "subjective." We are, throughout the tale within the tale, inside the narrator's mind, seeing the world as he sees it. Owing to the grotesquely distorted sets, Francis obviously sees things in an insane manner. Therefore, when we learn at the end of the film that he's mad, it should come as no great no surprise, since we have been given endless visual indications that this is the case.

Still, it invariably does surprise the first-time viewer. This constitutes the difference between a cheap-trick ending, in which the filmmakers withhold important information so that we'll be surprised, and a successful twist ending, in which they supply us with all the information we could ask for, yet somehow induce us into tricking ourselves.

Throughout his career, Hitchcock employed approaches and themes that originally appeared in *The Cabinet of Dr. Caligari*: the wrong man, voyeurism, doubles, murder by daylight, the issue of madness, and the common-man hero who takes on a dark conspiracy and, without the help of the authorities, wins in the end.

TRIVIA:

Fritz Lang was originally set to direct the film, but had to drop out when a serial that he was working on, *The Spider*, ran over schedule. Yet it was Lang who, before terminating his connection with *The Cabinet of Dr. Caligari*, suggested the epilogue and prologue be added to the script. The original version did not contain those scenes and played as more of a conventional horror story. Writers Janowitz and Meyer had intended to convey anti-authoritarian attitudes, but they were actually reversed in the finished film. Whereas they had hoped to show that people in power are crazy, the movie implies that those who think people in power are crazy are crazy.

ALSO RECOMMENDED:

The Cabinet of Dr. Caligari was the first of the great German Expressionist films. Among the most suspenseful that followed was Lang's own *M* (1931, #2). Hitchcock's *Spellbound* (1945) served as his unofficial remake of *The Cabinet of Dr. Caligari*, featuring the head of an institution who is far crazier than any of his patients. The name of the book that Hitchcock based his film on, *The House of Dr. Edwardes*, suggests the parallel. An exceptional B-movie turned cult film, Herk Harvey's Kansas-made *Carnival of Souls* (1962) will intrigue *The Cabinet of Dr. Caligari* fans.

99:

THE BLAIR WITCH PROJECT (1999)

Alliance Atlantis/Artisan Entertainment

> **"I'm scared to close my eyes;**
> **I'm scared to *open* them."**
> **—Heather Donahue**

CAST:

Heather Donahue (*Heather Donahue*); Joshua Leonard (*Joshua "Josh" Leonard*); Michael Williams (*Michael "Mike" Williams*); Bob Griffin (*Short Fisherman*); Jim King (*Interviewee*); Sandra Sánchez (*Waitress*); Ed Swanson (*Fisherman With Glasses*); Patricia DeCou (*Mary Brown*); Mark Mason (*Man in Yellow Hat*); Jackie Hallex (*Interviewee with Child*).

CREDITS:

Directors, Daniel Myrick and Eduardo Sánchez; screenwriters, Myrick and Sánchez; producers, Robin Cowie, Bob Eick, Kevin J. Foxe, Gregg Hale, and Michael Monello; original music, Tony Cora; cinematographer, Neal Fredericks; editors, Myrick and Sánchez; production design, Ben Rock; art director, Ricardo R. Moreno; running time, 87 min.; rating: R.

Thriller-vérité: the director as superstar in *The Blair Witch Project*.

THE PLOT:

Three young people, enrolled in film school, are assigned to pick a subject of interest and make a movie about it. They travel to Maryland, as one of the students has heard of a fascinating tale of the supernatural which has become a legend near Burkittsville. Supposedly, a witch haunts anyone foolish enough to wander into her domain. During the 1940s, several children disappeared without a trace, and most locals avoid the dark woods. Convinced this is only a silly superstition, though intrigued enough to want to record any hint that there may be some truth to the tale, Heather, Josh, and Mike camp out, hoping—via their student film—to prove or disprove the theory. They carry with them a 16mm camera, a Hi8 video camera, and a DAT recorder; as they wander, they record everything that happens.

The three never return. A year to the day that they set out, hikers discover the camera and screen the film the missing students were making. Heather, Josh, and Mike found small piles of stones in spots they passed the day before, noticing nothing then; though they try to travel in a straight line, they continually find themselves back where they started. Panic slowly sets in, though whether this is due to an actual witch or a projection of their own inner fears remains unclear. When Josh disappears, the two surviving members verge on madness. Then, Heather and

Mike spot an abandoned house and enter. Something terrible is inside, though just as we are about to get a look at it, the camera shuts off, the final aural entry being a scream of fear.

THE FILM:

Few films have created such immediate, intense, widespread fervor, only to be damned as a backlash shortly set in. If nothing else, *The Blair Witch Project* (originally to have been titled *The Black Hills Project*) must be admired as the greatest hoax since the Cardiff Giant. Myrick and Sánchez were themselves film students at the University of Central Florida, where they received an assignment to make a film as their thesis/project. The two decided that, in an age of reflexivity and deconstruction (concepts they had learned in theory classes), it might be fun to make a student movie about the making of a student movie, then insist the spooky results were the real thing. They titled their production company "Haxan Films" as an homage to *The Witches*, a documentary by Benjamin Christensen. They prepared an outline of slightly more than thirty pages, then improvised as they shot.

The Blair Witch Project was shot in and around Adamstown and Rockville, Maryland, including sequences at Patapsco State Park. In those scenes that depict them interviewing townspeople, the interviewees were rehearsed by the writer/directors as to what they should say, though the interviewers had no idea what was coming, to insure their reactions would be entirely real. Real, too, was the nausea experienced by theatregoers unused to the endless handheld camera movements. When production was finished, Myrick and Sánchez tried to sell their fiction as an actual document. The ruse went so far as to list the three main actors as "missing or dead" on the Internet. The film became a hit on the festival circuit, where such an offbeat experiment tickled the fancy of jaded cineastes who had seen one too many empty big-budget films. In 1999, *The Blair Witch Project* won the Award of the Youth at Cannes.

Immediately, spoofs appeared, including *The Blair Fish Project* (1999) and two adults-only features, *The Erotic Witch Project* (1999) and *The Bare Wench Project* (1999). Many youthful ticket-buyers—who knew nothing of the Festival circuit, but had heard this was "the" movie to see—felt ripped off by the inexpensive item. Now that the smoke has cleared and the dust has settled, *The Blair Witch Project* ought to be appreciated for its qualities. Those initial fans were not wrong in insisting this was one of the most imaginative student films ever made. Also, it serves as the ultimate rendering of what the legendary Val Lewton once insisted would be the ultimate thriller—ninety minutes of a black screen, with eerie noises on the soundtrack.

TRIVIA:

The film has been entered into the *Guinness Book of World Records* as the most profitable (measuring gross against cost) ever made. Budgeted at $35,000, the film had brought in an estimated $140,530,114 in the United States alone by November, 1999. Sam Barber, whose name did not originally appear, sued (and won) to have his name added, since he had actually suggested the concept in the first place.

ALSO RECOMMENDED:

Fans of low-budget filmmaking by enthusiastic film students will want to catch Francis Ford Coppola's *Dementia 13* (1963) and Peter Bogdanovich's *Targets* (1968) with Boris Karloff.

98:

HOMICIDAL (1961)

Columbia Pictures

"Who wears the pants in *this* family?"
—tag line for 1960 release

CAST:

Glenn Corbett (*Karl*); Patricia Breslin (*Miriam Webster*); Jean Arless (*Emily*) Eugenie Leontovich (*Helga*); Alan Bunce (*Doctor Jones*); Richard Rust (*Jim Nesbitt*); James Westerfield (*Mr. Adrims*); Gilbert Green (*Lt. Miller*); Wolfe Barzell (*Olie*); Ralph Moody (*Clerk*); William Castle (*Narrator*).

CREDITS:

Director, William Castle; screenplay, Robb White; producers, Castle and Dona Holloway; original music, Hugo Friedhofer; cinematographer, Burnett Guffey; editor, Edwin H. Bryant; art director, Cary Odell; running time, 87 min.

THE PLOT:

A little girl plays with her doll. Her brother enters the room, grabs the doll, and smashes it, causing her to cry. Twenty years later, Emily, a stunning blonde checks into a hotel, then tells the bellboy she wants him to marry her, for a few days only. She offers to pay him and, overwhelmed, he accompanies her to a chapel, where they are to be married. Suddenly insulted by something the officiator says, she yanks a knife from her handbag and slashes the bellboy to death. Then she takes off in the bellboy's car and heads home to a mansion owned by Helga, where Emily verbally abuses the wheelchair-bound elderly woman. A brunette friend of Emily, Miriam, and Karl's, who secretly loves Miriam, visits Emily. Shortly, Emily is joined by her brother, who moves into the mansion and attracts the attentions of Miriam, much to Emily's chagrin. Emily is unmasked as Warren, a transvestite who masquerades as his deceased sister.

Low-budget Hitchcock: a mysterious blonde (Jean Arless, far right) may not be precisely what she seems in William Castle's schlock-masterpiece, *Homicidal.*

THE FILM:

No study of the suspense film would be complete without a nod to William Castle (1914–77), born "William Schloss" in New York City. A con man from day one, he talked his way into a Broadway show, then headed for Hollywood in 1937, directing low-budget thrillers in the *Boston Blackie* series. In time, Castle worked his way up to the head of Columbia's B-movie unit, knocking out thrillers in the *Whistler* and *Crime Doctor* franchises. Though he did work with Orson Welles on *The Lady From Shanghai* (1948), Castle felt more at home with inexpensive exploitation flicks, leaving the major studios to direct and produce on his own.

Though he aspired to be the B-budget Hitchcock, Castle came far closer in approach to P.T. Barnum, taking that old showman's adage that there's a sucker born every minute to the motion picture industry. Simultaneous with Roger Corman, Castle realized that in the mid-to-late 1950s, an immense youth audience had emerged, looking for movies to catch at Saturday matinees or the local drive-ins. If Corman made better movies, Castle put on a grander show. When *Macabre* (1958) opened, the audience had the option of taking out insurance policies in case someone died during the screening. Many people consider *The Tingler* (1959) to be Castle's pièce de résistance; whenever the tingling creature appears onscreen, wires attached to theatre seats delivered a mild electric shock that set viewers screaming.

With *Homicidal*, Castle stopped the film five minutes before the ending in order to allow for a "fright break," in which the faint-hearted could get their money back by leaving before the film resumed. But teenagers out-conned the con man by attending the early show, remaining seated during the intermission, then watching the movie a second time and, having already seen the finale once, left during the second showing's "Fright Break" to get their ticket money back. When the "live" gimmicks were removed for TV showings, most of the Castle films appeared tepid, *Homicidal* being the notable exception. Though an obvious rip-off of *Psycho* (1960, #1), the film managed to score as a first-rate imitation, with a marvelous pace and far more intense suspense than in any of the director's other projects.

Decades before such a "revolutionary" film as *The Crying Game* (1992), Castle dared to challenge the censors by unmasking a supposed woman as a man. It's worth noting, though, that the director of *The Crying Game*, Neil Jordan, borrowed one trick from Castle to keep his mid-movie twist from being spotted by those watching the credits carefully: Jaye Davidson was as ambiguous a name as had been Jean Arless. Indeed, in the case of Castle's film, most moviegoers could not figure out whether the actor playing the male transvestite was, in fact, a man or a woman.

TRIVIA:

The lead performer was a twenty-nine-year-old woman, formerly known as Joan Marshall, a Chicago native who had been a Windy City showgirl before heading first to Vegas, then Hollywood. She played Dane Clark's love interest in the *Bold Venture* (1959–60) series. She was married for a while to filmmaker Hal Ashby, who based his film *Shampoo* (1975) almost entirely on his wife's recollections of her "experiences" in la-la land. She also appeared in the film's opening beauty parlor sequence. The gimmicky style of William Castle was heralded in Joe Dante's *Matinee* (1993), starring John Goodman as a thinly disguised version of the famed producer/director. Before his death, Castle produced the far more ambitious thriller *Rosemary's Baby* (1968, #19).

ALSO RECOMMENDED:

Among the best of Castle's creep-show features are *The Tingler* (1959), with Vincent Price as a man driven mad by strange high-pitched sounds, *Strait-Jacket* (1964) with Joan Crawford as a woman who fears she may be a homicidal maniac, and *I Saw What You Did* (1965), about a pair of teenage girls who, while babysitting, make creepy phone calls in which they shout out the phrase that lends the film its title, but then make the mistake of saying it to a man (John Ireland) who has just murdered a woman (Joan Crawford). And, for an intriguing comparison, do catch Neil Jordan's *The Crying Game* (1992).

97:

WINTER KILLS (1979)

Avco Embassy Pictures

> **"Your brother, the president of these United States, has just been assassinated."**
> —Pa Kegan to Nick Kegan

CAST:

Jeff Bridges (*Nick Kegan*); John Huston (*Pa Kegan*); Anthony Perkins (*John Cerruti*); Eli Wallach (*Joe Diamond*); Sterling Hayden (*Z.K. Dawson*);

Dorothy Malone (*Emma Kegan*); Tomas Milian (*Frank Mayo*); Belinda Bauer (*Yvette Malone*); Ralph Meeker (*Gameboy Baker*); Toshirô Mifune (*Keith*); Richard Boone (*Keifitz*); David Spielberg (*Miles Garner*); Brad Dexter (*Captain Heller One*); Michael Thomas (*Ray Doty*); Joe Spinell (*Arthur Fletcher*); Kim O'Brien and Candice Rialson (*Beautiful Blondes*); Tisa Farrow (*Nurse*); Camilla Sparv, Erin Gray, and Andrea Claudio (*Elegant Women*); Berry Berenson (*Morgue Attendant*); Elizabeth Taylor (uncredited, *Lola Comante*).

CREDITS:

Director, William Richert; screenplay, Richert, from a book by Richard Condon; producers, Daniel H. Blatt, Fred C. Caruso, and Leonard Goldberg; original music, Maurice Jarre; cinematographer, Vilmos Zsigmond; editor, David Bretherton; production design, Robert F. Boyle; art director, Norman Newberry; special effects, Jim Danforth; running time, 97 min.; rating, R.

THE PLOT:

When President Kegan is assassinated, his younger brother Nick is initially too stunned to do anything at all, and merely waits for the CIA or FBI to disclose the identity of the killer. But time goes by, and nothing happens. Nick cannot believe these two massive intelligence investigating units are truly unable to come up with any leads, so Nick informs his all-powerful father that he himself will seek out the culprit. Horrified, old Pa Kegan warns the youth against any such dangerous activity, though Nick ignores his advice. No sooner does Nick pursue his investigation than he comes in contact with a seductive beauty, Yvette, who may be either his best hope or an enemy agent sent to stop him at any cost. In time, Nick comes to realize that the answers to his questions may be known only by a Hollywood movie star who was his late brother's mistress.

THE FILM:

If ever there were a potential cult film that has somehow failed to achieve full cult status, certainly *Winter Kills* is that movie. *Dr. Strangelove* by way of *The Manchurian Candidate* (it is based on a novel by Richard Condon, who also wrote the latter paranoid masterpiece), this is a full-throttle dark comedy about not only the Kennedy assassination but also a wild satire on all the far-fetched conspiracy theories that emerged over the following decade and a half. Everything onscreen is played with a slightly surreal touch, much like the believable yet neatly overstated performances in the legendary Stanley Kubrick film, yet this movie remains

Jeff Bridges, son of a Joseph Kennedy-like icon (John Huston), attempts to rescue his father from a precarious position that purposely recalls such Hitchcock films as *Vertigo* and *North by Northwest*.

just barely within the bounds of possibility, more on the order of the John Frankenheimer opus. If *The Manchurian Candidate* dared suggest that right-wing Senator Joseph McCarthy was actually a Communist agent, then this Condon tale goes that thriller one better, implying that the assassination of Jack Kennedy might have been engineered by his own father, Joseph. "Very fine Strangelovian fantasy that sank without a trace in 1979," Dave Kehr wrote in the *Chicago Reader* at the time of the film's belated rerelease, as the head of a Kennedy-like clan sets out to investigate the assassination of his president brother, but becomes enmeshed in a "web of darkly comic paranoia, spun by an endless parade of iconographically aggressive guest stars. . . . Richert's visual style balances flamboyant comic-book colors and intelligent wide-screen framing." This strategy of "restrained excess" kept the picture continually on edge. The film is funny, but it's "frightening and vertiginous, too—a complex tone that apparently left audiences baffled" during its original theatrical release when viewers were unable to grasp "its oddball humor and (edgy) intelligence."

TRIVIA:

The film was shot on a $6,500,000 budget, quite considerable at the time for the minor-league and ever-struggling Avco Embassy company. Locations included Death Valley, Los Angeles, New York City, and Philadelphia. Though a financial bust in America (as well as a film that confounded most critics), *Winter Kills* developed a cult following in Europe, where it was marketed under a bizarre series of alternative titles: *Muertes de Invierno* (Spain), *Philadelphia Clan* (West Germany), *Rebus per un Assassinio* (Italy), *Salaliitto* (Finland), and *Viimeinen Viesti* (Finish TV title). Director William Richert never felt satisfied with the American release print, for he hadn't received the all-important "final cut." In 1983, Richert had the opportunity to re-edit the film and restore his original conception for the ending, at which time, according to Leonard Maltin, *Winter Kills* was at last "newly appreciated as a black comedy, which not everybody recognized the first time around." Elizabeth Taylor plays a character modeled on Marilyn Monroe. The part of a morgue attendant is played by Berry Berenson, the wife of one of the film's stars, Anthony Perkins. She's the sister of Marisa Berenson, who played the female lead in Stanley Kubrick's *Barry Lyndon* (1975). The film concludes with an homage to the vertigo-inspiring finale in Alfred Hitchcock's *North by Northwest* (1959, #8). Indeed, had Hitchcock and Kubrick decided to co-direct a fictionalized film about the Kennedy assassination, from a Condon scenario, this most likely would have been it. Here is a minor masterpiece awaiting rediscovery!

ALSO RECOMMENDED:

Obvious cross-references are to Frankenheimer's *The Manchurian Candidate* (1962) and Kubrick's *Dr. Strangelove* (1964, #4), as well as Rod Lurie's *The Contender* (2000, #48), in which Jeff Bridges plays a United States president. Bridges fans will want to catch him in George Sluizer's effective suspense thriller *The Vanishing* (1993).

96:

THE CAT AND THE CANARY (1939)

Paramount Pictures

> **"I'm so scared, even my goose pimples**
> **have goose pimples!"**
> **—Wally Campbell**

CAST:

Bob Hope (*Wally Campbell*); Paulette Goddard (*Joyce Norman*); John Beal (*Fred Blythe*); Douglass Montgomery (*Charles Wilder*); Gale Sondergaard (*Miss Lu*); Elizabeth Patterson (*Aunt Susan*); George Zucco (*Lawyer Crosby*); Nydia Westman (*Cicily*); John Wray (*Hendricks*); George Regas, Chief Thundercloud (*Indian guides*).

CREDITS:

Director, Elliott Nugent; screenplay, Walter DeLeon and Lynn Starling, from the play by John Willard; producer, Arthur Hornblow Jr.; original music, Ernst Toch and Andrea Setaro; cinematographer, Charles Lang; editor, Archie Marshek; art directors, Hans Dreier and Robert Usher; running time, 72 min.

THE PLOT:

Cyrus Norman Crosby, an eccentric millionaire, passes away. A bizarre clause in his will states that no relative may touch the family fortune for a full ten years. During that decade, several of the people who might inherit part or all of the money like-

Bob Hope and friends cringe in tongue-in-cheek fear.

wise meet their makers, some under dubious circumstances. At last, the long awaited day arrives. An aloof lawyer calls the survivors together in the New Orleans mansion, now spooky owing to the fact that no one has entered it for ten years, for the long-awaited reading of the will. Pretty Joyce Norman is named as the only heir to everything. However, there is a cryptic clause that may keep her from enjoying the fortune. Insanity has always been a major problem in the family, and if Joyce should show any symptoms of mental illness, a second will awaits, naming an alternative heir.

This does not seem likely, for Joyce appears normal. Nonetheless, a maid, Miss Lu, announces that one of the houseguests will die that very night. Shortly thereafter, a man named Hendricks shows up at the door, explaining that a crazed killer, nicknamed "The Cat," has escaped from jail and is somewhere in the area. They could all leave, if they chose, but all are too greedy to pass up the opportunity in case Joyce shows signs of madness. So they remain, even as a previously unseen masked figure steps out of the shadows. Meanwhile, complicating matters further is another recent arrival, glib wiseguy Wally Campbell, who has fallen in love with Joyce and hopes to protect her from her enemies so he can enjoy her considerable charms—and share the money.

THE FILM:

During the early years of the twentieth century, big city theatregoers paid little attention to prestigious playwrights of that time, Eugene O'Neill chief among them, preferring lurid melodramas with broadly drawn characters and arch situations that were, more often than not, set in haunted houses. One of the most durable of these cheesy chestnuts was John Willard's *The Cat and the Canary*, which kept audiences on the edges of their seats for several decades. Initially, the popular item was not filmed because that would have exposed to virtually everyone the trick ending (it is, incidentally, a trick of the most obvious sort, rather than a true Hitchcockian twist), destroying the play's potential as an ongoing moneymaker.

At last, the play was filmed in 1927 by esteemed European director Paul Leni who, like numerous other German, French, and Russian filmmakers, had been imported by studios to class-up the product. The ploy worked. With his remarkable skills for creating a tense pace and eerie atmosphere, Leni redeemed the relatively superficial material through stylish treatment. But if it is true that familiarity breeds contempt, then *The Cat and the Canary* finally had become so well known that it lost its ability to strike fear into the hearts of the public. When the show was staged again during the 1930s, most people found it necessarily to stifle giggles at unintentionally risible situations. It seemed likely the play would be put away in a drawer, like so many other shows that become dated as the public moves on to more sophisticated divertissements.

Then, a uniquely gifted director, Elliott Nugent, appeared on the scene. Son of famed writer J.C. Nugent, he had the inspired idea to openly play the piece for laughs. With this end in mind, Nugent cast Bob Hope, a London-born (1903) comedian, as Wally. Virtually unknown at the time, Bob (real name, Leslie Townes Hope) had been appearing on stage, radio, and in East Coast filmed shorts for Vitagraph, making his feature film debut in *The Big Broadcast of 1938*, where he first sang "Thanks for the Memory." Nugent felt that Hope's sly, tongue-in-cheek delivery could undercut the old-fashioned lines with modern humor, winking at the audience, always letting them know the filmmakers were as aware as viewers that this was being played for suspense *and* fun. Nugent and his collaborating writers stuck with the original plot but peppered it with endless gags. Among the most memorable:

Cicily: Don't big empty houses scare you?
Wally: Not me, I used to be in vaudeville.

TRIVIA:

Bob Hope often cited this as his favorite among the many films in which he had appeared.

ALSO RECOMMENDED:

The film's success led to a repairing of Hope and Goddard under the direction of George Marshall less than a year later. In *The Ghost Breakers* (1940), they maintain the delicate balance between scariness and silliness. This was a predecessor to the highly popular *Ghostbusters* (1984). Perhaps the most successful attempt to recreate the original film's charm was Michael Ritchie's *Fletch* (1985). By all means, catch Leni's 1927 silent *The Cat and Canary*; however dated, it remains an excellent archetype of this appealingly unique sub-genre of suspense thrillers.

95:

NIAGARA (1953)

20th Century Fox

"For a dress like that, you've got to start laying plans when you're about thirteen."
—Polly, as her husband eyeballs Rose

CAST:

Marilyn Monroe (*Rose Loomis*); Joseph Cotten (*George Loomis*); Jean Peters (*Polly Cutler*); Casey Adams (*Ray*); Denis O'Dea (*Inspector Starkey*); Richard Allan (*Patrick*); Don Wilson (*Mr. Kettering*); Lurene Tuttle (*Mrs. Kettering*); Harry Carey Jr. (*Taxi Driver*); Minerva Urecal (*Landlady*).

CREDITS:

Director, Henry Hathaway; screenplay, Charles Brackett and Walter Reisch, from a story by Richard L. Breen; producer, Brackett; original music, Sol Kaplan; cinematographer, Joe MacDonald; editor, Barbara McLean; art directors, Maurice Ransford and Lyle R. Wheeler; running time, 89 min.

THE PLOT:

Embittered George Loomis wanders along the Canadian side of Niagara Falls early one morning, masochistically enjoying the way in which the natural wonder heightens his own sense of smallness. Eventually, he heads back to the motor hotel, where George's considerably younger wife, Rose, sleeps. That day, Polly and Ray Cutler, a Midwestern couple on their belated honeymoon, arrive. While checking in, Polly learns that Mr. Loomis has just been released from a mental hospital.

As the honeymooners tour the falls, Polly spots Rose in the arms of Patrick, Rose's lover. That night, Rose makes a spectacle of herself, dancing wildly in her bright red dress. George makes a scene, cutting himself while breaking a record. While bandaging his hand, Polly learns that Rose is a slut that George picked up in a bar. Under her spell, though, he can't break up with her. According to Rose's plan, Patrick tries to kill George for his money. George, however, foils the plan and kills Patrick. He then stalks

Henry Hathaway's film showcases the natural wonders of Marilyn Monroe *and* Niagara Falls.

Rose, eventually strangling her in the bell tower, even as chimes play her favorite song, "Kiss." George tries to escape in a small boat, taking Polly as his hostage. But they veer out of control, heading toward the falls. A helicopter rescues Polly as George goes over the falls and dies.

THE FILM:

Niagara has the feel of a script left over from the immediate postwar era when, like Loomis, many male characters suffered from shell shock: William Bendix in George Marshall's *The Blue Dahlia* (1946), John Hodiak in Joseph L. Mankiewicz's *Somewhere in the Night* (1946), et. al. Eight years after the Armistice, such types had all but disappeared from the cinematic scene. In terms of technique, however, *Niagara* is certainly a movie of its time. To compete with television, the Fox Studio filmed almost every project in their own rich, vivid, glossy color process, and shot on actual locations. This was true for romances, such as Jean Negulesco's *Three Coins in the Fountain* (1954), as well as thrillers.

Almost every Hitchcockian element is found here, including the theme of a marriage so stifling that it leads to murder. The presence of Joseph Cotten as the sympathetic killer serves as a Hitchcock connection, for he was Hitchcock's favorite actor. The name of Cotten's character presages "Sam Loomis" in Hitchcock's *Psycho* by seven years. Niagara Falls is employed much in the same manner that Hitchcock used the British Museum in *The Man Who Knew Too Much* (1934), the Statue of Liberty in *Saboteur* (1942), and Mt. Rushmore in *North by Northwest* (1959, #8). All are immense icons that dwarf tawdry human affairs. There is a musical MacGuffin, the song that Rose loves and is played on the immense chimes, suggesting her imminent murder. Also, there is the contrast between the good-if-conventional brunette and the bad-but-irresistible blonde, most notable in Hitchcock's contrast between Barbara Bel Geddes and Kim Novak in *Vertigo* (1958).

Why didn't Hitchcock direct *Niagara*? Doubtless he would have been happy to do so if the character of Rose were played as originally written. It was not Monroe he minded (he would probably have been happy to have had her for the supporting part in *Strangers on a Train*), but that Fox now considered her their great new star. Producers built up her role (even giving her a song to sing) to exploit Marilyn's star potential—to the detriment of the other characters, who are less than fully developed—making room for more scenes, many of them unnecessary in terms of plot and/or character, featuring Marilyn. Nonetheless, the film remains powerful. A first-rate studio director, Henry Hathaway, brought his strong sense of craftsmanship to the material, particularly in the overwrought but ravishing suspense sequence in which Rose is stalked by her jealous husband in the

Moment of Passion: Illicit lovers spark the fuse in *Niagara*.

bell tower. It is, simply, one of the greatest Hitchcock-type sequences not shot by the master himself.

TRIVIA:

"Casey Adams" was the name that Fox's image-makers came up with for actor Max Showalter. He played character roles for years, then was dropped from their list of contract players. Despising that moniker, he returned to his original name for future credits, including his small but memorable role as a priest in Blake Edwards's *10* (1979). Originally, *Niagara* was planned as a star vehicle for Anne Baxter, who had recently won an Oscar for *All About Eve* (1950). When she realized the project was turning into a vehicle for Marilyn Monroe, whose part was bigger with each new draft of the script, Baxter withdrew and was replaced by Jean Peters.

ALSO RECOMMENDED:

Monroe fans should catch her in Roy Ward Baker's *Don't Bother to Knock* (1952), in which she convincingly plays a mentally disturbed babysitter. Director Hathaway's other suspense classics include *Call Northside 777* (1948), with James Stewart as a journalist fervently attempting to keep an innocent man (Richard Conte) from being executed.

94:

GASLIGHT (1944)

Metro-Goldwyn-Mayer

"It's all dead in here; the whole place smells of death."
—Paula

CAST:

Charles Boyer (*Gregory Anton*); Ingrid Bergman (*Paula Alquist*); Joseph Cotten (*Brian Cameron*); Dame May Whitty (*Miss Thwaites*); Angela Lansbury (*Nancy Oliver*); Barbara Everest (*Elizabeth Tompkins*); Emil Rameau (*Maestro Mario Guardi*); Edmund Breon (*General Huddleston*); Halliwell Hobbes (*Mr. Muffin*); Tom Stevenson (*Williams*); Heather Thatcher (*Lady Dalroy*); Lawrence Grossmith (*Lord Dalroy*); Jakob Gimpel (*Pianist*); Judy Ford (*Paula as a child*).

CREDITS:

Director, George Cukor; screenplay, John Van Druten, Walter Reisch, and John L. Balderston, from the play *Angel Street* by Patrick Hamilton; producer, Arthur Hornblow Jr.; original music, Bronislau Kaper and (piano solos) Jakob Gimpel; cinematographer, Joseph Ruttenberg; editor, Ralph E. Winters; art directors, Cedric Gibbons and William Ferrari; special sound effects, Joe Edmondson; special visual effects, Waren Newcombe; running time, 114 min.

THE PLOT:

During the Victorian era, a highly regarded opera singer, Alice Alquist, is strangled to death at 9 Thornton Square. Her young niece, Paula, who was living with the performer, found the body in front of the fireplace. Paula is taken from the dark scene and raised in Italy by a kindly maestro who asks Paula to try and forget the terrible memories. He attempts to turn her into a great singer like her aunt, though after ten years, Paula considers leaving the profession to marry and live a normal life with suave, handsome Gregory Anton. While making up her mind, Paula journeys to Lake Como by train and is befriended by an eccentric elderly lady, Miss Thwaites, who is always either reading murder-mystery novels or talking about them.

Paula marries Gregory and they move into the London home of her late aunt, whose murder has never been solved. Quickly, though, their dream life goes awry, as Paula comes to believe the house is haunted. Things seem alright when Gregory is there to comfort her, yet whenever she is alone, Paula notices that the gaslights turn themselves down, while eerie noises can be heard throughout the home. At first, Gregory laughs off her superstitions. In time, he begins to fear his wife is mad. When he gives Paula a beautiful brooch as a token of his great love, she immediately loses the valuable item, and she's too terrified to tell him, fearing he will have her committed to an asylum.

Scotland Yard's Brian Cameron learns of the situation from Miss Thwaites and begins an unofficial investigation of his own. In time, he realizes Paula—now on the edge of absolute madness—is gradually being driven insane by her husband. Gregory planned to eventually marry and then murder Paula ever since that day, ten years earlier, when he killed Alice Alquist, with whom he had become infatuated. More recently, he planned to eliminate his wife in order to now share the mansion with his mistress, Nancy Oliver, though Cameron and Thwaites put an end to his plot.

THE FILM:

During the early 1940s, Hollywood went quite mad for Alfred Hitchcock. His first directorial effort for producer David O. Selznick, *Rebecca* (1940), had won the Oscar for Best Picture of the Year, and the best of his English movies, most notably *The Lady Vanishes* (1938), had been imported and were hugely popular. Every major studio wanted its own faux Hitchcock thriller about a beautiful young woman in peril, and *Gaslight* (1944) was MGM's entry in the suspense sweepstakes. The plot device of a beautiful young woman verging on madness while in the company of a handsome but mysterious husband had been the premise of *Rebecca*. The notion of a young woman being befriended by a chatty elderly woman played by Dame May Witty had provided the central metaphor for *The Lady Vanishes* and *Suspicion* (1941). MGM even borrowed two contract players from Selznick, Ingrid Bergman and Joseph Cotten; the latter had already starred for Hitchcock in *Shadow of a Doubt* (1943) while the former would shortly become one of his favorite leading ladies in such films as *Spellbound* (1945) and *Notorious* (1946).

The actual director was George Cukor, famed as "the woman's director" thanks to his expert helming of such projects as *Little Women* (1933), Hollywood's only all-female film *The Women* (1939), and numerous other movies. Here, Cukor effectively employed the suspense approach that characterized Hitchcock's female-in-distress thrillers while adding a level of sympathy for the heroine that exceeds our emotional response in the similarly themed Hitchcock movies.

TRIVIA:

Ingrid Bergman won her first Oscar for her portrayal of Paula, while Angela Lansbury (who was nominated in the best supporting category) made her debut in this film. The story had been filmed four years earlier in England under the title of Patrick Hamilton's stage play, *Angel Street*. MGM—terrified that some enterprising distributor might import that film and release it before their own was completed—tried (without success) to destroy every existing print and the original neg-

The Tables are Turned: Charles Boyer finds himself threatened by Ingrid Bergman, his supposed victim.

ative. When *Gaslight* was released in England, the title was changed to *The Murder in Thornton Square* to avoid confusion.

ALSO RECOMMENDED:

Fortunately, Thorold Dickinson's excellent 1940 version survives and, despite its lack of star-power (Anton Walbrook and Diana Wynyard play the leads) or the opulence that was the hallmark of MGM, the English version is far more attentive to the Victorian-era atmosphere and emerges as an even more thrilling, if considerably less sumptuous, production. Fans of Bergman in such roles should not miss Hitchcock's *Spellbound* (1945), in which her wide-eyed heroine is matched with an irresistibly dangerous Gregory Peck.

93:
HOUSE OF WAX (1953)

Warner Bros.

"Why be afraid, my dear? I am going to make you immortal!"
—Prof. Jarrod to bound, naked Sue Allen
as he prepares to cover her in hot wax

CAST:

Vincent Price (*Professor Henry Jarrod*); Frank Lovejoy (*Lieutenant Tom Brennan*); Phyllis Kirk (*Sue Allen*); Carolyn Jones (*Cathy Gray*); Paul Picerni (*Scott Andrews*); Roy Roberts (*Matthew Burke*); Angela Clarke (*Mrs. Andrews*); Paul Cavanagh (*Sidney Wallace*); Dabbs Greer (*Sergeant Jim Shane*); Charles Bronson as Charles Buchinsky (*Igor*); Reggie Rymal (*The Barker*).

CREDITS:

Director, André De Toth; screenplay, Crane Wilbur and Charles Belden; producer, Bryan Foy; original music, David Buttolph and Maurice De Pack; cinematographers, Bert Glennon and Peverell Marley; editor, Rudi Fehr; art director, Stanley Fleischer; special makeup effects, George and Gordon Bau; running time, 88 min.

THE PLOT:

Gentle genius Henry Jarrod, who creates brilliant wax tableaus in his Victorian-era New York City showroom, is obsessed with his beautiful Marie Antoinette figure. When his corrupt business partner Burke decides to burn the place down to cash in on insurance, the distraught Jarrod is trapped inside and, so far as anyone knows, killed. Some time later, he re-emerges, apparently unscathed in terms of appearance, though now wheelchair-bound. Jarrod opens a new house of wax featuring even more lifelike figures than before. Meanwhile, the city's streets are menaced by a mysterious cloaked killer, who abducts beautiful women and kills off Jarrod's old enemies. When pretty showgirl Cathy Gray disappears, her roommate and friend Sue Allen wonders if perhaps Cathy hasn't been covered with wax, for the new Marie Antoinette looks suspiciously like Cathy.

The mysterious phantom menaces Phyllis Kirk.

At night, Sue slips inside and discovers she was right. She's captured by Jarrod (the wheelchair was a ruse and his seemingly normal face is actually a wax mask that covers scarred skin) and his brutish assistant, Igor. As they are about to cover Sue with hot wax and decapitate her boyfriend Scott with a guillotine, a police lieutenant and his team barge in and rescue them, and Jarrod falls to his death in boiling wax.

THE FILM:

The 3-D craze hit theatres in 1953, when a low-budget action-thriller called *Bwana Devil* had most everyone in America donning uncomfortable glasses to see (according to studio hype) "a lover in your arms, a lion in your lap!" Unlike widescreen formats, devised the following year (likewise, to lure viewers away from their TV sets), 3-D shortly wore out its welcome, as it proved to be more a gimmick than a valid storytelling technique. What Warners hailed as "the first 3-D feature by a major studio" also turned out to be the last. *House of Wax* was also the best, taking a sturdy, worthwhile tale and enhancing its thriller impact via images of hot wax being poured directly into the audience. "You've never been scared until you've been scared in 3-D!" the advertising tag line rightly bragged.

Studio-hand André de Toth created an effectively eerie mood, conveyed in vivid color. At the time, it was widely believed that a thriller ought to be shot in black and white. Most historians cite Hammer's *Horror of Dracula* (1958) and Roger Corman's *House of Usher* (1960) as early experiments which proved how effective color can be in horror movies; though *House of Wax*—five years ahead of its time in that respect—made color's potential abundantly clear.

TRIVIA:

Turn-of-the-century New York is made to appear like a combination of Paris, with its macabre theatrical performances, and London, as fog constantly drifts in. The plot is a reworking (and unofficial remake) of *The Phantom of the Opera* (1925), combined with elements drawn from the original thriller, *The Cabinet of Dr. Caligari* (1919). In fact, when released in West Germany, where that legendary film remains a part of the popular consciousness, *House of Wax* was retitled *Das Kabinett des Professor Bondi*. The story had been filmed before, as *Mystery of the Wax Museum* (1933). This was the first film in which Vincent Price played an over-the-top figure of horror. John Brahm's *The Mad Magician* (1954)—similar if less ambitious—was released simultaneously, establishing Price as the logical heir to Lugosi. In addition to top-billed Price, the film was filled with attractive young people, all hoping to become major movie stars. When that didn't happen, all of them achieved a middling level of success on series television: Phyllis Kirk (*The Thin Man*), Frank Lovejoy (*Meet McGraw*), Carolyn Jones (*The Addams Family*), and Paul Picerni (*The Untouchables*). Had anyone suggested then that the grotesque-looking fellow who played "Igor" would in due time become the world's biggest box-office attraction, the obvious reaction would have been laughter. Shortly, though, Charles Buchinsky changed his last name to Bronson and went on to accomplish precisely that. The film features an innovative deconstruction device, when an onstage barker wielding a paddleball threatens to knock the popcorn bag out of the hand of an onscreen spectator, then whams it beyond that man and into the audience watching *House of Wax* in 3-D. All across the country, viewers screamed and held tight their own bags of popcorn.

ALSO RECOMMENDED:

Like the better known remake, *Mystery of the Wax Museum* (1933) featured an innovative (and remarkably early!) use of color in a horror thriller. Directed by the esteemed Michael Curtiz, that film had been shot in the original two-hue Technicolor process some six years before *Gone With the Wind* and *The Wizard of Oz*. Lionel Atwill and Fay Wray (queen of the screamers) are the stars in an effectively eerie if notably understated version of the tale.

92:

THE USUAL SUSPECTS (1995)

PolyGram Filmed Entertainment

> **"This guy is protected from up on high**
> **by the Prince of Darkness."**
> **—Jeff Rabin, on Keyser Soze**

CAST:

Gabriel Byrne (*Dean Keaton*); Kevin Spacey (*Roger "Verbal" Kint*); Stephen Baldwin (*Spencer McManus*); Chazz Palminteri (*Dave Kujan*); Pete Postlethwaite (*Kobayashi*); Kevin Pollak (*Todd Hockney*); Benicio Del Toro (*Fred Fenster*); Suzy Amis (*Edie Finneran*); Giancarlo Esposito (*Jack Baer*); Dan Hedaya (*Jeff Rabin*); Paul Bartel (*Smuggler*); Scott B. Morgan (*"Keyser Soze"* in flashback).

CREDITS:

Director, Bryan Singer; screenplay, Christopher McQuarrie; producers, Singer and Michael McDonnell; original music, John Ottman; cinematographer, Newton Thomas Sigel; film editor, John Ottman; running time, 105 min; rating, R.

THE PLOT:

Forlorn, crippled con-man Verbal Kint is dragged into a police precinct, where he tells the investigating officers about a waterfront explosion he witnessed and somehow survived. A boat that exploded on the San Pedro pier took twenty-seven people down with it, though ninety-one million dollars in drug money was found after the smoke cleared. Six weeks earlier, five diverse men had been hauled in by the police for a line up—they, the usual suspects of the title—and questioned about a crime none had committed. However, they threw in their lot together, gradually realizing their meeting was not accidental—this was either a stroke of fate or planned by some devious character. A subsequent hijacking incident leads directly to the deadly occurance now being investigated.

Among those men is Keaton, a charismatic but dangerous born leader of activities, mostly criminal in nature. Once a cop, Keaton was dropped from the force for corruption and swears to one and all he only wants to go straight. Still, he's desperate enough for cash to allow himself to be talked into participating in one final heist. Unseen during all this is mastermind Keyser Soze. As Verbal tells the cops, "You think you can catch Keyser Soze? You think a guy like that comes this close to getting caught, and sticks his head out? If he comes up for anything it'll be to get rid of me. After that . . . my guess is you'll never hear from him again." Finally, the police allow Verbal to crawl out of the precinct. No sooner is he gone—picked up by a mysterious limo—than officer Kujan begins to wonder if perhaps Verbal might have been Keyser.

The Line-up: Kevin Spacey (far right) and fellow lowlifes (left to right) Kevin Pollak, Stephen Baldwin, Benicio Del Toro, and Gabriel Byrne, in *The Usual Suspects*.

THE FILM:

While on a lunch break at a solicitor's office, would-be writer Chris McQuarrie studied the notice board on the wall and constructed a plot from bits and pieces of information listed there. Most people assume that Chaz Palminteri's character is correct in assuming, at the end, that the seemingly harmless Verbal Kint was the monstrous Keyser Soze. Just before leaving the precinct, he is given back all the belongings he had to check on arrival. They include a gold watch and gold cigarette lighter, leading us to believe he's the mystery man, since Keyser employed both items in flashbacks. Moreover, the word "Soze" means "talks incessantly" in Turkish, which would suggest Verbal, who cannot keep quiet, is the man. However, when first-nighters asked Gabriel Byrne who he believed Keyser Soze to be, the actor replied, "During shooting and until watching the film tonight, I thought *I* was!" One theory, advanced by die-hard cineastes, is that the man who drives Verbal away at the end is Keyser, while Verbal is a lackey who has done and said all at Kesyer's bidding. This is upheld by two memorable tag lines: "In a world where nothing is what it seems you've got to look beyond" and "The greatest trick the Devil ever pulled was convincing the world he didn't exist."

Audiences delighted in the plot reversals, particularly the film's final shot, which have their origin in *The Cabinet of Dr. Caligari* (1919) and Hitchcock's oeuvre. The Academy honored the film with an Oscar for Best Original Screenplay. It's worth noting, though, that several influential critics did not agree with this estimation. Leonard Maltin insists that "if you think about it, the final twist negates the entire film!", claiming that the "highly-praised" movie was "too clever for its own good." Roger Ebert agreed; "There was less to understand than the movie at first suggests. The story builds up to a blinding revelation, which shifts the nature of all that has gone before, and the surprise filled me not with delight," rather with the feeling that the filmmakers were guilty of audience manipulation in place of character motivation.

TRIVIA:

The screenwriter and producers created the role of Verbal for Kevin Spacey. He was at that time still relatively unknown but greatly respected as a character actor. Spacey won the Best Supporting Actor Oscar for his role and immediately was catapulted to superstar status. The horrific Keyser Soze was inspired by a real-life murderer named John List. The film's title is inspired by one of Claude Rains's lines from *Casablanca* (1942). Also in deference to that classic is the fact that the production company for *Usual Suspects*, The Blue Parrot, derives from Sydney

Greenstreet's African nightclub. Though by the mid-nineties, most films were edited electronically and then transferred to film, John Ottman insisted on editing on film in the old-fashioned tradition.

ALSO RECOMMENDED:

Like Quentin Tarantino's *Reservoir Dogs* (1992) and so many recent films about an odd assortment of loners embarking on a crime, *The Usual Suspects* is in part inspired by John Huston's legendary film *The Asphalt Jungle* (1950), starring Sterling Hayden and featuring Marilyn Monroe.

91:

VILLAGE OF THE DAMNED (1960)

Metro-Goldwyn-Mayer

"Beware the stare that will paralyze the world!"
—advertising tag line

CAST:

George Sanders (*Gordon Zellaby*); Barbara Shelley (*Anthea Zellaby*); Michael Gwynn (*Alan Bernard*); Laurence Naismith (*Doctor Willers*); John Phillips (*General Leighton*); Richard Vernon (*Sir Edgar*); Jenny Laird (*Mrs. Harrington*); Richard Warner (*Harrington*); Carlo Cura, Lesley Scoble, Mark Milleham, Roger Malik, Elizabeth Munden, Theresa Scoble, Janice Howley, Paul Norman, Robert Marks, John Bush, Billy Lawrence, Peter Preidel, Peter Taylor, Howard Knight, and Brian Smith (*"The Children"*).

CREDITS:

Director, Wolf Rilla; screenplay, Rilla, Stirling Silliphant, and George Barclay, from the novel *The Midwich Cuckoos* by John Wyndham; producer, Ronald Kinnoch; original music, Ron Goodwin; cinematographer, Geoffrey Faithfull; editor, Gordon Hales; art director, Ivan King; special makeup effects, Tom Howard; special photographic effects, Eric Aylott; running time, 78 min.

The perfect . . . too perfect . . . children of Midwich.

The Plot:

On a seemingly normal day, the small, remote village of Midwich undergoes a strange experience. Everyone suddenly falls asleep in the mid-afternoon. When they eventually wake, no one appears any the worse for wear. Within a few months, however, all the women in the village find themselves pregnant. Each in time gives birth to a beautiful child that grows up looking like a member of some super-race: blonde, intelligent, though aloof, with strange, penetrating eyes. These children share a singular vision and congregate together, with no sense of loyalty to family. One by one, the villagers come to believe the women were impregnated by alien beings during that long ago period of afternoon slumber, but all are afraid to say anything to outsiders for fear they would be considered crazy.

When a motorist accidentally almost runs down one of the children, the others surround him and telepathically cause the man to lose control. Purposefully, he crashes his car into a wall. When that man's brother arrives and attempts to kill one of the children with a shotgun, the others gather around again and stare at him until he instead turns the gun on himself. Professor Gordon Zellaby argues against the military officers who want to isolate the children for the protection of the community, hoping to reason with the strange beings. Gradually realizing that they intend to take over the world, he takes it on himself to destroy them by visiting them with dynamite while he concentrates on a brick wall. The children focus on melting down his mental wall, but before they can, they are killed in the ensuing explosion.

THE FILM:

MGM planned to shoot *The Midwich Cuckoos* in the United States, until the Catholic Legion of Decency protested. The organization feared that the novel's vision, if brought to a wider audience via motion pictures, would corrupt the country. The Catholic hierarchy insisted all belief in aliens went against Biblical teachings, and that this particular sci-fi story was particularly odious, mocking the idea of virgin birth. Producer Ron Kinnoch and director Wolf Rilla, dedicated to bringing John Wyndham's subtle mid-thirties thriller to the screen, headed for England, where they could shoot entirely in a quaint village called Letchmore Heath. This leant their movie a unique, timeless quality, removing the film's mise-en-scène from ordinary American settings that had become de rigueur for B-budget sci-fi flicks during the passing decade. The British setting also cemented a relationship with the master of suspense for, as Les Wright has noted, "The film's effectiveness emerges from implied horror, the signature 'veiled threat approach' of Hitchcock." Recently, Dennis Schwartz added, "By keeping everything elementary and not relying on gimmicks or special effects, *Village of the Damned* remains an intelligent creepy tale that has not lost its luster over time."

This was the most innovative alien-invader movie since *Invasion of the Body Snatchers* (1956), likewise achieving its impact by eschewing monsters with zippers running up their costumed backs for the implied scariness of the unknown. *Village* relates to *Invasion* in yet another way: Once again, those who have been taken over by the seeds from space are less monstrous in any conventional sense but, ironically, "perfect"—without any cruelty or rage yet devoid of all other human emotion as well. Even when we do see "the creatures," the effect is entirely original, for adorable little children in every sense but one—their glow-in-the-dark eyes—project the terror that ordinarily would derive from something huge and ugly.

TRIVIA:

The original novel's title refers to the habit of the cuckoo bird to drop its eggs in the nests of other birds and allow them to nurture its young. Though the film looks like a carefully mounted A-budget production, the entire cost of filming was a mere $300,000, with George Sanders the only "name" star. He took the part largely because this was one of the rare heroic roles he was offered, having been typecast as a villain, most notably in Alfred Hitchcock's *Rebecca* (1940).

ALSO RECOMMENDED:

Village of the Damned set the pace for an entire cycle of suspense-thrillers in the 1970s that focused on demonic children, the most famous being *The Exorcist* (1973) and Richard Donner's *The Omen* (1976), in which Gregory Peck must, like George Sanders here, attempt to kill his own adorable child. Another great British sci-fi/thriller from the same era is Val Guest's *The Day the Earth Caught Fire* (1961), starring Janet Munro. Fans of Sanders will want to catch his other heroic role as the title character in *The Falcon* series of B-movie detective-thrillers; the third and best is *The Falcon Takes Over* (1942), from a Raymond Chandler novel.

90:
BLUE VELVET (1986)

De Laurentiis

"I'm seeing something that was always hidden."
—Jeffrey Beaumont

CAST:

Isabella Rossellini (*Dorothy Vallens*); Kyle MacLachlan (*Jeffrey Beaumont*); Dennis Hopper (*Frank Booth*); Laura Dern (*Sandy Williams*); Hope Lange (*Mrs. Williams*); Dean Stockwell (*Ben*); George Dickerson (*Detective John D. Williams*); Priscilla Pointer (*Mrs. Beaumont*); Frances Bay (*Aunt Barbara*); Jack Harvey (*Tom Beaumont*); Ken Stovitz (*Mike*); Brad Dourif (*Raymond*); Jack Nance *(Paul)*.

CREDITS:

Director, David Lynch; screenplay, Lynch; producer, Fred Caruso and Richard Roth; original music, Angelo Badalamenti and Lynch; cinematographer, Frederick Elmes; editor, Duwayne Dunham; production designer, Patricia Norris; special makeup effects, Dean Gates; running time, 120 min.; rating: R.

THE PLOT:

Lumberton is a small logging town town that appears to have popped out of a Norman Rockwell painting. Jeffrey Beaumont, a naive college student who has returned to town to visit his dying father, happens upon a severed human ear while taking a shortcut through an empty lot. Dutifully, Jeffrey delivers the ear (in a paper bag) to Detective Williams. That night, while his mother and aunt watch mysteries on TV, Jeffrey slips out to visit the dark side of town that he either never knew existed—or, if he did know, he had made it a point to avoid. Jeffrey can no longer do that. What he discovered has awoken within him the long-repressed desire to know by experience the full, terrible reality of what he envisioned as a sacrosanct place, one not tinged by the corruption that has turned big cities into styes. Accompanying him on this journey from innocence to experience is the detective's pretty blond daughter, Sandy, a timeless variation on Sandra Dee from 1950s iconography. Sandy tells Jeffrey about Dorothy Vallens, a mysterious singer who remains housebound nearby, and the two curious teenagers decide to investigate on their own.

The following night, Jeffrey and Sandy catch Dorothy's act (a variation on Marlene Dietrich as The Blue Angel) at a retro-art deco nightclub. While Dorothy performs, Jeffrey sneaks into her apartment, hiding when she re-enters. Dorothy strips down to luridly exotic underwear, talking on the phone with a perverted killer, Frank, who has kidnapped Dorothy's family to hold her as a sex slave. Discovering Jeffrey in the closet, Dorothy turns the tables and makes him her slave, forcing the youth at knifepoint to strip. Then the terrifying Frank shows up and Jeffrey must hide again. While Frank forces Dorothy to have twisted, kinky sex, Jeffrey voyeuristically watches, too terrified to move, too fascinated to look away. When Frank leaves, Jeffrey tries to console Dorothy, but she insists he abuse her, too.

Though he hurries off to the wholesome Sandy, Jeffrey feels compelled to return to Dorothy's apartment and becomes her lover. Gradually, the once innocent Jeffrey realizes he is the monstrous Frank in embryo, becoming more and more like that human-monster all the time. Finally, he kills Frank, less to save Dorothy and others from this madman than to destroy what he fears is a twisted mirror image of himself.

The film ends with Frank's gang smashed by the police, Dorothy reunited with her child, and Jeffrey and Sandy together. In the final scene, we see the two of them gazing at a red robin, which is perched on the windowsill with a large black insect dangling from its beak. This is a reference to Sandy's earlier dream about robins bringing the "Blinding Light of Love" and ridding the world of all the bad things, all the Franks. But what is interesting about this robin is that it is clearly fake, a puppet. The "robin of love" isn't real; it's a dream. In the last line of dialogue in the film, Sandy says, "It's a strange world, isn't it?" and Jeffrey nods in agreement.

The film ends by replicating the beginning, with earlier images playing in reverse order: yellow tulips before a white picket fence, a red fire truck moving slowly down the street with a fireman waving, red tulips against a white fence. We then see little Donny running with his arms outstretched toward Dorothy who is seated on a park bench. As she cradles her son in her arms, tears form in her eyes and she is heard singing in the background: "And I still can see Blue Velvet through my tears." The camera pulls upward and loses focus as it fills the screen with blue sky and then dissolves into undulating blue velvet.

THE FILM:

About Alfred Hitchcock's *Shadow of a Doubt* (1943), John Russell Taylor has written: "Hitch particularly relished giving violence and menace a local habitation ... setting extraordinary happenings against very humdrum, everyday surroundings. And, too, he was fascinated by the omnipresence of evil, the fact that there was no refuge from it ... murder, evidently, was something happening just down the street, behind the most respectable facade. Every little town has its share of evil, and a sleepy backwater is not exempt, even if it seems like a paradise of innocence." Those words just as effectively describe *Blue Velvet*. It's difficult to believe that Lynch did not

Deadlier Than the Male: Kyle MacLachlan falls under the spell of Isabella Rossellini in *Blue Velvet*.

consciously create this as his own updated *Shadow*, taking the dark ideas that Hitchcock had left as subtexts and bringing them to the surface.

Most students of Hitchcock have noted that, despite the supposed realism of such films as *Shadow*—shot on actual locations for absolute authenticity—he is something of a surrealist. Hitchcock employed the formal elements of film—lighting, angles, camera movements, music and sound—to warp the experience of watching what appears to be actual people in the real world. He transformed his objective mise-en-scène into a highly subjective, subtly distorted vision of life. *Blue Velvet* continues and furthers that approach. The movie's "world" is cinematically painted in garish strokes and florid coloring, unlike anything seen since the golden age of Douglas Sirk, particularly *Written on the Wind* (1957). The setting emerges as Thornton Wilder's *Our Town* by way of L. Frank Baum's *Oz*.

TRIVIA:

Filming locations were in Lumberton and Wilmington, North Carolina. When the film premiered (September 12, 1986) at the Toronto Film Festival, it was greeted by equally intense cheering and booing by the audience of film buffs and movie reviewers. The first name of Isabella Rossellini's character is an homage to *The Wizard of Oz*, David Lynch's favorite film, other than the Hitchcock classics. She even wears ruby red slippers at one point. Dennis Hopper reportedly read the script and announced, "I've *got* to play Frank because I *am* Frank." Jack Nance, who plays a supporting role, starred in Lynch's first major movie, *Eraserhead* (1978). Brat-packer Molly Ringwald turned down the role of "Sandy" and Val Kilmer passed on "Jeffrey."

ALSO RECOMMENDED:

Many Lynch fans believe *Mulholland Drive* (2002) to be his most effectively suspenseful work since *Blue Velvet*. Certainly, it is his other best exercise in the thriller genre.

89:

D.O.A. (1949)

United Artists

"I want to report a murder—*mine*!"
—Frank Bigelow (opening line)

CAST:

Edmond O'Brien (*Frank Bigelow*); Pamela Britton (*Paula Gibson*); Luther Adler (*Majak*); Beverly Campbell (*Miss Foster*); Lynn Baggett (*Mrs. Philips*);

William Ching (*Halliday*); Henry Hart (*Stanley Philips*); Neville Brand (*Chester*); Laurette Luez (*Maria*).

CREDITS:

Director, Rudolph Mate; screenplay, Russell Rouse, Clarence Green, and (supervision) Arnold Laven; producers, Leo C. and Harry M. Popkin; music, Dimitri Tiomkin; cinematographer, Ernest Laszlo; art direction, Duncan Cramer; running time, 83 min.

THE PLOT:

Police officers in a San Francisco precinct are having a rather quiet day when a distraught man wanders in, looks at them nervously, then tells the detectives that he wants to report a murder—his own. Initially, they are in a state of disbelief. Then Frank Bigelow begins to explain the bizarre events that occurred over the past two days. A certified public accountant in the small town of Banning, he'd left his secretary (and lover) Paula behind when he headed to San Francisco for several days of rest and relaxation. That first night, he visited a jazz club. In a flashback, the viewer sees what Frank does not: a man in the shadows slips something into Bigelow's drink. The following morning, he wakes up feeling ill and visits a doctor. The stunned medical man informs Bigelow he's been poisoned and has less than forty-eight hours to live. Hysterical, Bigelow runs down streets of this vertigo-inducing city, as though by doing this, he might somehow escape the poison deep inside him.

Realizing there is no antidote for his situation, he decides to catch those who sealed his fate before death overtakes him. As he's a nasty man, often involved in shady dealings, there are many people to suspect. At one point, he even begins to believe Paula, whom he has treated shabbily, may have ordered the "hit." Meanwhile, an assortment of shady characters, including a brutal psycho killer named Chester, attempt to keep Bigelow from discovering what has happened. In time, though, he and Paula (constantly conversing on the phone) realize that several months ago, Frank signed a routine form allowing a shipment of iridium to pass from one company to another. After learning that the owner of an L.A. firm that handled the transportation has died in precisely the same manner, Bigelow realizes he has not been targeted for any of the sordid things he has done in his life. Instead, he's part of a large group of people who are being killed because they had played some small part in the illegal shipment. The powers behind the conspiracy plan to murder every single person who might possibly reveal their identity. This plan led them to small-timer Bigelow, who, most likely, would never have checked those files again.

With time running out, Bigelow tracks down Mr. Big, an upscale sleazy character named Majak, and enacts his own justice. Then, he wanders off to police headquarters. After relating his strange story, he drops dead before their eyes. When an officer asks the lieutenant what they should label the corpse, he tells them to mark Bigelow "Dead on Arrival."

THE FILM:

An independently financed film (A Popkin Production) released on a limited basis late in 1949, it later received wider distribution from United Artists. *D.O.A.* beautifully characterizes the style known as film noir—"films of the night." Those

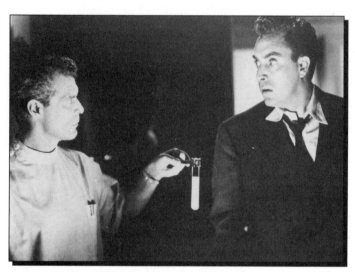

Edmond O'Brien gets the bad news in *D.O.A.*

postwar melodramas concern shifty loners walking the mean streets of some menacing city, threatened by deliciously deadly women, rough urban rednecks, and silky-suited villains with aristocratic manners and base motives. Is *D.O.A.* the best noir ever? That's debatable, though there's no question that this is the most *suspenseful* noir-genre entry, owing to a ticking clock that actually outdoes the later and more famous one in *High Noon* (1952). As Carl Macek has noted, "*D.O.A.* is a prime example of a thriller accentuated by factors of cynicism, alienation, chaos, and the corrupt nature of society to convey a dark vision of contemporary America. . . . It typifies the hopeless plight of people manipulated by forces they are unable to control or comprehend," leading to an "existential outlook." Also significant is that the new and experimental forms of jazz, pioneered during the postwar period, are incorporated into *D.O.A.* This element introduced the public at large to the sound that would characterize edgy music during the upcoming Beat Generation era.

TRIVIA:

Though most often described as a unique piece of Hollywood filmmaking, *D.O.A.* was actually a remake of a fine (if little known) German film by Robert Siodmak called *Der Mann der seinen Mörder sucht* (1931). Many German films of the twenties and early thirties, with their shadowy worlds and sense of conspiracy, serve as predecessors to the Hollywood noirs of the late forties and fifties, when our society would become as paranoid as Germany had been twenty years earlier. Numerous German-Jewish directors had left their country when Hitler rose to power, migrating first to England, then America. Most worked first for Carl Laemmle at Universal (he had emigrated earlier), then later for numerous other studios.

ALSO RECOMMENDED:

Robert Siodmak was responsible for noir classics with great thriller appeal such as *The Dark Mirror* (1946) with Olivia de Havilland as twins—one normal, the other crazy and potentially homicidal. Another classic is *The Killers* (1946), from the Ernest Hemingway short story, featuring Ava Gardner (at her femme fatale best) and Burt Lancaster (in his first film role). In *Cry of the City* (1948), Victor Mature and Richard Conte fight over Shelley Winters and the unofficial control of New York City.

88:

THE LAST OF SHEILA (1973)

Warner Bros.

> **"My mouth is so dry they could shoot *Lawrence of Arabia* in it."**
> **—Christine**

CAST:

Richard Benjamin (*Tom*); Dyan Cannon (*Christine*); James Coburn (*Clinton Green*); Joan Hackett (*Lee*); James Mason (*Philip*); Ian McShane (*Anthony*); Raquel Welch (*Alice*); Yvonne Romaine (*Sheila Green*); Pierre Rosso (*Vittorio*); Serge Citon (*Guido*); Roberto Rossi (*Captain*).

CREDITS:

Director, Herbert Ross; screenplay, Anthony Perkins and Stephen Sondheim; producers, Ross and Stanley O'Toole; original music, Billy Golden-
berg; cinematographer, Gerry Turpin; editor, Edward Warschilka;
production design, Ken Adam; art director, Tony Roman; running time,
120 min.; rating, PG.

THE PLOT:

One year ago, someone killed Sheila—the beautiful wife of movie producer Clinton Green—in a hit-and-run accident. On the anniversary of that incident, Green
invites six "friends" to join him on his luxury yacht, which is named after the
deceased lady, for a week of cruising along southern France's coastline. Rising star
Alice is always oblivious while talent agent Christine delivers brittle, bitchy bon
mots with dispassionate cruelty. Past-his-prime director Philip considers all the
others from his world-weary outlook. Once aboard, each guest realizes he or she
was selected for a sinister reason. Any might have been the person who killed
Sheila, by accident or on purpose. But to abandon ship would be tatamount to
admitting guilt, so each guest continues on, playing a clever little game.

Each guest receives a piece of paper that relates a long-hidden secret from the
past of one of the other guests. One, we learn, is an alcoholic, another a homosexual, a third a child molester, and so on. Each is to try and deduce, from clues
hidden everywhere, which secret applies to which fellow traveler. The tone, however, remains genteel while the Cote d'Azur surroundings are elegant. As a series of
murders plague the guests, mystery writer Tom and his wife Lee try to solve them
by treating the situation as if it were one of his own thriller scripts. All the while,
Green watches and listens, knowing that in revealing each other's hidden pasts,
the members of his entourage will eventually—if inadvertently—reveal Sheila's
killer. Until, that is, he turns up dead, and the others must continue trying to solve
the puzzle without him.

THE FILM:

In the late sixties and early seventies, critics and audiences alike lauded the new
freedom of the screen, which had led to such unsparingly realistic films as *Midnight Cowboy* (1970) and *Carnal Knowledge* (1971). Shortly, though, they would
mourn the death of old-fashioned entertainments, particularly those sophisticated
mystery-thrillers mounted with all-star casts, upscale international settings, witty
dialogue, and a touch of class. Though many believed such movies would never

Cruise to Terror: James Coburn (third from left) welcomes his guests (left to right) James Mason, Raquel Welch, Joan Hackett, Ian McShane, Dyan Cannon, and Richard Benjamin, in *The Last of Sheila*.

again appear, two unlikely fans of the labyrinthian suspense thriller—actor Anthony Perkins and composer Stephen Sondheim—decided to do something about it. They collaborated on a film that gently spoofed the genre while wholeheartedly reviving it. They also added modern touches—an overt sexuality and dollops of graphic violence not possible in previous incarnations. In so doing, they created a bridge between the high-camp approach of the sixties and the post-modernism of the eighties.

Owing to the writers' inside knowledge of the film industry, past and (then) present, *The Last of Sheila* provides accurate, on-target portraits of Hollywood types at that time. Arguably, there was no need to caricature such people since they were already living caricatures. As Vincent Canby noted, "They are beautiful but edgy people, the kind who greet good jokes with a rating ('That's beautiful') rather than laughter . . . even casual conversation can be a form of competition. The wisecrack is the weapon." Like many other critics at the time, Canby likened the film to an after-dinner party game played by self-consciously sophisticated (some might say pseudo-sophisticated) people who trip themselves up with their virtuoso displays of cleverness. "More important to me," he continued, "was the generally festive air in which all this mayhem takes place, as well as the charming

Agatha Christie manners that are observed. As plot points are explained, people get themselves drinks from the bar. If someone is murdered, the pall of gloom lasts for a maximum of five minutes. Beautiful people, after all, haven't got time to be nice."

TRIVIA:

Sondheim and Perkins were inveterate game players, and they devised the film's plot as a means of sharing their passion with the public. Joel Schumacher, later to emerge as a major Hollywood director, designed the film's costumes. Those who love to play spot the "movie goofs" note a real whopper in this film. At one point, the guests all stand in front of the good ship *Sheila* and pose for a group photo; Christine is wearing her sunglasses. However, when the photo is seen later in the movie, she is no longer wearing them.

ALSO RECOMMENDED:

Fans of director Herbert Ross will want to see his other seminal thriller, *The Seven-Per-Cent Solution* (1976), based on a novel by Nicholas Meyer and featuring an off-beat story about Sherlock Holmes (Nicol Williamson) and Dr. Watson (Robert Duvall). They join forces with Sigmund Freud (Alan Arkin) to apprehend evil Moriarty (Laurence Olivier). Fans of *Sheila* should also catch Sidney Lumet's *Murder On the Orient Express* (1974), in which a similar group of upscale characters (this time set in the Victorian age) likewise confront the murderer among them.

87:

SCREAM (1996)

Dimension

> **"Horror movies are always about some big-breasted blond who can't act, running upstairs when she should run out the door."**
> **—Sidney Prescott**

CAST:

Neve Campbell (*Sidney "Sid" Prescott*); Skeet Ulrich (*William "Billy" Loomis*); Courteney Cox (*Gale Weathers*); David Arquette (*Deputy Dwight*

"*Dewey*" *Riley*); Drew Barrymore (*Casey Becker*); Rose McGowan (*Tatum Riley*); Matthew Lillard (*Stuart "Stu" Macher*); Jamie Kennedy (*Randy Meeks*); W. Earl Brown (*Cameraman Kenny Jones*); Joseph Whipp (*Sheriff Burke*); Liev Schreiber (*Cotton Weary*); Henry Winkler (*High School Principal*); Linda Blair (*Reporter*).

CREDITS:

Director, Wes Craven; screenplay, Kevin Williamson; producers, Cary Woods and Cathy Konrad; original music, Marco Beltrami; cinematographer, Mark Irwin; editor, Patrick Lussier; art director, David Lubin; special makeup effects, Howard Berger and Kamar Bitar; running time, 110 min.; rating, R.

THE PLOT:

Home alone one night, Casey Becker receives a strange phone call, at once threatening and provocative. At first, she plays along with the game, eventually wondering if it is indeed a game. Finally, Casey realizes she really is being watched and stalked. Following Casey's death, Sid Prescott spends a long weekend alone. Her father is away, and Sid is overcome by memories of her mother, murdered a year ago. She is visited by her boyfriend, who slips in the window to keep her company, though Sid remains a virgin. At school the next day, all the kids talk about a masked serial killer who models himself after the fiends in such films as *Halloween*, *Friday the 13th*, *The Texas Chainsaw Massacre*, and *Nightmare on Elm Street*.

As everyone knows from watching those films, virgins are the least likely girls to get killed by such knife-wielding attackers. Still, Sid is scared, and soon begins to suspect everyone from her boyfriend to her father, among others, of being her mother's killer, who is now out to get her. Jerky deputy Dewey may be less harmless than he seems, while pretty TV reporter Gale Weathers might actually be performing the violent acts to have something of interest to bolster the station's ratings.

THE FILM:

With *Nightmare on Elm Street* (1984), Wes Craven helped invent the modern horror movie in which teenage girls are menaced by ferocious males in masks. Whereas most of his colleagues from that era—Tobe Hooper, Sean S. Cunningham, eventually even John Carpenter—found themselves unable to move beyond that level, Craven evolved. A decade later, he invented the post-modern thriller, even as the Grand Guignol with which he'd made his reputation diminished in popularity. A hipper, more knowing genre emerged in the mid-nineties. Characters in the new movies were obsessed with movies. In *Scream* and its sequels and imitations, the teenagers are movie addicts, watch thrillers endlessly, and attempt to solve crimes by referencing movie murders.

As Roger Ebert wrote, "*Scream* is *about* knowledge of the movies . . .'Don't say I'll be right back,' one kid advises a friend, 'because whenever anybody says that, he's *never* right back.'" The film is informed by concepts of deconstruction and reflexivity, which argue that the ultimate in sophistication is for a film to regularly admit it is a film. The most effective way to involve the audience is to make a movie about what it means to be an audience. Kevin Williamson's script proves itself smart, pulling the rug out from under Craven's edge-of-your-seat tension. A line like, "I was attacked and nearly filleted last night" could have been an embarrassing retread of stuff heard in previous horror films. But these characters self-consciously speak like those earlier characters because the current events in their "real" world begin to imitate beloved flicks.

In the ultimate deconstruction device, one female character—played, of course, by an actress—wonders about who would play her if this incident ever becomes a film, sighing, "I see myself as sort of a young Meg Ryan. But with my luck, I'll get Tori Spelling." The ultimate reflexivity gag occurs when a child watches *Halloween*, calling out to a potential victim to watch out for the stalker behind her, even as a stalker comes up behind the kid. Despite such bits of knowing humor, which are virtually constant, the sharp comedy does not undercut the suspense.

Drew Barrymore as the first victim.

TRIVIA:

The leading role, Sid, was supposed to have been played by Drew Barrymore, who had to pass owing to previous commitments. When Neve Campbell replaced her, Drew offered to do an extended cameo for the film's opening sequence. The name Loomis was purposefully chosen for Billy, as it references two classic horror movies, John Gavin in *Psycho* (1960) and Donald Pleasence in *Halloween* (1978). Wes Craven plays Fred, the school janitor. One more smart reference: Craven modeled the killer's mask after the famed Edvard Munch painting *The Scream*. The voice of the killer on the phone was supplied by actor Roger L. Jackson. The film's original title was *Scary Movie*, which was eventually used for a parody of *Scream*.

ALSO RECOMMENDED:

All the rage in 1979 but largely forgotten (except by film cultists) today is Fred Walton's *When a Stranger Calls* (1979), with Carol Kane as a terrorized babysitter. The opening of *Scream* serves as an extended homage to that effectively creepy film. *Scream 2*, the 1997 sequel, in which a film (*Stab*) is made about the incidents in the original *Scream*, equals the original in inventiveness and originality. *I Know What You Did Last Summer* (1997), also scripted by Williamson, is another strong example of post-modernist suspense.

86:
FROM RUSSIA WITH LOVE (1963)

United Artists

"Shaken, not stirred."
—James Bond

CAST:

Sean Connery (*James Bond*); Daniela Bianchi (*Tatania Romanova*); Pedro Armendariz (*Kerim Bey*); Lotte Lenya (*Rosa Klebb*); Robert Shaw (*Red Grant*); Bernard Lee (*M*); Eunice Gayson (*Sylvia Trench*); Walter Gotell (*Morenzy*); Nadja Regin (*Bey's Mistress*); Lois Maxwell (*Miss Moneypenny*); Aliza Gur (*Vida*); Martine Beswick (*Zora*); Desmond Llewelyn (*Major Boothroyd*, aka 'Q').

CREDITS:

Director, Terence Young; screenplay, Richard Maibaum and Johanna Harwood, from the novel by Ian Fleming; producers, Harry Saltzman and Albert R. Broccoli (for 'Eon Productions'); music, John Barry and Lionel

Bart; cinematographer, Ted Moore; editor, Peter Hunt; production design, Syd Cain; special effects, John Stears; stunt coordinator, Peter Perkins; main title design, Robert Brownjohn; running time, 118 min.

THE PLOT:

Agent James Bond is assigned to embark on a dangerous mission involving Tatiana Romanova. Word has reached London that the young woman, employed as a cypher clerk in the Soviet Union, will defect, taking with her Lektor, a state of the art cypher machine that could tip the balance of world power. There is a catch—she will only surrender to Bond, with whom she has become obsessed. Though he suspects a Russian trap, 007 cannot resist the temptation. A secret criminal organization, known as SPECTRE, becomes aware of the negotiations. The shadowy Blofeld sends various agents, including Krebb, an elderly lesbian, and Grant, an immense killing machine, to stop Bond and seize Lektor. However, Bond has been equipped with various devices by the charming curmudgeon "Q." These help trip up the villains as they intercept him and his lovely companion at various stops on that legendary train, the Orient Express. Also fundamental in avoiding the villains is Kerim Bey, Bond's Istanbul contact. Unfortunately, this agreeable hedonist is killed while helping Bond escape. Eventually, Bond persuades Tatania—who was indeed a double-agent—to defect, thanks to his gift for seduction.

THE FILM:

Devout fans of Albert "Cubby" Broccoli's James Bond film franchise love the big-scale action and special effects, often citing *Goldfinger* (1964) and *The Spy Who Loved Me* (1977) as the best. Those who wish that the films had stayed closer to Ian Fleming's literary conception hail this, the second entry, as their favorite. Terence Young, who had directed the first Bond film, *Dr. No* (1963), guided this intelligent exercise in suspense, something that's not experienced by the audience while watching most Bond movies. Once established as a superhero, Bond could—like a jaded Superman—be trusted to always win. The outcome was never in doubt, rendering suspense impossible.

Fortunately, the series wasn't yet that formulaic when *From Russia With Love* was made. The film adheres to the book's plot more closely than any other Bond film. The filmmakers did set the conventions into place here. This is the first Bond to feature an exotic and elegant opening credits sequence designed by Maurice Bender, with an accompanying pop song that could be marketed into a major hit. It was first time "Q" was allowed to gleefully provide Bond with a virtual armory in an attaché case, allowing us to see the remarkable potential of each weapon,

Sean Connery and Daniela Bianchi create their own predecessor to perestroika.

then wait with patient delight for each to be used in the subsequent story. We watch, for the first time, Bond deliver a cruel, nasty bon mot immediately after dispatching one of his enemies. Finally, the film marked the first time that an "extra" fight (with Klebb) was added to the action after what we had wrongly believed was the last great conflict (with Grant) had concluded.

The Bond-Grant match, aboard a coach as the train roars across Eastern Europe, rates as one of the all-time greatest *mano e mano* movie fight sequences. The combat goes on for an extraordinarily long time without becoming repetitive, tiresome, or forced. The difficult romance between Bond and Tatania always keeps us guessing. We are never sure when, or if, either of the principles is "acting," and we sense that they are in the very same bind. The two are so attractive, though, that we remain spellbound by the liaison, waiting to see if, at the end, they will kill or kiss one another. The story is character-driven, despite elaborate fights, set pieces, great gadgetry, and gorgeous backgrounds, including diverse international settings and what shortly would come to be called "the Bond girls." Those who loved the original books—which, if never realistic, were at least believable—can't help but cite *From Russia With Love* as a model of what the series could, and perhaps should, have been.

TRIVIA:

In an early sequence, Eunice Gayson appears as "Sylvia Trench," the first woman to be seduced by Bond in *Dr. No*. Originally, Albert "Cubby" Broccoli had intended to have Bond in bed with Sylvia immediately following the title sequence of each movie, further developing their relationship from film to film. However, this device was dropped when it did not fit into the scheme for the opening of the next 007 epic, *Goldfinger* (1965).

ALSO RECOMMENDED:

Fans of romantic, believable spy films will want to catch Michael Powell's *The Spy in Black* (1939). In it, Conrad Veidt and Valerie Hobson find themselves in a situation that's notably similar to the one in the second Bond movie, only with the sexual roles reversed and Germany taking Russia's place. Connery shines in Richard C. Sarafian's *The Next Man* (1976), in which his Saudi Arabian diplomat is targeted and seduced by hit-woman Cornelia Sharpe, recalling the Luciana Paluzzi character from *Thunderball* (1965).

85:

THE MOST DANGEROUS GAME (1932)

RKO Radio Pictures

> **"The most dangerous game is man!"**
> **—Richard Connell**

CAST:

Joel McCrea (*Bob Rainsford*); Fay Wray (*Eve*); Leslie Banks (*Dr. Zaroff*); Robert Armstrong (*Martin*); Noble Johnson (*Ivan*); Steve Clemento (*Tartar*); Dutch Hendrian, James Flavin, and Hale Hamilton (*Shipmates*); William Davidson (*Captain*).

CREDITS:

Directors, Irving Pichel and Ernest B. Schoedsack; screenplay, James Asmore Creelman, from the short story by Richard Connell; producers,

Merian C. Cooper and David O. Selznick; original music, Max Steiner; cinematographer, Henry Gerrard; editor, Archie E. Marshek; art director, Carroll Clark; running time, 63 min.

THE PLOT:

On a cabin cruiser churning through unknown waters in the South Pacific, famed adventurer Robert Rainsford beguiles his companions with stories about hunting big game all over the world. He knows the thrill of the kill, particularly when the animal he's following is dangerous. Often, he's wondered what might be the most dangerous game. Rainsford is about to find out, for the buoys near an uncharted island are misleading, causing the ship to run aground and sink. Sharks appear, devouring the crew, though Rainsford is powerful enough to outswim them. Rainsford is relieved to see a light and heads for an island. He spots a castle on top of the highest hill. Once there, Rainsford meets Dr. Zaroff, a cryptic gentleman who extends every courtesy, as he has done to

Fay Wray and Joel McCrea stumble through a set left over from *King Kong*.

a beautiful young woman named Eve, who also was shipwrecked. Despite the civilized aura, Rainsford gradually comes to realize that Zaroff is a madman who purposefully causes passing ships to sink, allowing the fittest members of the crew to enter his home and recuperate. Then, he—a hunter himself—turns these people loose, with a knife and one day's head start, and tracks and kills them. Any person who refuses to play the prey is tortured to death. Eve chooses to run with Rainsford rather than remain. The two devise various traps to try and stop Zaroff, but he outguesses them. They run into the swamps and hide, Zaroff following with his men and dogs. Apparently, Rainsford is killed in a fight with a dog, both falling from the cliff into the raging waters below. However, when Zaroff drags Eve back to the castle, Rainsford awaits them. He fights Zaroff and escapes with Eve. As a result of the experience, it is unlikely that Rainsford will ever again take pleasure from hunting.

THE FILM:

As executive producer at RKO, David O. Selznick had okayed the big-budget production *King Kong* (1933), knowing it was a risky move for a one-of-a-kind film that might make or break the studio during those difficult days of the Great Depression. It would prove to be a huge hit, then and forever. Without that advance knowledge, however, Selznick needed a way to hedge his bet. He convinced produer Cooper and director Schoesdack to simultaneously film a tightly-budgeted movie, using *King Kong* sets when the crew for that film temporarily left for other locations. This left Selznick with a B-movie that boasted A-movie production values. Featuring a highly suspenseful script, a twenty-four-hour ticking clock story punctuated by well-staged action sequences, *The Most Dangerous Game* proved highly popular on a double-bill, coupled in various locations with comedies and westerns.

TRIVIA:

In addition to the *King Kong* sets, numerous cast and crew members also appear in this quickly shot programmer. Max Steiner is listed as composing the music, though mainly he allowed the filmmakers to use extra material that had been cut from the *King Kong* soundtrack, with several additional pieces filling out the score. Robert Armstrong and Noble Johnson, who played the Barnumlike showman and the Native Chief, joined female star Fay Wray. The two films, released in rapid succession, earned her the reputation as "the queen of the screamers." Why Bruce Cabot was replaced by Joel McCrea is unknown; what is known, however, is the identity of McCrea's stunt double—Buster Crabbe, an Olympian swimming star who had originally auditioned for the lead, though the producers weren't certain if he would be effective as an actor. Shortly, Crabbe moved over to Universal, where he became the star of such outer-space cliffhangers as *Buck Rogers* and *Flash Gordon*, highly popular in the thirties and considered camp classics ever since. Lon Chaney, Jr.—then known by his birth name, Creighton Chaney—is believed to be onscreen briefly, playing one of the shipmates, though this has never been confirmed for certain. Incidentally, there is no beautiful girl in Connell's short story, which is strictly a man-to-man conflict. A lovely blonde was hastily added to pad the film out to a little more than sixty minutes, while also adding the requisite romantic subplot for a Hollywood movie of that time. The film has been remade, officially or unofficially, at least twenty times, with variations including *A Game of Death* (1945), *Bloodlust!* (1961), *Woman Hunt* (1972), *Slave Girls From Beyond Infinity* (1987), and *Hard Target* (1993), just to name a few.

ALSO RECOMMENDED:

By far, the best remake was *Run For the Sun* (1956), directed by Roy Boulting, best known for his famous Ealing comedies of the 1950s. Here, he proves himself the equal of his old friend Hitchcock at doing edge-of-your-seat suspense. Richard Widmark is the hero, Trevor Howard the villain, and Jane Greer the beautiful girl in this far more subdued version of the thriller. The understated performances and actual locations add a strong dose of realism to what, in the original, was strictly Grand Guignol.

84:

SUSPIRIA (1977)

Seda Spettacoli

> **"You're pretty, very pretty indeed."**
> **—Madame Blanc, eyeing Suzy**

CAST:

Jessica Harper (*Suzy Bannion*); Stefania Casini (*Sara*); Flavio Bucci (*Daniel*); Miguel Bosé (*Mark*); Barbara Magnolfi (*Olga*); Susanna Javicoli

(*Sonia*); Eva Axén (*Patty "Pat" Hingle*); Rudolph Schündler (*Prof. Milius*); Udo Kier (*Prof. Frank Mandel*); Alida Valli (*Miss Tanner*); Joan Bennett (*Madame Blanc*); Margherita Horowitz (*Teacher*); Jacopo Mariani (*Albert*); Fulvio Mingozzi (*Taxi Driver*); Franca Scagnetti (*Cook*).

CREDITS:

Director, Dario Argento; screenplay, Argento and Daria Nicolodi, from the book *Suspiria de Profundis* by Thomas De Quincey (uncredited); producers, Claudio Argento and Salvatore Argento; original music, (Dario) Argento and The Goblins; cinematographer, Luciano Tovoli; editor, Franco Fraticelli; production design, Giuseppe Bassan; special effects, Germano Natali; running time, 92 min; rating, R.

THE PLOT:

A pretty young American ballet dancer, Suzy Bannion, leaves her homeland to study at the faraway school she's heard so much about, a celebrated academy in Freiburg called Tanzakademie. Once there, her life becomes ever less connected to reality, as the situations and images around her all appear to be drawn out of fairytales.

The headmistresses, Madame Blanc and Miss Tanner, remind Suzy of the evil stepmother in *Cinderella*, while the girls (other than sweet Sara) recall the evil stepsisters. Many such legends were set here, in the Black Forest. Dimly-remembered horror stories transform into frightening dream-like experiences, all terrifyingly real to Suzy, who can no longer discern where dreams leave off and her current reality begins.

The blind piano instructor, Daniel, is attacked and eaten by his dog. Then the mean headmistresses take the girls flying through the air. Suzy clings to words called out by another girl, Patty, as the heroine arrived in a torrential rainstorm: the phrase "secret iris" will somehow save Suzy if she utters this incantation at the right moment.

THE FILM:

Following his apprenticeship as a screenwriter, Dario Argento invented a uniquely Italian form of Hitchcockian suspense, dubbed the *giallo* or "yellow," symbolizing fear. With *Suspiria*, he moved away from that relatively realistic genre into more supernatural territory. Argento intended this film to be the first installment in an uncompleted trilogy he'd planned to call *The Mothers*. *Suspiria* was hailed as a minor masterpiece, outdistancing in quality his already well-received exercises in

Barbara Magnolfi finds herself the victim of a malevolent force.

the realm of the "everyday thriller." In *Slant* magazine, Ed Gonzalas referred to Argento's style as "deliriously artificial," claiming that the director owes "as much to German Expressionism as to Jean Cocteau and Grimm fairy tales." He also noted that "an impressive manipulation of mise-en-scène lies in the film's door handles; in their higher than usual positions, (they) emphasize the youth and stature of the film's characters in relation to their grotesquely overwhelming doll house."

Suspiria opens with the words, "Once upon a time . . ." With these same words, Luis Buñuel and Salvador Dalí began their equally anti-narrative work, *Un chien andalou* (1926). That silent was considered offensively avant-garde by the era's mainstream, yet the film that set the pace for the post-modern iconoclastic thrillers. As Ted Prigge has written, *Suspiria*'s story is so incompetent that "one actually wonders if the point of the film is to diss all of the so-called 'qualities' of [conventional] story in favor of a [work] that is undeniably and totally *about* style [and a self-consciously purposeful denial of] substance."

Trivia:

One source for the film was a work of fiction by De Quincey, whose most famous work, *Confessions of an Opium Eater*, remains a cult novel to this day. Argento actually drew more on reality than anyone guessed at the time. He had become intrigued with the Waldorf Schools opened by Rudolf Steiner. Steiner was an Austrian who had been widely accused of teaching the occult to impressionable young girls under the auspices of providing them with an eccentric though liberal education.

The film was shot almost entirely in Munich and Bavaria, with several key shots completed at Villa Capriglio in Turin and Piedmont, Italy.

Argento was one of Sergio Leone's collaborators on his mytho-poetic epic, *Once Upon a Time . . . in the West* (1969). Jessica Harper turned down a supporting role in Woody Allen's *Annie Hall* (1975) to play the lead. In addition to their talent, Alida Valli and Joan Bennett won their roles in part owing to their connection with classic thrillers. The former appeared in Alfred Hitchcock's *The Paradine Case* (1948), the latter in Fritz Lang's *The Woman in the Window* (1944).

Argento insisted the ultimate homage here was to Walt Disney's *Snow White and the Seven Dwarfs*, which he'd seen as a child. That film had obsessed him all his life, and Argento considers it the most frightening movie ever made. The color scheme in *Suspiria* is an attempt to precisely reproduce the one in the Disney film.

Also Recommended:

Dario Argento's oeuvre includes several classics of the often unappreciated sub-genre of terror called the *giallo*. Most notable is *The Bird With the Crystal Plumage* (1969), a Hitchcockian thriller that, like so many masterpieces of suspense, deals with an initial misperception on the part of the film's hero that is finally corrected. Also, for a far more violent film, *Deep Red*, a.k.a. *The Hatchet Murders* (1975) is among Argento's most admired works.

83:

CHARADE (1963)

Universal-International

> **"You know what's wrong with you? Absolutely *nothing*!"**
> **—Reggie to Peter**

CAST:

Cary Grant (*Peter Joshua*); Audrey Hepburn (*Regina "Reggie" Lambert*); Walter Matthau (*Hamilton Bartholomew*); James Coburn (*Tex Panthollow*); George Kennedy (*Herman Scobie*); Ned Glass (*Leopold Gideon*); Jacques Marin (*Inspector Edouard Grandpierre*); Paul Bonifas (*Felix*).

CREDITS:

Director, Stanley Donen; screenplay, Peter Stone, from the story "The Unsuspecting Wife" by Stone and Marc Behm; producer, Donen; music, Henry Mancini and Johnny Mercer; cinematographer, Charles Lang; editor, James Clark; art direction, Jean d'Eaubonne; main title, Maurice Binder; running time, 113 min.

SYNOPSIS:

Someone tosses a man named Lambert to his death from a speeding train. His wife, "Reggie," has little time to mourn, since shortly she's hounded in Paris by dangerous characters, all convinced she knows the whereabouts of $250,000 that her late husband—a member of an illegal international operation—has hidden.

Reggie takes refuge in the arms of Peter Joshua, a handsome stranger she met at a ski resort, until a series of circumstances make her believe Peter may be a part of the conspiracy. Desperate, Reggie turns to the frumpy American consulate, Hamilton Bartholomew, for help.

The conclusion comes when Reggie, alone at night under the arches of the Paris Opera, notices Peter and Hamilton approaching from either side. Both claim to be her savior, yet each is capable murdering Reggie. Lost in love, she rushes to Peter, who saves Reggie from the killer (and faux consulate). As it turns out, Bartholomew had been after the rare stamp in which Reggie's husband had invested the money.

Cary Grant attempts to convince Audrey Hepburn that she should trust him.

THE FILM:

Lesley Brill has written extensively about "Hitchcockian romance." The films that constitute this unique sub-genre of the master's work achieve a balance between thrills and humor, emphasizing the love story, though always containing it within a suspenseful framework. In time, Hitchcock abandoned the genre and turned to a much darker type of film with *Psycho* (1960). Throughout the sixties and early seventies, he avoided repeating his earlier successes and pushed in new directions with ever more unpleasant films, most notably *Marnie* (1964). Meanwhile, other filmmakers took up the slack. These were competent craftsmen who lacked Hitchcock's visionary status, but were able to handsomely mount the kinds of movies he no longer made yet which the public still hungered for. The best by far was *Charade* (1963), dazzlingly brought to the screen by Stanley Donen. This director was rightly revered for such delightful musicals as *Singin' in the Rain* (1952), which he co-directed with star Gene Kelly.

The rare postage stamp, that remains constantly in view but is ignored by everyone, is a perfect example of what Hitchcock called the MacGuffin: that simple object which propels all the wild running around but which, ironically, appears so insignificant that the people who covet it fail to recognize the object of their search even when staring directly at it. Cary Grant is employed much as Hitchcock had used him in *Suspicion* (1941), effectively playing his character with a double-edged sword so that we believe throughout he may or not be revealed as the killer in the final moments. *Charade*'s conclusion is likewise totally Hitchcockian. Alone at night, Reggie must quickly choose between Peter and Hamilton. The former is a man she has fallen romantically in love with but has good reason to fear, owing to circumstantial evidence suggesting he is her potential killer. The latter is a man she has no reason to mistrust but whom she finds unappealing. Her choice is between logic and emotion. Convinced she will likely die, Reggie impulsively rushes into the arms of her lover. In *Charade*, as in Hitchcock and films by other people he inspired, the heart is always more correct than the head. There is, then, another and deeper meaning to the term "romantic" when applied to such a film than the obvious element of a love story. However civilized we have become, we must finally reach back to something more natural in our makeup—the "noble savage" in each of us—if we are to find salvation.

It's worth noting that Audrey Hepburn had the good fortune to inherit many of the roles that otherwise would have gone to Grace Kelly, who had retired from films after meeting and marrying Prince Rainier of Monaco while filming *To Catch a Thief* (1955). Hitchcock stumbled at this point in his career, making a noble but doomed *Vertigo*-like attempt to transform Tippi Hedren, a bland brunette, into a cool, classy blonde of the Grace Kelly order. He would have done far better to follow the example of Donen and, several years later, Terence Young, who likewise directed Hepburn in a successfully Hitchcock-like film version of the acclaimed suspense play *Wait Until Dark* (1967), when Hitchcock himself unwisely turned that project down.

Trivia:

Grant's studio contract insisted that, no matter how suspicious his character seemed, he could not be the killer at the end. Though Grant had been the first choice to play Grace Kelly's murderous husband in Hitchcock's *Dial M for Murder* (1954), negotiations fell through when it was deemed impossible for him to turn out to be innocent at the end. At that point, Ray Milland assumed the role.

Also Recommended:

Other Hithcock "knockoffs" of high quality include Mark Robson's *The Prize* (1963) with Paul Newman and Elke Sommer, and Arthur Hiller's *Silver Streak* (1976) with Gene Wilder and Jill Clayburgh. Both were box-office successes, and the latter introduced Richard Pryor to a wide movie-going audience for the first time, while also setting the pace for future Wilder/Pryor vehicles. Grant fans will want to catch his similar role in Hitchcock's aforementioned *Suspicion* (1941) and *To Catch a Thief* (1955) opposite Grace Kelly, and of course the legendary *North by Northwest* (1959).

82:

MEMENTO   (2001)

Newmarket

> **"I can't remember to forget you."**
> **—Leonard Shelby**

CAST:

Guy Pearce (*Leonard Shelby*); Carrie-Anne Moss (*Natalie*); Joe Pantoliano (*John Edward "Teddy" Gammell*); Mark Boone Junior (*Burt Hadley*); Russ Fega (*Waiter*); Jorja Fox (*Catherine Shelby*); Stephen Tobolowsky (*Sammy Jankis*); Harriet Sansom Harris (*Mrs. Jankis*); Thomas Lennon (*Doctor*); Callum Keith Rennie (*Dodd*); Kimberly Campbell (*Blonde*); Marianne Muellerleile (*Emma the Tattooist*).

CREDITS:

Director, Christopher Nolan; screenplay, Nolan, from a story by Jonathan Nolan; producers Jennifer Todd, Suzanne Todd, and Chris J. Ball; original music, David Julyan; cinematographer, Wally Pfister; editor, Dody Dorn; special effects, Andrew Sebok; running time, 115 min.; rating, R.

THE PLOT:

The opening image is a Polaroid snapshot that does precisely the opposite of what we expect, dissolving before our eyes rather than taking an ever more vivid form. This sets in place the bizarre adventure of Leonard, who suffers from short-term memory loss. The last thing Leonard can remember is the murder of his wife. Despite his problem, he attempts to solve that crime, hoping this may cure his mental block.

Leonard constantly jots down notes on what's happening so he can refresh himself moments later. Adding to the intrigue, the story unfolds in reverse time, each sequence occurring before the one that follows. This forces the audience into a position at once analogous to and opposite of the hero's dilemma; while he lacks the ability to remember and must forever move forward, we possess it but are forced to trace the events in a backward direction. An edge-of-your-seat quality is enhanced by our constant frustration in attempting to mentally rearrange everything we see, even as our on-screen hero does more or less the same thing by talking fast so that he'll be able to make it through a conversation without forgetting who it is he's talking to, or why.

Cryptic Teddy Gammell, who may be Leonard's savior or the culprit, points out to the troubled hero that even if Leonard manages to enact revenge, he won't be able to remember it a moment later. Leonard responds by insisting that this doesn't matter: she deserves retribution, and he will enact it, no matter what.

Leonard would be completely lost if he didn't have objects that anchor him in reality. One is a photo of a pretty girl, Natalie, on which he's noted, "She has also lost someone." But we aren't sure if she is with or against Leonard. Also interspersed is an ongoing series of revelations about a case Leonard investigated while working for an insurance company. He came face-to-face with a man named Sammy, who also suffered from a similar memory problem, causing us to realize the two seemingly disparate cases will come together in some way. Finally, there's the possibility that Leonard himself is the killer. Will he unmask himself, Oedipus-like, when he solves the crime? If this is the case, then his memory loss serves as the ultimate denial tactic his mind has developed to avoid dealing with such a horrible possibility.

Guy Pearce reveals his modus operandi.

Leonard becomes strangely sympathetic as he faces the motel clerk who sneeringly insists he has just charged Leonard for two rooms, and will get away with it because Leonard will forget what he's just heard before he can do anything. As the conclusion (opening?) nears, we suspect Teddy who, more than any other character, has come to appear ambiguous, at one moment ready to help Leonard, though later (earlier) out to hinder the uncovering of truth.

THE FILM:

Budgeted at five million dollars, and returning five times that investment in grosses, *Memento* put then-unknown Newmarket Capital Group on the map as a key distributor of intriguing indies. Like other postmodernist thrillers, *Memento* is about perception and reality and the distinction between the two. Roger Ebert complained about the concept: "The film's deep backward and abysm of time is for our entertainment and has nothing to do with (Leonard's) condition. It may actually make the movie too clever for its own good." Ebert saw the film twice and, the first time through, felt that he needed a second viewing if he were to fully comprehend the concept. But during the second viewing, he came to believe that even as he acquired a greater grasp on the plot mechanics, he sensed that the texture and theme were less complex than he'd originally believed, leading him to conclude, "Once is right for this movie. Confusion is the state we are intended to be in." Ebert's criticism of the film as gimmicky provides a back-handed compliment, suggesting that *Memento* is successful on the level that it was intended to work.

Other reviewers were far kinder, hailing *Memento* as a minor classic in reverse suspense, a one-of-a-kind movie. Besides offering the tautness we expect from a first-rate thriller, *Memento* is surprisingly funny, as when the hero encounters a man who's been beaten to a pulp:

> Leonard Shelby: Who did this to you?
> Dodd: *You* did.

At another point, Leonard sees Dodd running:

> Leonard Shelby: I'm chasing this guy.
> (Dodd turns and fires a gun at Leonard)

> Leonard Shelby: Nope. He's chasing me.
> (Leonard turns and runs).

TRIVIA:

"Teddy" tells Leonard that his phone number is 555-0134; this is the same phone number as the one that Marla Singer has in *Fight Club*. When Leonard parks his Jaguar at the motel, the white Honda Civic in the next parking place belongs to filmmaker Christopher Nolan. *Memento* was eligible for the Best Original Screenplay category in all film competitions, even though it was based on an already-existing short story by the screenwriter's brother, Jonah. This was because the short story had not been published at the time when the film was shot.

ALSO RECOMMENDED:

Betrayal (1983), based on a play by Harold Pinter, is the only other feature film to have each sequence precede in story time the scene that it follows in running time. Nolan has since gone on to direct *Insomnia* (2002), another stark thriller, this one starring Al Pacino. After that, catch the original Norwegian version by Erik Skjold-bjaerg, which is far better.

81:
HORROR OF DRACULA (1958)

Warner Bros.

> **"The notion that vampires can transform
> into bats and wolves is only folklore."**
> —Van Helsing

CAST:

Christopher Lee (*Count Dracula*); Peter Cushing (*Van Helsing*); Melissa Stribling (*Mina Holmwood*); Michael Gough (*Arthur Holmwood*); Carol Marsh (*Lucy*); Charles Lloyd Pack (*Dr. Seward*); Valerie Gaunt (*Vampire Woman*); Olga Dickie (*Gerda*); Miles Malleson (*Undertaker*).

CREDITS:

Director, Terence Fisher; screenplay, Jimmy Sangster, from *Dracula* by Bram Stoker; producer, Anthony Hinds; music, James Bernard; cinematographer, Jack Asher; editor, Bill Lenny; production designer, Bernard Robinson; running time, 82 min.

SYNOPSIS:

Jonathan Harker arrives at the Transylvanian castle of Count Dracula, presumably to work as the elegant gentleman's secretary. In fact, Harker is part of a secret society dedicated to destroying the Count and his cult of the undead. Harker is sorely tested when one of the beautiful brides of Dracula attempts to seduce him. The following day, Harker finds the lair of the vampires and kills the vampire woman first, realizing that Dracula has risen from the grave and escaped. Having glimpsed a photograph of Jonathan's betrothed, Lucy, the Count travels to their home city and claims her, in vengeance, for his bride. Also, he decides to seduce her relative, Mina Holmwood, though here he overextends himself. Mina's husband, Arthur, alerts vampire hunter Van Helsing. Together, they trail the Count back to his home. There, Van Helsing enters into a one-on-one duel with Dracula and at last destroys the Count by exposing him to rays of sunlight.

THE FILM:

In 1955, England's Hammer studio rated as a minor league undertaking that produced black-and-white "programmers," rarely exported to other countries. Down on their luck, they had to fold or try something entirely new. Studio-head Michael Carreras decided on the latter. He was aware that during the past ten years, Hollywood's Universal Studio had ceased making their once lucrative gothic horror films, having run the genre into the ground. Instead, they were concentrating on newly popular science-fiction flicks. Carreras and company decided to film Mary Shelley's *Frankenstein* with an entirely new approach. When the movie proved surprisingly popular, even imported for the lucrative American market, they went that route again with *Horror of Dracula*.

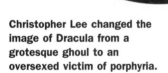

Christopher Lee changed the image of Dracula from a grotesque ghoul to an oversexed victim of porphyria.

The result was a masterpiece, not of horror but of suspense. This was due to the significant decision to eliminate all supernatural elements, most notably Dracula's ability to transform into a bat or a wolf. Such stuff may have been potent material when first presented in Stoker's novel, and all previous Dracula movies from F.W. Murnau's German classic *Nosferatu* (1922) through Todd Browning's early sound version (1931), both of which presented the title character as a ghoul. Between 1930 and 1950, this had degenerated into cliché. Here, Dracula is not a monster but a man, suffering from a real disease, porphyria, believed by many to produce an obsessive need to consume blood.

Once this decision was made, director Terence Fisher responded by creating an entirely new mise-en-scène. Instead of having cinematographer Jack Asher shoot the story on Grand Guignol studio-sets, which suggest an exaggerated fairy-tale for grown-ups, the movie was filmed in muted color and on actual locations. Though a handsomely mounted period-piece, Hammer's *Dracula* conveys from its opening shot a sense of immediacy and, with it, urgency. Despite Victorian costumes and medieval castles, the tale unfolds in a frighteningly contemporary manner. Christopher Lee's stunning approach to the Count—he conveys a subtle charisma in disarming contrast to Lugosi's cackling fiend—furthers the notion of a realistic (therefore thrilling) threat rather than a fantastical diversion into the horror-movie genre.

Other cast members, though relatively unknown, were veterans of England's various Shakespearean companies. Director Fisher encouraged them to maintain their sophisticated approach to character rather than assume that, since they were appearing in a B-budget horror movie, they ought to go "over the top." Fisher also heightened the story's sexual subtext. Various Victorian women, faithful wives and virginal fiancées, open their bedroom windows for the darkly handsome Count to enter and unbutton their bodices. Vampirism, for the first time on screen, is unabashedly portrayed as a sexual metaphor in which repressed women erotically explode at first sight of a dangerous stranger, willingly inviting the elegantly fatal Count into their boudoirs while hurriedly unlacing their bodices.

Likewise, screen violence was extended. *Horror of Dracula* played two years before *Psycho* and in many respects paved the way for Hitchcock's landmark film. The opening is case in point. The camera slowly dollies in on the grave of Dracula, appearing in purposefully subdued color. Then, bright drops of blood drip down on the stone. The image, mild by today's standards, proved revolutionary at the time, creating a controversy over explicit screen violence that would continue to build during the sixties, with such films as *Bonnie and Clyde* (1967) and *The Wild Bunch* (1969). Each of the Hammer sequels, beginning with *Brides of Dracula* the following year, grew more violent than the last. By concentrating on heightened suspense undercut by sensual tension, Fisher transformed what had been perceived as a conventional monster movie into a psycho-sexual thriller.

TRIVIA:

Christopher Lee appears onscreen for only eleven minutes. Lee chose not to appear in the sequel, Fisher's *Brides of Dracula* (1960) for fear of typecasting, though he eventually returned to the fold.

ALSO RECOMMENDED:

Brides of Dracula is, in many ways, the equal of the first Hammer vampire film, and fans of Lee will want to catch him in Freddie Francis's *Dracula Has Risen From the Grave* (1968), Peter Sasdy's *Taste the Blood of Dracula* (1970), and, best of all, Roy Ward Baker's *Scars of Dracula* (1970).

80:

A SHOT IN THE DARK (1964)

United Artists/Mirisch Company

"I suspect everyone. And no one."
—Inspector Jacques Clouseau

CAST:

Peter Sellers (*Inspector Jacques Clouseau*); Elke Sommer (*Maria Gambrelli*); George Sanders (*Benjamin Ballon*); Herbert Lom (*Charles Dreyfus*); Tracy Reed (*Dominique Ballon*); Graham Stark (*Hercule Lajoy*); Moira Redmond (*Simone*); Vanda Godsell (*Madame LaFarge*); Maurice Kaufmann (*Pierre*); Burt Kwouk (*Kato*); Ann Lynn (*Dudu*); André Maranne (*Fran*).

CREDITS:

Director, Blake Edwards; screenplay, Edwards and William Peter Blatty, from the Harry Kurnitz play of the same name, in turn adapted from Marcel Achard's *L'Idiot*; producers, Edwards and Cecil F. Ford; original music, Henry Mancini; cinematographer, Christopher Challis; editor, Bert Bates and Ralph E. Winters; production design, Michael Stringer; running time, 101 min.

THE PLOT:

Investigators discover Swedish bombshell Maria Gambrelli sitting on a bed in the château of wealthy Benjamin Ballon, holding a smoking gun over the body of the

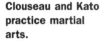

Clouseau and Kato practice martial arts.

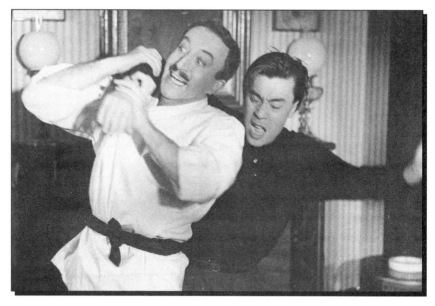

Spanish chauffeur, Miguel. The door was locked from the inside. Clearly, she—the millionaire's mistress—murdered this employee, who had worn out his welcome as her secret lover. Yet one lone voice cries out in the wilderness. Inspector Jacques Clouseau, fresh from solving the Pink Panther jewel-heist case, insists that lovely Maria is innocent and sets out to prove this is so. His actions infuriate Chief Inspector Charles Dreyfus, who hoped to quickly close the case. Dreyfus had been driven to distraction by Clouseau's ever more outlandish theories and oddly effective strategies. The Chief hysterically claims, "Give me ten men like Clouseau, and I could destroy the world."

Maria's innocence becomes more difficult to argue when police find the gardener mangled, with Maria standing beside the body holding bloody shears. Constantly, Clouseau fights off attacks by Kato, his loyal houseboy, assigned to do this in order to reinforce Clouseau's awareness that enemies are everywhere. Clouseau tracks Maria to a nudist colony, eventually discovering the aloof millionaire was seen crawling down the château wall on the night of the killing. Clouseau wraps up the case with the following words, "I submit, Ballon, that you arrived home, found Miguel with Maria Gambrelli, and killed him in a rit of fealous jage!"

THE FILM:

As Damian Cannon has noted, "Clouseau blunders about, blissfully unaware of ensuing chaos, naive and innocent in a peculiar way." Certainly, most of the film's gags derive from the awkwardness of Clouseau, and Sellers' gifts as a physical comedian—some critics claim he was the equal of silent greats Chaplin, Keaton, and Lloyd. The situation, in Cannon's words, "imbues Clouseau with a special aura, a feeling that somehow everything will turn out alright despite the errors made along the way." This, of course, is precisely what so maddens Dreyfus, whose own logical approach to crime pales, in terms of effectiveness, when compared with Clouseau's inspired anarchy. Varied comedic styles from broad physical slapstick to the subtlest delivery of one-liners enhance rather than diminish the surprisingly suspenseful murder-mystery plot.

Indeed, it's difficult to believe this was never intended to be a Clouseau caper, though that happens to be the case. Edwards had devised his pet project, *The Pink Panther* (1964), as a vehicle for actor Peter Ustinov. When shooting began, it became apparent that actor and character did not jell. Ustinov politely chose to withdraw, at which point Sellers agreed to play the dogged detective. Clouseau was to be a supporting role in a film showcasing old Hollywood hands David Niven and Robert Wagner, as well as then-emerging sex symbols Capucine and Claudia Cardinale. A glitzy diversion, *The Pink Panther* became wildly popular largely because audiences fell in love with Sellers, sensing that they'd discovered the greatest physical clown of his generation.

Producers then cast Sellers in an adaptation of the popular stage play by Harry Kurnitz that involved a pair of bumbling detectives (the other was to have been played by Walter Matthau). Sellers, always a perfectionist, expressed his dissatisfaction with the project and threatened to leave. Executives at United Artists, aware of how happily Sellers and Edwards had collaborated, begged Blake to take over the troubled film. Realizing that nothing other than a complete rewrite would satisfy Sellers, Edwards shelved the Matthau character and concentrated on a funny/scary version of Hitchcock's favorite theme: the desire for the fall—a male hero falls for a beautiful woman, seemingly a murderess, less because he believes she is innocent than that he would enjoy becoming her next victim.

Audiences who had loved *The Pink Panther* but longed for a greater focus on Clouseau flocked to *A Shot in the Dark* (1964). United Artists released the film little more than four months after the original wowed the world.

TRIVIA:

The character of Kato was based—some would say stolen—on the longtime sidekick of *The Green Hornet*. Perhaps to avoid legal problems, "Kato" would be changed to "Cato" in all future films. The character of Maria Gambrelli reappeared in *Son of the Pink Panther* (1993), this time played by Claudia Cardinale, who had played Princess Dala in the original. When Sellers left the series after two films (he would return to the role a decade later), Alan Arkin—sometimes called "America's answer to Peter Sellers"—assumed the role in *Inspector Clouseau* (1968). Elke Sommer also embodied the era's image of a Swedish sexpot in another thriller, *The Prize* (1963), opposite Paul Newman. Despite the popular perception of her, Elke was, in fact, German.

ALSO RECOMMENDED:

In addition to the original, *The Pink Panther Strikes Again* (1976) also effectively conveys the balance between suspense and humor that made *Shot in the Dark* an instant classic. Edwards's other memorable thriller is *Experiment in Terror* (1962); in it, Glenn Ford attempts to protect Lee Remick and Stefanie Powers from a serial rapist.

79:

THE PHANTOM OF THE OPERA (1925)

Universal Pictures

> **"Feast your eyes! Glut your soul on my accursed ugliness!"**
> **—Erik/The Phantom**

CAST:

Lon Chaney (*Erik/The Phantom*); Mary Philbin (*Christine Daae*); Norman Kerry (*Vicomte Raoul de Chagny*); Arthur Edmund Carewe (*Ledoux*); Gibson Gowland (*Buquet*); John Sainpolis (*Comte Philip de Chagny*); Snitz Edwards (*Florine Papillon*); Mary Fabian (*Carlotta, in 1929 re-edited version Only*) Virginia Pearson (*Carlotta's Mother, in 1929 re-edited version*); Olive Ann Alcorn (*La Sorelli*); Alexander Bevani; (*Mephistopheles*); Edward Cecil (*Faust*); Chester Conklin (*Orderly*); Bruce Covington (*M. Moncharmin*); Ward Crane (*Count Ruboff*); George Davis (*Guard at Christine's Door*); Cesare Gravina (*Manager*); Carla Laemmle (*Prima Ballerina*); Edward Martindel (*Comte Philip de Chagny*); John Miljan (*Valentin*); William Tyroler (*Director of Opera Orchestra*).

CREDITS:

Director(s), Rupert Julian and (uncredited) Lon Chaney and Edward Sedgwick; screenplay, Elliott J. Clawson (adaptation), Tom Reed (title cards), Frank M. McCormack, and Raymond L. Schrock, from the novel by Gaston Leroux; producer, Carl Laemmle (Sr.); original music (for 1925 release), Gustav Hinrichs; (for 1929 reissue), David Broekman, James Dietrich, Heniz Roemheld, Domenico Savino, and Bernhard Kaun; (for 1996 restoration rerelease print), Carl Davis; cinematographers, Milton Bridenbecker, Virgil Miller, and Charles Van Enger; editors, Maurice Pivar and Gilmore Walker; art directors, Charles D. Hall and E.E. Sheeley; special makeup effects, Chaney; consulting artist, Ben Carr; various running times, 79 min. (1925 release) and 101 min. (1929 re-release).

Man of a Thousand Faces: Lon Chaney, Sr.

THE PLOT:

A cryptic character called the Phantom has been sending threatening notes to the manager of the Paris Opera House, insisting that terror will shortly strike unless the female lead in the current show is replaced by her understudy, the talented but inexperienced Marguerite. When such warnings are initially ignored, a phantom in white mask and black cloak strikes, swinging on chandeliers over performances in progress, horrifying the audience. The Phantom kidnaps the lovely Marguerite, dragging her down to the hidden chambers in a labyrinthian space beneath the opera house. Her fiancé, a military man, dares all to enter the Phantom's lair and save his lady-love from the scarred creature who has become obsessed with the frightened beauty.

THE FILM:

"The man of a thousand faces" is the nickname that Universal employed to hype its greatest, if most troublesome, silent performer. At a time when the star-system was being developed around performers who played virtually the same part over and over again—William S. Hart, the all-American cowboy; Doug Fairbanks (Sr.), the all-purpose swashbuckler; Charlie Chaplin, the lovable little clown; Rudolph Valentino, the Latin lover—Chaney pioneered screen *acting* by popping up in various genres. Chaney always appeared in such an entirely new guise that audiences could not recognize him from one film to the next. He thus set the stage for such future "character leads" as Paul Muni, Dustin Hoffman, and Robert De Niro. In truth, though, Chaney will always be best remembered for his thrillers. *The Phantom of the Opera* remains the most beloved, largely because Chaney's presence was effectively augmented by the ambience. As Scott M. Keir has noted, "the passages, hidden places behind the walls and the secret lair created by Ben Carre, are almost a supporting player."

For total authenticity, *Phantom* was filmed entirely on location in Paris. This constituted a rarity at a time when most films, even those with specific European settings, were made on studio backlots. Though shot and edited by the end of 1923, the film was not released for two years, because the studio feared that Chaney's horrific effects might be too much for audiences. When Laemmle finally did allow the movie to be shown, he predicted a box-office and critical disaster. What he got was an unexpected success. Reviewers and the public alike ecstatically greeted what would become one of the most famous of all silent movies.

TRIVIA:

Gibson Gowland, a well-regarded character actor, would achieve iconic status when, later that year, Eric von Stroheim cast him as "McTeague" in *Greed* (1925), one of the abiding masterpieces of silent cinema. The small role of the opera-house orderly went to Chester Conklin, beloved silent clown known for his squat frame and walrus moustache. He too appears in *Greed*, as Gowland's father-in-law. The role of the Prima Ballerina was portrayed by the daughter of Carl Laemmle, the film's producer and head of Universal studios. *Phantom* has been filmed and refilmed more times, for theatres and television, than any other story, with the possible exception of *The Three Musketeers* (1921, original). Eventually, of course, (Sir) Tim Rice and (Lord) Lloyd Webber brought the story to life as one of the most lavish and well-loved of all modern stage musicals.

ALSO RECOMMENDED:

Chaney fans—particularly those who relish thrillers—will want to catch his equally absorbing if (by today's standards) unsubtle work in Wallace Worsley's *The Hunch-*

back of Notre Dame (1923). The film is yet another Parisian thriller, in which Chaney's even more sympathetic creature harbors an equally intense obsession for Patsy Ruth Miller. He also starred for director Todd Browning in *London After Midnight* (1927), a silent vampire film by the man who would eventually introduce Bela Lugosi to the world as Dracula. Lugosi would play Chaney's role in Browning's 1935 remake of his earlier silent classic, this time titled *Mark of the Vampire*. As for *Phantom*, the best remake is Universal's 1943 version with Claude Rains in the title role, directed by Arthur Lubin. Also worth watching is Brian De Palma's *Phantom of the Paradise* (1974), a comedy thriller that resets the tale in a contemporary rock club.

78:

DIE HARD (1988)

20th Century Fox

> **"Now I have a machine gun. Ho, ho, ho."**
> **—John McClane**

CAST:

Bruce Willis (*John McClane*); Bonnie Bedelia (*Holly Gennaro McClane*); Reginald Veljohnson (*Sgt. Al Powell*); Paul Gleason (*Dwayne T. Robinson*); De'voreaux White (*Argyle*); William Atherton (*Thornburg*); Hart Bochner (*Ellis*); James Shigeta (*Takagi*); Alan Rickman (*Hans Gruber*); Alexander Godunov (*Karl*); Bruno Doyon (*Franco*); Andreas Wisniewski (*Tony*); Clarence Gilyard Jr.(*Theo*); Joey Plewa (*Alexander*); Lorenzo Caccialanza (*Marco*); Gérard Bonn (*Kristoff*); Dennis Hayden (*Eddie*); Hans Buhringer (*Fritz*); Robert Davi (*Big Johnson*); Grand L. Bush (*Little Johnson*); Mary Ellen Trainor (*Gail*); Rebecca Broussard (*Hostage*).

CREDITS:

Director, John McTiernan; screenplay, Jeb Stuart and Steven E. de Souza, from the novel *Nothing Lasts Forever* by Roderick Thorp; producers,

Charles Gordon, Lawrence Gordon, and Joel Silver; original music, Michael Kamen; cinematographer, Jan De Bont; editors, John F. Link and Frank J. Urioste; production design, Jackson DeGovia; art director, John R. Jensen; special effects, William Aldridge; special visual effects, Mike Chambers; running time, 124 min.; rating, R.

THE PLOT:

East coast cop John McClane heads for Los Angeles, where his estranged wife (and their children) now live. She works for Nakatomi, an international corporation run by Japanese executives. McClane joins Holly for her company's Christmas party at a lavish thirtieth-floor suite in a Century City high-rise, hoping to convince her to return home. A team of terrorists takes over the building, holding party-goers hostage. The leader is Hans Gruber, a nattily-dressed man of intellect who plans to steal a fortune in negotiable bonds. McClane becomes a one-man army to save his wife

Bruce Willis as John McClane.

and the others, suddenly striking against the terrorists like some avenger in the night. Outside, a sympathetic policeman, Sgt. Powell, maintains communication via radio and attempts to aid McClane, though other officials and the media only interfere with McClane's private war. One by one, McClane eliminates the terrorists and rescues his wife; we are left with the impression that she will drop her job and hurry home with McClane.

THE FILM:

Die Hard appeared on the scene as action movies starring Arnold Schwarzenegger (*Conan the Barbarian*, 1982) and Sylvester Stallone (*Rambo*, 1985)—highly popular during the early eighties—were beginning to lose box-office steam. Those performers had encapsulated the Reagan-era mindset by presenting rugged individu-alists who express more contempt for bureaucrats than Clint Eastwood's "Dirty Harry" Callahan. By decade's end, their escapades had become tiresome. One key element was missing: suspense. Clearly, these were impregnable superheroes, and there never even seemed to be anything so potent as Kryptonite around to give them pause. In time, the elaborate stunts—however well-executed—failed to pro-vide any true thrills, for there was no way either Stallone's or Schwarzenegger's character could lose. Watching their supposedly perilous adventures boiled down to a case of a detached audience waiting to see how the hero, who never seemed to sweat, would get the job done.

Die Hard provided an antidote to all that. Willis likened his character to one of his own personal favorites, William Holden in *The Bridge on the River Kwai* (1957). Willis described that character and his own thusly, "an ordinary man rising to heroic stature under extraordinary circumstances." On some level we know McClane will win. This is, after all, a Hollywood movie. Still, we feel (at least within the suspension of disbelief so necessary if we are to "buy in" to any motion picture) that McClane may not be able to make it out, just as audiences wondered, back in 1952, whether or not Gary Cooper really would be able to defeat all four evil gunslingers in *High Noon* (1952). This allows for an edge-of-your-seat ele-ment that was not possible in epics of the early eighties. Whereas *Rambo* and *Conan* were essentially action films, *Die Hard* is a thriller with great action sequences.

Whereas early eighties films rate as "modern" action flicks, *Die Hard* can be considered "postmodern," owing to elements of reflexivity and deconstruction. There are constant movie references intended to remind us this is, indeed, a movie, part of an ongoing tradition of which the main character is himself aware:

> Hans Gruber: This time John Wayne does not walk off into the sunset with Grace Kelly.
>
> John McClane: That was Gary Cooper, asshole.

Trivia:

The terrorist/villain in James Coburn's first starring vehicle, *Our Man Flint* (1966), was also named Hans Gruber. The first draft of Steven E. De Souza's script was an intended sequel to his earlier *Commando* (1985). When Arnold Schwarzenegger decided not to appear, the screenwriter rewrote it, creating a more vulnerable and human character. At that time, the producers envisioned Richard Gere as McClane. The plot is based on a novel, *Nothing Lasts Forever*; its hero was the same character that Frank Sinatra portrayed in *The Detective* (1968). Bruce Willis made his debut in that film in a bit part as a bar patron. German importers rewrote the dialogue to make the terrorists "vaguely European" rather than "specifically German." At one point in the film, music from James Horner's score for *Aliens* (1986) appears on the soundtrack. One of the stuntmen—Paul Picerni, Jr.—is the son of actor Paul Picerni; see *House of Wax* (1953, #93).

ALSO RECOMMENDED:

Director John McTiernan was also responsible for *Predator* (1987). It's an effective Schwarzenegger thriller since the large-scale action sequences are contained within a suspenseful plot that suggests Arnold's hero is not so invulnerable after all.

77:
DIABOLIQUE (1955)

Vera

> **"Paul's back—back from the dead!"**
> **—Nicole**

CAST:

Simone Signoret (*Nicole Horner*); Vera Clouzot (*Christina Delasalle*); Paul Meurisse (*Michel Delassle*); Charles Vanel (*Inspector Fichet*); Jean Brochard (*Plantiveau*); Noël Roquefort (*Herboux*); Thérèse Dorny (*Mme. Herboux*); Pierre Larquey (*Drain*); George Chamarat (*Loisy*); Michel Serrault (*Raimond*).

CREDITS:

Director, Henri-Georges Clouzot; screenplay, Jérôme Geronimi, Frédéric Grendel, René Masson, and Clouzot, based on a novel by Pierre Boileau and Thomas Narcejac; producer, Clouzot; music, Georges Van Parys; cinematographer, Armand Thirard; editor, Madeleine Gug; running time, 115 min.

THE PLOT:

Schoolmaster Michel Delassale holds a strange power over two beautiful women. He treats his sickly wife Christina terribly, yet she's too intimidated to leave him. Likewise, he badly uses his beautiful mistress, Nicole. She, too, finds herself unable to break away. In an act of incredible self-assurance, Michel invites his mistress to share the home he and his wife inhabit. Incredibly, both women accept this situation and gradually form a close relationship. Finally, neither can stand Michel's outrageous behavior any more. Now best friends, they decide to kill him.

Christina and Nicole drug Paul, drown him in the bathtub, then bury the body. Briefly, the two relax, enjoy their lives, and run the school, telling neighbors that Michel deserted them both. Then, strange things begin happening. Michel's ghost appears to haunt them, as objects appear and disappear. Finally, Michel does appear, as a horrible visage, advancing toward Christina. Terrified, she suffers a heart attack and dies. Michel relaxes, wipes the dirt off his coat, and joins Nicole in celebration of the two of them having pulled off the perfect murder.

THE FILM:

Diabolique has its source in a 1952 novel, *Celle qui n'était plus*, published in America as *The Woman Who Was No More* in 1954. The collaborators, Pierre Boileau and Thomas Narcejac, were Gallic writers who idolized Alfred Hitchcock and hoped to write for him. Since they had no access to the master of suspense, they decided to create a series of novels, all in the Hitchcock style. The books would prove so perfectly suited to what Hitchcock did best that, sooner or later, he would (hopefully) come across them and option one for a film.

Their first effort caught the attention of Henri-Georges Clouzot, one of the many French auteurs of the 1950s and early sixties who likewise idolized Hitchcock. One of Clouzot's early directorial efforts had been 1943's *The Raven* (later filmed in Hollywood by Otto Preminger as 1951's *The 13th Letter*), about poison-pen letters in a small village. Now, though, Clouzot wanted to take a step further in the Hitchcock direction, fashioning films for an icy blonde he admired as much as Hitchcock did Grace Kelly. In Clouzot's case, this was his wife Vera. He announced his future plans in the very name of his own production company, Vera Films. Though Hitchcock had not picked up on the Boileau/Narcejac novel, Clouzot knew upon reading it that his own Hitchcockian abilities in the suspense-thriller genre, as well as his need for a vehicle for his wife, made this book a prime possibility for the next project. The result was hailed by more than one observer as "the best Hitchcock-type thriller *not* made by Hitchcock himself."

Upon seeing the movie, Hitchcock apparently expressed his admiration mixed with regret that he had not happened on the novel before Clouzot. Hitchcock requested that his assistant, Joan Harrison, learn what their next book would be. Already, the collaborators had begun work on a follow-up Hitchcock-inspired epic, *Back From the Dead*, which upon publication did quickly find its way into the master's hands. The result was what many consider to be his greatest—or, at least, most personal—film, *Vertigo* (1958, #11). Finally, the collaborators got what they had wanted all along!

TRIVIA:

In the original novel, Michel is a traveling salesman, not a schoolmaster, and the relationship of the women is more clearly of a lesbian nature. Though this is hinted at in Clouzot's movie, it was toned down in order to avoid censorship problems when the film was eventually screened in America. Still, *Diabolique* was daring enough that, on its initial release in the United States, between seven and nine minutes were considered too risqué and edited out. The film has since been fully restored. It has also been

A Woman's Face: Vera Clouzot was idealized on film by her director husband.

remade numerous times. These include a 1974 version by John Badham, called *Reflections of Murder*, starring Tuesday Weld as the mistress, Joan Hackett as the wife, and Sam Waterston as the husband. Shot in Canada, it's long been considered one of the top ten made-for-television movies of all time. This TV version compares surprisingly well to the original in terms of everything from the level of acting to the intensity of the suspense. The same cannot be said of Jeremiah Chechik's 1996 theatrical remake, with Sharon Stone, Isabelle Adjani, and Chazz Palminteri. An utter disaster, this update veers awkwardly (and at times embarrassingly) between a "straight" remake and a high camp, over-the-top spoof of a thriller.

ALSO RECOMMENDED:

The aforementioned *Reflections of Murder* is nearly as suspenseful as Clouzot's film, which is high praise indeed. Also catch *Le Salaire de la peur* (*The Wages of Fear*, 1953). The effect of watching a motley group transport deadly nitroglycerin across rural Guatemala inspired Bosley Crowther of the *New York Times* to admiringly insist that "you sit there waiting for the theatre to explode." It was disappointingly remade by William Friedkin in 1977 as *Sorcerer*.

76:

THE OTHERS (2001)

Miramax Films

"Sooner or later, they *will* find you."
—Mrs. Mills

CAST:

Nicole Kidman (*Grace Stewart*); Fionnula Flanagan (*Ms. Bertha Mills*); Alakina Mann (*Anne Stewart*); James Bentley (*Nicholas Stewart*); Christopher Eccleston (*Charles Stewart*); Eric Sykes (*Mr. Edmund Tuttle*); Elaine Cassidy (*Lydia*); Réné Asherson (*Old Psychic*); Keith Allen (*Mr. Marlish*); Michelle Fairley (*Mrs. Marlish*); Alexander Vince (*Victor Marlish*); Aldo Grilo (*Gardener*).

CREDITS:

Director, Alejandro Amenábar; screenplay, Amenábar; producers, Fernando Bovaira, Eduardo Chapero-Jackson, Park Sunmin, and Jose Luis Cuerda; original music, Amenábar; cinematographer, Javier Aguirresarobe; editor, Nacho Ruiz Capillas; production design/art director, Benjamin Fernández; special visual effects, Félix Bergés; running time, 101 min.; rating, PG-13.

Single Mom: Nicole Kidman, Alakina Mann, and James Bentley.

THE PLOT:

As the Second World War winds to a close, Grace Stewart packs up her children and heads for Jersey, where she's rented a secluded mansion. Her son, Nicholas, is easily frightened but her older child, Anne, remains in good humor. Grace patiently awaits the return of her husband from the front lines. Frightened during the night, the servants run away, leaving the three alone. Shortly after Grace posts an advertisement letter to the newspaper for a new household staff, several potential candidates arrive, including Mrs. Mills, a middle-aged Irish woman who once ran the place, Lydia, her mute helper, and Mr. Tuttle, the gardener. Grace grows suspicious about their presence when she realizes that her advertisement was never printed. Desperately in need of assistance, she nonetheless keeps them on.

She informs the servants that her children suffer from a strange and unique disease. The shades must be kept down at all times, since the merest touch of sunlight will cause them to become ill. Grace sets up a bizarre series of rules for all to live by, most significant that a door must never be opened until the previously opened one has been closed. Despite such precautions, Grace becomes convinced she and her little ones are threatened, perhaps by ghosts of former residents. What may be spirits are seen—or, more correctly put, felt and almost seen—hurrying down the staircase; a Chopin waltz plays on a piano, though no one is in the room. Grace's daughter feels the presence of a strange little boy in the house, and she terrifies her brother with stories of his existence.

At one point, Grace's husband briefly joins her, then leaves, leading to the possibility that he was himself a ghost. Finally, Grace comes in contact with "the others," those different beings who inhabit the mansion along with herself and family. At last, Grace realizes that she and her children are the ghosts, while "the others" whom she has feared are actually normal people, who have, likewise, become aware they live in a mansion inhabited by "others."

THE FILM:

Following the box-office and critical success of *The Sixth Sense* (1999, #24), Hollywood became swept up by a craze for ghost movies. Most were abominable attempts to ape a great film's magic, including an embarrassing remake of Robert Wise's classic *The Haunting* (1963, #26) and a redux of that old William Castle B-movie clunker, *The House on Haunted Hill* (1958). Finally, though, one filmmaker did manage to come up with a classic. Numerous critics noted that director Amenábar chose the 1940s style of filming ghost stories—oblique and suggestive— which perfectly fit the period-piece trappings. Lawrence Toppman rightly tagged *The Others* "the most sophisticated and satisfying ghost story on film since *The Sixth Sense*" in his *Charlotte Observer* review.

"Like *Sense*," he added, "it begins with an eight-year-old who claims to see dead people. But the mystery deepens quickly, and the long-delayed payoff will catch you off-guard." Some critics—and audiences—complained that the pace was too slow. Considering that *The Others* was a thriller, not enough happened for every taste. But this is a self-consciously old-fashioned movie, part of a tradition in which that was the way suspense gradually built to a climax.

"Certain things should be taken slowly," Toppman added, "exquisite meals, the adagios in Mahler symphonies and especially ghost stories. Horror films provide blunt shocks, but spooky tales need to build gradually to a stunning climax." That sums up the film's remarkable ability to pull off its haunting effect, leaving us wondering at the end how we managed to miss all the hints—some pretty obvious—that could lead to no other possible conclusion.

TRIVIA:

Though set in rural England, the movie was shot in Madrid, Spain and Oheka Castle, New York. Tom Cruise, who was still married to Nicole Kidman at the time, served as executive producer. Cinematographer Javier Aguirresarobe shot the film by candlelight to create the proper mood, a technique not employed for an entire motion picture since Kubrick's *Barry Lyndon* (1975). At the Academy of Science Fiction, Fantasy & Horror Films (2002), *The Others* won the coveted Saturn Award and Amenábar was honored as Best Writer. The London Critics Circle picked Kidman as Best Actress of the Year. This was the film that proved Nicole was a heavyweight actress as well as a great screen beauty.

ALSO RECOMMENDED:

A fine ghost story which fans of this film will want to catch is Lewis Allen's *The Uninvited* (1944). In it, Ray Milland is more curious than terrified as he realizes his home is haunted by a distraught spirit. Also not to be missed is Jack Clayton's *The Innocents* (1961), with Deborah Kerr as a governess unsure whether her house is haunted or if she's mad. The film, coscripted by Truman Capote, is a variation on Henry James's *The Turn of the Screw*. Amenábar fans must catch *Open Your Eyes* (1998), in which Penelope Cruz essays the same role she later played in the American remake, *Vanilla Sky* (2001).

75:
PICKUP ON SOUTH STREET (1953)

20th Century Fox

"Who cares?"
> **—Skip McCoy, about communist spies**

CAST:

Richard Widmark (*Skip McCoy*); Jean Peters (*Candy*); Thelma Ritter (*Moe*); Murvyn Vye (*Capt. Dan Tiger*); Richard Kiley (*Joey*); Willis B. Bouchey (*Zara*); Milburn Stone (*Winoki*); Henry Slate (*McGregor*); Ray Stevens (*FBI Agent*).

CREDITS:

Director, Samuel Fuller; screenplay, Fuller, from a concept by Dwight Taylor; producer, Jules Schermer; music, Leigh Harline and Lionel Newman; cinematographer, Joe Macdonald; editor, Nick De Maggio; art directors, Lyle Wheeler and George Patrick; running time, 83 min.

THE PLOT:

On a New York City subway, professional pickpocket Skip McCoy spots a potential mark, a pretty young woman who may have something of value in her purse. He slips close and, at the right moment, steals the purse's contents. Back in his sleazy waterfront abode, McCoy considers what appears to be a worthless piece of micro-film. What Skip doesn't realize is that it contains coveted government secrets. The girl, Candy, was the mistress of a Communist. Three-time-loser lowlife Skip is now in possession of materials that both federal agents and Russian spies will do any-thing to get their hands on.

Feds who were tailing Candy contact the police and tell their tale of being beaten to the punch by a pickpocket. Capt. Tiger guesses who this must have been, helping the feds track down Skip. An elderly lady of the streets named Old Moe confirms to the authorities that Skip does have the invaluable object. When Com-munist agent Joey approaches her, Moe lets him beat her to death rather than hurt her country by telling what she knows to a Soviet spy. Her life on the line, Candy tracks down Skip. The Commies have told her that she must bring back the micro-film or suffer the consequences. An awkward romance ensues.

Though Candy comes into possession of the microfilm, her patriotism is re-ignited and she works with the feds. This is the catalyst that finally causes cyn-ical Skip to do the right thing. Morally reawakened, he tails Joey and confronts him on the subway, bringing the spy to justice.

THE FILM:

During the early 1950s, the film noir style that had dominated Hollywood drama for five years began to wane. First, however, it gave birth to an intriguing—if by today's standards, bizarre—sub-genre: the anti-Communist propaganda film.

River Rats: Jean Peters and Richard Widmark

These ranged from tacky low-budget affairs like Republic's *The Red Menace* (1949) to major studio extravaganzas such as *My Son John* (1952) starring lofty talents Helen Hayes and Robert Walker. Most are insufferable today and are rarely, if ever, shown. The one exception is *Pickup,* a suspense thriller that triumphs owing to writer-director Sam Fuller's ability to transcend the dubious sub-genre's obvious limitations.

Significantly, we don't learn an awful lot about what exists on that microfilm. This follows Hitchcock's key rule for the MacGuffin: the less that the audience knows about what's inside the pumpkin, the better. This approach works well today: the vagueness of what's inside the much-desired suitcase was essential to the appeal of Quentin Tarantino's *Pulp Fiction* (1994). Blake Lucas has noted that *Pickup* passes the test of time as an exercise in pure form: "Fuller is never stylistically redundant. Long takes, such as the moving shot that stalks Candy as Joey assaults her, alternate with rhythmically cut sequences. Intense close-ups often dominate, but at other times the camera glides over the action, coming to rest and resuming movement at unexpected intervals." The Fuller vision is nowhere more effectively conveyed than in this film. Those people whom respectable Americans barely notice—the Bowery bums of that time and the street people of Times Square—are the ones who sacrifice everything to do what is right, giving of themselves in a way that (at least in Sam Fuller films) respectable middle-class people never do.

The great character arc is the one that Skip must navigate. Initially, he seems a fitting symbol of the early fifties syndrome known as "the lonely crowd," an inner-directed rugged individualist in the worst sense of the term—interested only in himself. Through the love of a flawed but worthwhile woman who has herself gone through a great deal to try and do the right thing, his morality is reawakened. Thus, Skip's initial cynicism is not shared by the writer-director, but perceived and portrayed as a natural product of the times. Such cynicism has to be overcome as part of his reclamation of the last remaining spot of goodness that still existed somewhere deep within.

As to Skip's willingness to punch Candy one moment and caress her the next, that makes him a strong example of the new breed of screen antiheroes then making their mark. He set the pace for, among others, Ralph Meeker as Mike Hammer in Robert Aldrich's adaptation of Mickey Spillane's *Kiss Me Deadly* (1955).

TRIVIA:

Though the film is ultra-conservative in its attitudes, star Widmark was actually a bleeding-heart liberal. Star Jean Peters was the long-time mistress of Howard

Hughes. Character actor Milburn Stone was spotted by the producers of an upcoming TV western and awarded the role of "Doc" on *Gunsmoke*.

ALSO RECOMMENDED:

Other top Red Scare thrillers include Victor Saville's *Conspirator* (1949), in which Elizabeth Taylor realizes that husband Robert Taylor is an enemy agent, and Gordon Douglas's *I Was a Communist for the F.B.I.* (a.k.a., *The Woman on Pier 13*, 1951), with Frank Lovejoy excellent as a double-agent. Widmark also shines in another Fuller thriller, the submarine adventure *Hell and High Water* (1954).

74:

MARATHON MAN (1976)

Paramount Pictures

> **"You're not afraid of the dentist, are you, little boy?"**
> **—Szell to Babe before torturing him**

CAST:

Dustin Hoffman (*Babe*); Laurence Olivier (*Szell*); Roy Scheider (*Doc*); Marthe Keller (*Elsa*); William Devane (*Janeway*); Fritz Weaver (*Prof. Biesenthal*); Richard Bright (*Karl*); Marc Lawrence (*Erhard*); Allen Joseph (*Babe's Father*); Tito Goya (*Melendez*); Ben Dova (*Szell's Brother*); Lou Gilbert (*Rosenbaum*); Jacques Marin (*LeClerc*); James Wing Woo (*Chen*).

CREDITS:

Director, John Schlesinger; screenplay, William Goldman, from his novel; producers, Robert Evans and Sidney Beckerman; original music, Michael Small; cinematographer, Conrad Hall; editor, Jim Clark; running time, 125 min.; rating, R.

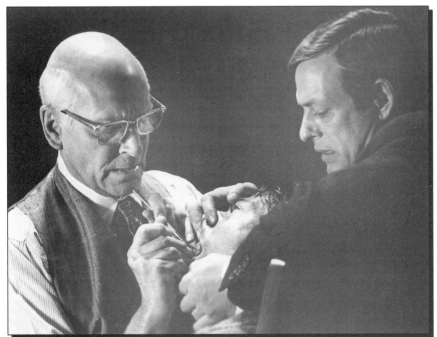

In *Marathon Man*, Dustin Hoffman undergoes a form of torture first suggested in the early Hitchcock thriller, *the Man Who Knew Too Much.*

THE PLOT:

Two elderly New York drivers find themselves locked in a duel as they cruise the city's mean streets. The drag-racing situation escalates, as people scatter out of the way, until a terrible crash instantly kills one man. The dead man is the brother of Szell, a onetime Nazi concentration camp boss. His brother was serving as the American custodian of a fortune that Szell, a dentist by trade, extracted from Jewish inmates. Quite literally, he pulled the gold out of their teeth, later transferring the fortune to diamonds that are locked away in a Manhattan safe-deposit box that only his brother had access to. Now, that precious connection is gone. This necessitates that Szell come out of hiding, and into conflict with an American agent, Scylla. Eventually, the agent is shot, and he shows up at the apartment of his younger brother. Babe is an intense student who had no idea that his sibling (known to him as "Doc") was in any way involved with international intrigue. Shortly, the men who murdered Scylla/Doc are after Babe, who falls in love with a beautiful, mysterious woman of European descent. Soon, though, Babe wonders whether she may, in fact, be less an innocent new acquaintance than a part of the evil Szell's plan to learn precisely what Babe does or does not know about the hidden fortune.

As the forces of evil close in, Babe realizes that his hobby—training for the marathon—may save his life, for he must flee on foot and literally run for his life. First, though, he must suffer the most horrific day at the dentist's anyone ever suffered (including Jack Nicholson in Roger Corman's *The Little Shop of Horrors*!) as Szell employs his dental equipment to torture Babe.

THE FILM:

Along with *The Holocaust* mini-series on NBC television and another thriller, *The Boys From Brazil* (1978) also starring Olivier, *Marathon Man* represented part of a mini-boomlet of significant works about "the final solution"—the Nazi plan to exterminate the Jews—to appear during the seventies. Writer Goldman (*Butch Cassidy and the Sundance Kid*, 1969) effectively combined a serious consideration of history (Babe is haunted by memories of his father's blacklisting during the McCarthy era of the fifties) with top-notch thriller techniques. John Schlesinger (*Midnight Cowboy*, 1969), an English director who often worked in America, neatly paired two of the era's greatest performers: Hoffman, the American "method" actor who works from the inside out, and Olivier, the British "technique" actor who works from the outside in. The former must always find a link between himself and the character; the latter claims that picking the right tie can set a role in place.

TRIVIA:

A legendary (if perhaps apocryphal) behind-the-scenes story claims that Dustin, knowing that he must appear harried for an upcoming scene and always eager to live his role—stayed up all night, then ran around the block several times. Finally certain that he looked awful enough to make the scene convincing, he showed up on the set where Olivier patiently waited. "Dustin, dear boy," the old Brit supposedly quipped, "why don't you just try . . . *acting*?" At the time of the film's release, critics were mixed in their reaction to the offbeat teaming of the stars. Robert Hatch of *The Nation* complained, "Dustin Hoffman does again his impersonation of a homicidal mouse, and Olivier, with the help of a pair of very thick lenses, attains the final pinnacle of the master criminal cliché." Contrarily, Jay Cocks of *Time* spoke for most fans of both stars when he wrote that "the movie offers Dustin Hoffman, giving one of his best performances, up against Laurence Olivier, who is in fine form playing an arch villain."

Though the film is exceptionally well paced and at times quite terrifying, one aspect of the novel—in fact, the device that made it so particularly powerful—could not be translated to the screen. While reading the book, we have no reason to believe that the spy Scylla and Babe's brother Doc are the same person. Their episodes are so distant in terms of the lives that they lead, we simply assume they are different people. Until, that is, Scylla is wounded by the Nazis and in desperation seeks out Babe, then collapses into his arms. But since a film, by its very nature, reveals what the characters look like, this unexpected plot reversal couldn't survive the transition to the screen.

ALSO RECOMMENDED:

Franklin J. Schaffner's 1978 *The Boys From Brazil* (from a novel by Ira Levin, who also penned *Rosemary's Baby*) depicts Nazi kingpin Joseph Mengele (Gregory Peck) attempting to clone a new Hitler. This time, Olivier gets to play the good guy, as an aged Nazi hunter. To see the sequence that inspired this film's dental-torture, catch the similar scene in the early Hitchcock thriller, *The Man Who Knew Too Much* (1934).

73:

FAIL-SAFE (1964)

Columbia Pictures

> **"It will have you sitting on the brink of eternity!"**
> **—original advertising tag line**

CAST:

> Henry Fonda (*The President*); Walter Matthau (*Professor Groteschele*); Dan O'Herlihy (*Brigadier General Warren Black*); Frank Overton (*General Bogan S.A.C.*); Ed Binns (*Col. Jack Grady*); Fritz Weaver (*Colonel Cascio*); Larry Hagman (*Buck*); William Hansen (*Secretary Swenson*); Russell Hardie (*General Stark*); Russell Collins (*Gordon Knapp*); Sorrell Booke (*Congressman Raskob*); Dom DeLuise (*Tech. Sgt. Collins*); Dana Elcar (*Mr. Foster*).

CREDITS:

Director, Sidney Lumet; screenplay, Walter Bernstein, from the novel by Eugene Burdick and Harvey Wheeler; producers, Lumet, Charles H. Maguire, and Max E. Youngstein; cinematographer, Gerald Hirschfeld; editor, Ralph Rosenblum; art director, Albert Brenner; set decorator, J.C. Delaney; running time, 111 min.

THE PLOT:

At the height of the Cold War, a series of random accidents and unavoidable bits of incompetence on both the Soviet and American sides turn the routine situation of nuclear surveillance into an ever-escalating situation that could result in the end of the world. First, U.S. security reports an unidentified aircraft apparently moving in the direction of the U.S.. In response, a quintet of bombers, each equipped with a nuclear warhead, is sent toward Moscow. Their orders are to strike if they do not receive further word from home base. Shortly, that previously unidentified aircraft is discovered to be a commercial plane. The base attempts to recall the bombers at once, only to discover their fail-safe mechanism won't work, owing to a technical failure.

The planes cannot be recalled, and will continue and bomb Moscow, leaving the Soviets with no other possible response than to strike back. While remaining

A frightened translator (Fritz Weaver) is carried out of the War Room.

in frantic communication with his counterpart, the Premiere, on the hotline, the American President desperately commands his military forces and political advisors to release U.S. fighter jets to shoot down the bombers. For one of the president's advisors, Dr. Gottschalk, this situation can be employed as a means of smashing the enemy once and for all. For General Black, it is a challenge to illustrate all of his talents at military strategy. When all realize that the bombers cannot be stopped in time by the jets, the president agrees to allow Russia to bomb New York City to compensate for the Soviet loss, thereby avoiding a retaliation that would lead to the end of the world. This "logical" compromise reveals the absolute madness of the then-current situation.

THE FILM:

Fail-Safe represented, along with the better known *Dr. Strangelove* (1964, #4), a final pair of bookends for a unique genre of the suspense thriller that had come into being fifteen years earlier. The realization that Soviet spies had spirited into enemy hands the secret of the atomic bomb created an immediate emotional letdown from the euphoria with which the war had ended. With the realization that nuclear weapons were pointed at America, even as American weapons were aimed at the Soviets, an altogether new, dark, paranoid mood fell over the country during the Eisenhower era. Hollywood reacted by producing a succession of films that played off and, in many cases, exploited our fears, including such notable dramas as *The World, The Flesh, and the Devil* (1959) and *On the Beach* (1959). By 1964, Stanley Kubrick could film a black comedy on the subject, subtitled "How I Learned to Stop Worrying and Love the Bomb." Such denial was challenged by *Fail-Safe*, perhaps the most worthy drama made on the subject. But if the public was ready to laugh at their onetime widespread fears, they had seen enough dramatic depictions over the years to feel sated. Ironically, what may be the finest dramatic depiction on the subject was also the least widely seen, despite a low-key approach that brought the situation vividly to life. While fervently anti-nuke, the film never becomes a polemic on the subject. Always, *Fail-Safe* communicates its ideas through the edgy entertainment of a political suspense thriller.

TRIVIA:

When Lumet approached the Department of Defense to ask for cooperation, the director/producer was coldly rebuffed. This necessitated that stock footage of a single Convair B-58 Hustler be employed for the diverse shots of our Vindicator bombers. Both of the great Cold War thrillers released in 1964, *Fail-Safe* and

Dr. Strangelove, were distributed by the same company, Columbia. Each film was shot on three sets, realistically designed, then shot with offbeat camera angles and surrealistic lighting to convey the sense of a nightmare scenario. Even the hideous professor played in this film by Walter Matthau is a less caricatured incarnation of the title figure in the other film. One major problem in distributing this film abroad was the title, which made no sense when removed from the American scene of the time. *Fail-Safe* was rechristened *A Prova di Errore* (*A Case of Error*) in Italy, *Bombs* in Sweden, and *Miss Suicida* in Portugal. A huge fan of the film, George Clooney produced a live-TV version in 2000, with Richard Dreyfuss playing the president.

ALSO RECOMMENDED:

Sidney Lumet's other memorable thrillers include *12 Angry Men* (1957), his directing debut, with Henry Fonda heading an all-star cast as a jury must decide the fate of a man accused of murder. Other than the opening and closing shots, the entire film takes place in a single room. For more Cold War nuke thrillers, catch *The Bedford Incident* (1965), with Sidney Poitier and Richard Widmark deciding whether to fire a nuclear weapon at a Soviet ship, and *Crimson Tide* (1995), with Denzel Washington and Gene Hackman in virtually the same situation.

72:
THE WICKER MAN (1973)

Warner Bros.

> **"We are the minions of the moon."**
> **—Willow**

CAST:

Edward Woodward (*Sgt. Neil Howie*); Christopher Lee (*Lord Summerisle*); Diane Cilento (*Miss Rose*); Britt Ekland (*Willow*); Ingrid Pitt (*Wicca*

Woman); Lindsay Kemp (*Alder MacGregor*); Russell Waters (*Harbor Master*); Aubrey Morris (*Gardener*); Ian Campbell (*Oak*); Geraldine Cowper (*Rowan*).

CREDITS:

Director, Robin Hardy; screenplay, Anthony Shaffer; producer, Peter Snell; music, Paul Giovanni; cinematographer, Harry Waxman; editor, Eric Boyd-Perkins; running time, 102 min.; rating, R.

THE PLOT:

In a Scotch harbor town, fellow police officers laugh at Sgt. Howie behind his back because he, and he alone, takes his job so seriously. A dedicated detective, Sgt. Howie is also a lay-preacher (of Puritan temperament) and a virgin who insists he will never know a woman until he is married. Then, an anonymous resident of a small island, Summerisle, contacts Howie, informing him that a child named Rowan Morrison had disappeared. The local authorities made no serious attempt to track her down. Shortly, Howie arrives on the island and realizes that the people live entirely out of time. This is a pagan place, where women still dance and copulate with various males under the moonlight; children still dance around a huge wooden phallic symbol in May Day rituals; the pagans still worship hares as the animal that signifies the magic of reproduction. Though the Lord of the island seems sophisticated and welcomes Howie, he insists their secrets are best left alone. Howie becomes convinced that Rowan has not (as he initially assumed) been murdered but was kidnapped. The crops have failed; pagans traditionally attempt to win over their angry gods by sacrificing an innocent, who attends the pagan rites by free will.

Though the island people attempt to keep Howie from learning where their spring ritual will be held, he does detective work and discovers the time and the place. On the morning that the blood sacrifice is to take place, he disguises himself and joins the parade of masked pagans. Decked out in the guise of beasts, they head for the appointed place by the seashore. When the pagans lead Rowan (who is indeed alive) to the sacrificial alter, Howie doffs his costume and rushes to save her, though Rowan gleefully throws herself into the arms of Lord Summerisle. Her disappearance was a ruse, designed to lure Howie to this place so the villagers could sacrifice a virgin Christian. The pagans place Howie in a huge "wicker man," where he is burned alive; as he dies, he sings the Puritan prayers while, around him, villagers chant their songs of sensuality.

Christopher Lee worships the Devil before the title object in *The Wicker Man*.

THE FILM:

At the Festival of Fantastic Films in Paris, 1973, the recently completed *The Wicker Man* received the Grand Prize as "the best new horror film." However, it is less a genre movie than a one-of-a-kind suspense film, and the most accurate ever made on the subject of witchcraft. Robin Hardy, the film's first time director, had once accidentally happened upon just such a pagan rite in a Cornish Village, and the incident haunted him thereafter. He persuaded producer Peter Snell to finance a film on the subject, and they were lucky enough to acquire the talents of writer Anthony Shaffer, who had penned the acclaimed suspense play and film *Sleuth* (1972, #41).

Danny Peary effectively explains *The Wicker Man*'s impact, "Because every episode that takes place along the way is presented with tongue seemingly in cheek, there is not a frightening moment before the horrifying sacrifice. Yet there is an accumulative effect whereby we become increasingly unnerved. By the end, we have stopped smiling." Also important to the impact is that, like *The Exorcist*— shot more or less simultaneous with *The Wicker Man*—this film offers an early example of "terror by daylight," thus rejecting the old shadow world format of earlier thrillers. Despite great care taken in presenting the world of Wicca, most modern pagans despise the film, claiming that—however effectively the individual symbols and rituals might have been—*The Wicker Man* leaves a viewer with the impression that all Wiccans, modern or ancient, are essentially violent and devious, whereas most employ their unique "arts" only for positive purposes.

TRIVIA:

Owing to a tight shooting schedule, the movie—set entirely in springtime—had to be shot in the dead of winter, 1972. This necessitated that the film crew spend hours cutting individual faux flowers out of colored paper, then pasting them everywhere in the forest before each scene was shot. Because of the film's uniqueness, producer Snell had great trouble in finding a distributor in the United States. Even Roger Corman turned *The Wicker Man* down, claiming that it was too steeped in genre elements (including the presence of the screen's current Dracula, Christopher Lee) to be marketed as an arthouse item, yet too arty to satisfy those who came for the cheap thrills of a typical Lee vehicle. Warner Bros. eventually distributed a butchered print, which left out the opening prologue, that establishes Howie's virginity, without which nothing else in the movie makes any sense. Though a full 102 min. version is now available on video, Hardy has often insisted even this does not capture the full impact of what he had originally shot.

ALSO RECOMMENDED:

For other fine examples of suspense films derived from the practice of witchcraft, see Roman Polanski's *Rosemary's Baby* (1968, #19) and his *Macbeth* (1971), as well as Edgar G. Ulmer's *The Black Cat* (1934, #32).

71:
THE LOST PATROL (1934)

RKO Radio Pictures

> **"Where are my men? *There* are my men!"**
> **—Victor McLaglen (The Sergeant), pointing to a dozen graves**

CAST:

Victor McLaglen (*The Sergeant*); Boris Karloff (*Sanders*); Wallace Ford (*Morelli*); Reginald Denny (*George Brown*); J.M. Kerrigan (*Quincannon*);

Billy Bevan (*Herbert Hale*); Alan Hale (*Matlow Cook*); Brandon Hurst (*Bell*); Douglas Walton (*Pearson*); Sammy Stein (*Abelson*); Howard Wilson (*The Aviator*); Paul Hanson (*MacKay*); Francis Ford (*Lonely Man*).

CREDITS:

Director, John Ford; screenwriters, Dudley Nichols and Garrett Fort, from a short story by Philip MacDonald; producers, Ford, Merian C. Cooper, and Cliff Reid; original music, Max Steiner; cinematographer, Harold Wenstrom; editor, Paul Weatherwax; art directors, Van Nest Polglase and Sidney Ullman; orchestration, Bernhard Kaun; running time, 73 min.

THE PLOT:

In 1917, on an arid stretch of desert in Mesopotamia, members of a British patrol rein in their horses for a brief rest. An Arab sniper fires a single shot, killing the lieutenant. The sergeant assumes command, allowing the most religious member of the squad, Sanders, to bury the officer and say a few words. The sergeant

Victor McLaglen (center) spots a plane attempting to land.

explains that he has no idea where they are or why; this was a secret mission and only the lieutenant knew the orders. Wandering north, they spot an oasis and stop to refresh themselves. A young soldier, Pearson, stands guard that night. In the morning, the others discover his dead body with a knife in the back. All their horses have been stolen. The Arabs who killed the lieutenant were also headed for the oasis. Like the British, they don't have enough water to reach the river without replenishing themselves. The tribesmen have no option other than to take the oasis by force.

The men bury Pearson, using his sword in place of a cross, then decide to make a stand. Trooper Brown suggests slipping out at night to find the snipers and slit their throats. Sanders goes berserk and has to be tied up, though he escapes and wanders into the desert, singing strange hymns, and carrying a huge makeshift cross. A plane attempts to rescue the remaining soldiers but snipers kill the pilot. Alone, the sergeant realizes that the tribesmen are so crazed with thirst that they will rush him en masse. He shoots them down with a machine gun. As crazed as Sanders now, the sergeant faces the relief column and points to the long line of graves, insisting that his patrol is ready to greet the reinforcements.

THE FILM:

John Ford always claimed to make "one for them, one for me," shooting a big-scale picture some studio wanted if that company would also finance a tightly-budgeted but highly personal film. *The Lost Patrol* (1934) is an example of the latter. The film is a labor of love featuring no big stars, but rather an excellent array of character actors playing finely-wrought men in complex relationships with one another. The budget was a mere $254,000, considerably less than Ford had to spend on such extravaganzas as *The Iron Horse* (1924) and *Drums Along the Mohawk* (1939). Every penny shows up onscreen, and the audience is convinced that it has been transported to some isolated exotic place, even though the company never left Yuma, Arizona. The result was the most suspenseful war movie ever made. As Sanderson Beck noted, "This bleak story exposes the futility and waste of war and the killing of enemies. . . . The enemy is unseen until the end when they are all killed, emphasizing the mysterious dehumanization of war." The enemy is, simply, the *other* of the thriller genre, barely glimpsed agents of death and danger that exist in the shadows on the edge of the screen.

Often derided as a jingoistic patriot, Ford fashioned this film between the two great World Wars. His film offers a harsh commentary on the waste of the first and a grim warning about our becoming involved in yet another conflict. The acting is dazzling, particularly in those scenes that feature McLaglen and Karloff in tandem. At the time, Boris was attempting to rid himself of the Frankenstein monster stigma, searching for strong character roles that would show his enormous talent to advantage. Though Ford did exploit the actor's ripe association with the macabre, the director allowed the actor to create a unique, eccentric performance, unlike anything Karloff—or, for that matter, anyone else—had ever done. Few films of any genre create and sustain such a remarkable aura of anxiety. *The Lost Patrol* involves us deeply with characters who are less than likable as individuals, yet whose fates nonetheless keep us on the edge of our seats throughout.

TRIVIA:

Previous versions of the story include one filmed in England in 1929. This was one of of that country's final silent films before the conversion to sound took place later that same year, by Hitchcock with his early masterpiece, *Blackmail* (1929). In the British silent, the role that Victor McLaglen plays in Ford's film went to Victor's older brother, Cyril.

ALSO RECOMMENDED:

The first official remake was a B-western by Lew Landers called *Bad Lands* (1939). *The Lost Patrol* was remade twice during World War II, and both films come close to equaling the original in terms of suspense. In Tay Garnett's *Bataan* (1943), Robert Taylor commanded a motley group of Americans. That same year, Zoltan Korda's *Sahara* reset the story in Africa, with Humphrey Bogart in command of a stranded tank crew. Also influencing this version was a similar Russian film, *Thirteen* (1937). Ford's other most impressive exercise in suspense is a little known gem, *The Fugitive* (1947), about a priest (Henry Fonda) on the run from political enemies in Mexico.

70:

CAT PEOPLE (1942)

RKO Radio Pictures

"Her kiss means death!"
—advertising tag line

CAST:

Simone Simon (*Irena Dubrovna*); Kent Smith (*Oliver Reed*); Tom Conway (*Dr. Judd*); Jane Randolph (*Alice Moore*); Jack Holt (*The Commodore*); Elizabeth Russell (*Cat Woman*); Theresa Harris (*Minnie*); Alec Craig (*Zookeeper*); Dot Farley (*Cleaning Lady*); Alan Napier (*Doc*); Steve Soldi (*Organ Grinder*).

CREDITS:

Director, Jacques Tourneur; screenplay, De Witt Bodeen; producer, Val Lewton; original music, Roy Webb; cinematographer, Nicholas Musuraca; editor, Mark Robson; art directors, Albert S. D'Agostino and Walter E. Keller; special sound effects, John L. Cass; special photographic effects, Linwood G. Dunn; running time, 73 min.

THE PLOT:

In New York, Oliver—a white-collar working stiff—visits the zoo on his day off and notices a beautiful, exotic, mysterious young woman sketching the black panther. Nervously, he strikes up a conversation and learns that she is Irena, a recent arrival from Serbia. Oliver is delighted when she agrees to date him. He tells his friends at work, including Alice Moore, who is happy for Oliver, though she always belelieved they would become a couple. While celebrating the engagement in a restaurant, a strange woman, whose features resemble that of a cat, stops by the table and with a look acknowledges Irena as her sinister sister. Nonetheless, the marriage takes place, though Oliver must deal with a unique problem. He cannot sleep with his wife, for she believes that any sexual contact will awaken a terrible beast within her that will destroy the man in her arms.

Oliver consults a psychiatrist, Dr. Judd, though he soon covets Irena and plans to seduce her. The marriage becomes increasingly strained, causing Oliver and Alice to become closer. Furious, Irena stalks Alice—first as she waits for a bus, and later as Alice swims in a basement pool at her apartment house. Finally, Irena turns into a panther, cornering Alice and Oliver at their office after hours. But the decent, human element in Irena will not allow her to kill people she cares about. So she returns home, where Dr. Judd awaits. When he attempts to kiss her, Irena tears him to shreds, though he wounds her with the blade he carries inside a walking stick.

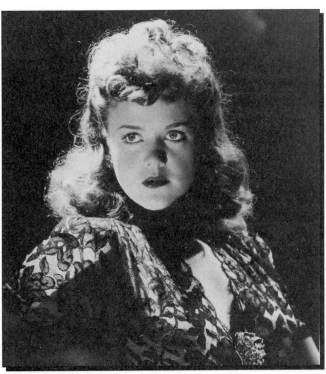

Kiss of Death: Simone Simon as Irena.

THE FILM:

Stephen King has claimed that *Cat People* "is almost certainly the best" thriller of the forties, an extreme but valid claim from a man who knows the genre well. It was the film that changed the notion of screen terror from the *seen* to the *unseen*, thereby bringing the genre out of the world of monster movies and into the realm of suspense. Writer Val Lewton came on board to head up the low-budget division at RKO Radio Pictures. His assignment was to make inexpensive movies with strong box-office potential, and the studio heads were convinced that macabre tales, which had done so well for Universal, could likewise be profitable for them. In part because there was little money available for special effects, and in part because he believed that revealing the monster would diminish rather than heighten the growing sense of terror, Lewton decided to show as little as possible, creating tension through tight cutting and keeping the creature—real or imagined—in the darkness at the edge of the frame.

According to Lewton, the ideal horror film would be ninety minutes of a black screen, accompanied by eerie but unrecognizable sounds. This would allow the audience to release their own deepest, darkest fears and project them onto the screen, seeing not what was there but what they feared and had always repressed. In this manner—what J.P. Telotte would call "the presence of absence"—Lewton and his directorial collaborators would, beginning with *Cat People*, literally reinvent the film of terror. They created a nightmare by daylight which encroaches on real, everyday settings. For budgetary reasons and in order to carefully control such effects as lighting and atmosphere, Lewton and Jacques Tourneur shot *Cat People* inside a studio—much as the Germans had done beginning with *The Cabinet of Dr. Caligari* (1919). This allowed Lewton to offer a unique double-vision; scary scenes, such as Irena stalking Alice at midnight, take place in what appears to be Central Park yet is not precisely that place. It is, instead, Central Park as it would appear in our worst collective nightmare.

Likewise, the film proved that in the unique realm of the suspense thriller, moviemakers could deal with then-forbidden subjects. Though the term is never mentioned during the drama, *Cat People* is actually about the issue of female frigidity, which in the tight restrictions of Hollywood's Production Code days could not have been approached in a more realistic melodrama.

TRIVIA:

The film was ahead of its time in featuring the concept of psychology, which would come to dominate the American cinema during the postwar years, beginning with Alfred Hitchcock's *Spellbound* (1946). *Cat People* is also out of time, for while it clearly takes place in the 1940s, there is no mention of the ongoing war in Europe. By contrast, almost every other movie of the period makes some acknowledgement of the conflict.

ALSO RECOMMENDED:

The sequel, *Curse of the Cat People* (1944) directed by Robert Wise, introduces the lonely daughter of Oliver and Alice. Irena's spirit visits the child; this thriller is ostensibly about autistic children. Also catch director Tourneur's fine English film, *Curse of the Demon* (1958), which likewise shows us as little of the title monster as possible.

69:

BASIC INSTINCT (1992)

TriStar

> **"So, are you going to charge me with smoking?"**
> **—Catherine Tramell**

CAST:

Michael Douglas (*Detective Nick Curran*); Sharon Stone (*Catherine Tramell*); George Dzundza (*Gus*); Jeanne Tripplehorn (*Elisabeth "Beth" Garner, Ph.D.*); Denis Arndt (*Lieutenant Walker*); Leilani Sarelle (*Roxy*); Bruce A. Young (*Andrews*); Chelcie Ross (*Captain Talcott*); Dorothy Malone (*Hazel Dobkins*); Wayne Knight (*John Correli*); Daniel von Bargen (*Nilsen*); Mitch Pileggi (*Internal Affairs Investigator*).

CREDITS:

Director, Paul Verhoeven; screenplay, Joe Eszterhas; producers, Alan Marshall and William S. Beasley; original music, Jerry Goldsmith; cinematographer, Jan de Bont; editor, Frank J. Urioste; production design, Terence Marsh; art directors, Mark Billerman and William Cruse; special effects, Rob Bottin; running time, 127 min. (original release print), 128 min. (director's cut); rating, R.

THE PLOT:

San Francisco Detective Nick Curran has a dark history. Accused of unnecessary brutality, he's currently being investigated by Internal Affairs for firing his gun too quickly and injuring innocent bystanders. Nonetheless, Nick and his partner Gus are assigned to investigate the bizarre murder of a music star killed with an ice pick while at the height of orgasm. Incredibly, the deceased man's lover, Catherine Tramell, recently wrote a book with precisely that plot. Is this an obvious confession before the fact? Or perhaps someone had reason to frame Catherine by killing the rocker in a way that would point a guilty finger at her.

Rather than attempt to clear herself, Catherine revels in the attention, particularly when it becomes obvious that Nick is attracted to her. The more the evi-

Femme Fatale: Sharon Stone as Catherine.

dence points to Catherine, the more attracted he becomes, particularly after he realizes she has set to work on a new novel about a police detective murdered by the suspect he becomes obsessed with. Catherine has a lesbian lover, Roxy, and Nick's old girlfriend, Beth, offers him respite from the ever more intense situation. But in his twisted state of mind, Nick convinces himself Beth was the killer and shoots her. Alone in bed with Catherine, he plans their future even as she reaches under the bed for an ice pick.

THE FILM:

In films as different as *Vertigo* and *Marnie*, Hitchcock offered audiences a psychologically troubled hero who becomes obsessed by a beautiful blonde, probably a killer, and an equally striking brunette, who offers him salvation. Even knowing all this, he cannot help but make the wrong choice and embrace the blonde. The theme, as the master of suspense described it, is the desire for the fall. The protagonist is like a male spider or praying mantis, understanding that the female of the species is far deadlier than the male. Yet he is caught up in the combination of death wish and desire for the ultimate sexual release.

Hitchcock's most vivid statement appeared in *The Paradine Case* (1948), in which barrister Gregory Peck fervently defends a client (Valli) accused of murder. Everyone else, however—including his loyal and loving wife—grasps that she is as guilty as sin. This only makes him more obsessed with somehow setting her free so that he can be her next victim. Unfortunately, the film was marred by the tamperings of producer David O. Selznick, causing the final split between the two long-time collaborators. Screenwriter Joe Eszterhas had tried a similar ploy in 1985's *Jagged Edge*, in which it was a female lawyer (Glenn Close) who was attracted to a dangerous male client (Jeff Bridges). Unfortunately, the at-best-ordinary direction of Richard Marquand failed to realize that script's potential. Luckily, the gifted Dutch director Paul Verhoeven—who had proved his abilities as a director of stylish, surealistic suspense thrillers with *The Fourth Man* (1983)—won the opportunity to bring the *Basic Instinct* script to the screen as the kind of twisted psycho-sexual "entertainment" that Hitchcock had been fascinated with toward the end of his career. Had he still been alive and working, Hitchcock would likely have found this project irresistibly attractive.

TRIVIA:

Kim Basinger, Greta Scacchi, and Michelle Pfeiffer had been sought for the role of Catherine, but turned it down, fearing it might wreck their careers. The role made a major star out of Sharon Stone, who won the Cannes Film Festival Award for Best Actress. All of Catherine's costumes are modeled on ones Kim Novak wore in *Vertigo* (1958, #11). Also, the fact that both movies take place in San Francisco is hardly coincidental. Gay rights activists picketed the movie, claiming that by having a bisexual character turn out to be the killer, *Basic Instinct* reinforced popular prejudices—i.e., supposedly implying that people with differing sexual orientations are dangerous. Most observers believed that without the controversy, the film never would have succeeded so well at the boxoffice.

Basic Instinct* would become the most often spoofed film of the nineties, with burlesques of its various gambits—particularly Sharon Stone's leg-crossing sans panties sequence—appearing in *Fatal Instinct* (1993), *Loaded Weapon 1* (1993), *Hot Shots! Part Deux* (1993), *Wayne's World 2* (1993), *The Silence of the Hams* (1994), and *The Game* (1997), which was not a spoof but a serious film with the same male star, Michael Douglas.

ALSO RECOMMENDED:

The aforementioned *The Fourth Man* features Renee Soutendijk as a European blonde who may or may not be a killer. Her deadly charms prove so seductive that a gay writer (Jeroen Krabbé) considers "changing teams" so he can die in her lovely arms. *Marnie* (1964), which people either love or hate more than any of Hitchcock's films, likewise deals with such disturbing themes, as does his final masterpiece, *Frenzy* (1972, #39).

68:

MAD LOVE (1935)

Metro-Goldwyn-Mayer

> **"He *likes* dead things!"**
> **—Marianne, about Dr. Gogol**

CAST:

Peter Lorre (*Dr. Gogol*); Frances Drake (*Yvonne Orlac*); Colin Clive (*Stephen Orlac*); Ted Healy (*Reagan the Reporter*); Sara Haden (*Marie the Maid*); Edward Brophy (*Rollo the Knife Thrower*); Henry Kolker (*Prefect Rosset*); Isabel Jewell (*Marianne*); Keye Luke (*Wong,*); May Beatty (*Françoise*); Cora Sue Collins (*Child Patient*); Nell Craig (*Nurse*); Ian Wolfe (*Henry*).

CREDITS:

Director, Karl Freund; screenplay, Florence Crewe-Jones, P.J. Wolfson, John L. Balderston, and Guy Endore, from the novel *Les Mains d'Orlac* by Maurice Renard; producer, John W. Considine Jr.; original music, Dimitri Tiomkin and (uncredited) David Snell; cinematographers, Chester Lyons and Gregg Toland; editor, Hugh Wynn; art directors, Cedric Gibbons and William A. Horning; running time, 69 min.

THE PLOT:

Stephen Orlac and his wife, Yvonne, are popular performers, though their mediums are notably different. While he appears in cities across the continent as a concert pianist, she performs at the Theatre of Cruelty. Nightly, Yvonne is bound and seemingly tortured during a bizarre scenario. One unlikely fan is Dr. Gogol, a noted surgeon obsessed with Yvonne. When the show closes and Yvonne leaves to pursue a normal life, the distraught Dr. Gogol purchases the life-size likeness of Yvonne that was used to advertise the show and worships his own Galatea, sensuously combing her faux hair when not otherwise involved with feeding bugs to his man-eating plants.

When Yvonne's husband loses his hands in an accident, Dr. Gogol grafts on those of a recently executed killer, insisting that he has merely restored and rebuilt

Peter Lorre as the obsessed doctor eyes his inamorata.

Stephen's own hands. But the pianist finds himself able to wield a deadly knife, at one point threatening his own stepfather, Henry Orlac. When Henry turns up dead, it's assumed Stephen committed the crime. Even he believes this to be true. Ever loyal, Yvonne takes the place of her likeness at Dr. Gogol's apartment, where she overhears the madman's boastful confession. Police arrive and rescue her moments before Dr. Gogol can engage in the ultimate insane act, exclaiming, "One always kills the thing one loves the most!"

THE FILM:

Though shot for a mere $257,502, *Mad Love* cannot correctly be considered a B-level movie. Though director Karl Freund (*The Mummy*, 1932), star Peter Lorre (he'd shortly play the lead in *The Face Behind the Mask*, 1941), and Colin Clive (of *Frankenstein* fame, 1931) were all associated with Universal's tightly-budgeted horror films, *Mad Love* was an MGM release. In those days, every studio liked to boast a full-slate of films, and this was their thriller for that year. This explains the lofty talents involved: cinematographer Greg Toland (who would photograph the films of Orson Welles, William Wyler, and John Ford), set designer Cedric Gibbons, J.L. Balderston (who penned the *Dracula* stage play), novelist Guy Endore (author of *The Werewolf of Paris*), and future Academy Award-winning composer Dimitri Tiomkin (*High Noon*). All were under contract at MGM, drawing weekly paychecks, so they were put to work between more lofty assignments on the studio's programmers—minor but high-quality pictures like this one.

Mad Love rates as a throwaway item from the past that plays far better today than many prestigious pictures from its time. A cult following has formed around this and other Lorre vehicles—Boris Ingster's *Stranger on the Third Floor* (1940) notable among them—while many blockbusters of that era are not released on video or DVD simply because few care to see them. Released as *The Hands of Orlac* in England, Freund's film is based on Maurice Renard's novel of that name.

Freund and his writing team employed only the merest outline of that story, for here, the poor fellow only *believes* his hands are out of control and forcing him to kill. Stephen has been brainwashed by Dr. Gogol to think he's now a murderer, whereas Dr. Gogol is the killer. This qualifies *Mad Love* as the earliest thriller to deal with Freudian psychology as a basis for its drama, introducing a theme that would dominate the postwar years and serve as the essence for the style known as film noir.

Freund grafted two fascinating elements onto Renard's story. First, the theatre where Madame Orlac works is the most vivid portrayal of Paris's Grand Guignol until *Interview With the Vampire* (1994). Second, the inclusion of a Pygmalion-Galatea plot adds a mythic element. Also striking is a macabre sense of black humor, inserted into even the most deadly serious scenes, as when American reporter Reagan trades bits of banter with the condemned Rollo moments before the guillotine comes down on Rollo's neck.

TRIVIA:

This was Lorre's first American film. He had achieved fame in the German thriller *M* (1931, #2). Then, Lorre hurried to England to escape the Nazis and appeared in *The Man Who Knew Too Much* (1934) for Hitchcock. As for Freund, despite the solid success of this and *The Mummy* (1932, #25) for Universal, the director—yet another German-Jewish émigré—had trouble securing jobs. During the early 1950s, he spent his final years as cameraman for the *I Love Lucy* series.

ALSO RECOMMENDED:

The aforementioned *Stranger on the Third Floor* (1940) is Lorre's other great thriller from this period. Lorre fans will also want to catch him as a good-guy detective in the Mr. Moto film series. The best entries are *Think Fast, Mr. Moto* (1937) and *Thank You, Mr. Moto* (1937). Fans of Bela Lugosi will want to catch him in a similar role (a brilliant but eccentric surgeon obsessed with an erotic dancer) in *The Raven*, released that same year.

67:

BLACK SUNDAY (1960)

American International Pictures/Galatea

—Demons of Hell in an Orgy of Horror!"
—tag line for American release

CAST:

Barbara Steele (*Katia Vajda/Princess Asa Vajda*); John Richardson (*Dr. Andre Gorobec*); Andrea Checchi (*Dr. Thomas Kruvajan*); Ivo Garrani (*Prince Vajda*); Arturo Dominici (*Javutich/Javuto*); Enrico Olivieri (*Constantin Vajda*); Antonio Pierfederici (*Priest*); Clara Bindi (*Inn Keeper*); Mario Passante (*The Coachman*); Germana Dominici (*Innkeeper's Daughter*).

CREDITS:

Director, Mario Bava; screenplay, Bava, Ennio De Concini, and Mario Serandrei, from a short story "The Vij" by Nikolai Gogol, with additional English dialogue by George Higgins; producers, Massimo De Rita and (U.S. version) Samuel Z. Arkoff; original music, Robert Nicolosi (Italian version) and Les Baxter (U.S. version); cinematographer, Bava; editor, Mario Serandrei; special artistic effects, Giorgio Giovannini (set design) and Bava; special sound effects (U.S. version), Robert Sherwood; running time, 83 min. (U.S. release).

THE PLOT:

In seventeenth-century Russia, beautiful Princess Asa degenerates into witchcraft. Finally, the humble people of her village can stand no more. They drag Asa to a stake and hammer a spiked mask onto her face before burning her alive. Dying, Asa screaches out a curse. She will return and wreak vengeance on the descendants of those who dared do this, particularly her brother.

Two hundred years to the date of her execution, a coach carrying Professor Choma Kruvajan and Dr. Andrej Gorobec veers off the rural road. Struggling to find their way, the companions come across an ancient chapel. They do not know the legend—and the threat—and so fail to realize the consequences of moving a cross. Its shadow kept evil Asa imprisoned in her tomb. Now she is free, and Asa stumbles out into the night. Her once beautiful face is intact, though grotesquely punctured by the mask's spikes. Shortly, she possesses her descendant and precise double, Princess Katia, employing the naive girl to destroy the families of her ancient enemies.

THE FILM:

Released in Italy and other Mediterranean countries in 1960 and the U.S. and U.K. a year later, *Black Sunday* composed one entry in a cinematic triad which would revolutionize the thriller genre. In England, Hammer Film Productions Limited had already begun revamping such classic tales as *Frankenstein* and *Dracula*. In America, Roger Corman had initiated his series of Edgar Allan Poe adaptations. In Italy, set designer Mario Bava (who had created the mythic worlds for the popular *Hercules* films starring Steve Reeves) rethought black-and-white cinematography in this, the first of a series of atmospheric thrillers that would become as identifiable for their unique style as were the in-color films of Hammer and Corman.

Bava and his endless imitators (Riccardo Freda, Antonio Margheriti, et. al.) adhered to the monochromatic vision that endured from Germany's Ufa studio through Universal's reclaiming of that approach during the thirties, exaggerating its forms to the point of purposeful caricature. Likewise, Bava graphically displayed masochism and necrophilia, dark themes that had only been suggested during an earlier age of heavy censorship. In addition to the striking starkness of the strange world created within Bava's films—a misty and mythic demimonde—he focuses on realistically lurid emotions that override the intellect and send seemingly civilized beings into a hell on earth.

Essential to the film's appeal was the incredible impact of Barbara Steele, at once breathtakingly beautiful yet somehow strange and unnerving. Aficionados hailed her "skull under the skin" beauty. Though a quietly elegant woman in real life, her features appeared distinctly evil when photographed, leading to typecasting as a gorgeous demon. Film historians who focus on the thriller and/or horror genres have noted that elements of bondage and sadism were more emphasized in these films than in their contemporary American and English counterparts. Italy's long period of repression exploded in an era that Federico Fellini would call la dolce vita.

Additionally, Bava's camera freely wandered into crypts and castles, plunging the viewer directly into the horrifying situations rather than letting him/her passively observe them. Most shocking was the opening sequence, in which the death mask is hammered into place while the camera assumes Princess Asa's point of

Witch in Bondage: Barbara Steele at the stake.

view. Having already achieved financial and critical success with Corman's Poe adaptations, Sam Arkoff of American International sensed the potential here and picked up the American distribution, adding an inappropriate jazz score and dreadfully dubbed dialogue. Even they failed to diminish the considerable thrills.

TRIVIA:

The original Italian title was *La Maschera del demonio*. The film was marketed under various titles, including *Le Masque du Demon* (Mexico and Spain) and *Revenge of the Vampire* (United Kingdom). The film was not released in England, however, until eight years after completion, owing to controversy over the on-screen depravity. Tim Burton has cited this as his favorite film. Though Steele became an international icon of terror, she resented such typecasting, having intended to become a "serious" actress. Her non-generic work can be seen in Federico Fellini's *8½* (1963) and Louis Malle's *Pretty Baby* (1978). In 1989, *Black Sunday* was limply remade as *Black Sabbath*.

ALSO RECOMMENDED:

Those interested in catching other excellent showcases for Steele's formidable screen presence should seek out *The Pit and the Pendulum* (1961, #61), Riccardo Freda's *The Horrible Dr. Hitchcock* (1962), and Mario Caiano's *Nightmare Castle* (1965). Most highly recommended among Bava's other films are *Black Sabbath* (1963), *Kill, Baby . . . Kill!* (a.k.a. *Curse of the Living Dead*, 1966), *Blood and Black Lace* (1964), and *Hatchet for a Honeymoon* (1966). The latter two leave Italian-Gothic behind and enter into another sub-genre of continental thriller, the *giallo*, the Italian word for "yellow"—which is the color of fear.

66:
SLEEPY HOLLOW (1999)

Paramount/Mandalay Pictures

"Truth is appearance, but appearance isn't always truth."
—Ichabod Crane

CAST:

Johnny Depp (*Ichabod Crane*); Christina Ricci (*Katrina Anne Van Tassel*); Miranda Richardson (*Mary Van Tassel/The Western Woods Crone*); Michael Gambon (*Baltus Van Tassel*); Casper Van Dien (*Brom Van Brunt*); Jeffrey Jones (*Reverend Steenwyck*); Christopher Lee (*Burgomeister*); Richard Griffiths (*Magistrate Samuel Philipse*); Ian McDiarmid (*Thomas Lancaster*); Michael Gough (*James Hardenbrook*); Marc Pickering (*Masbath*); Lisa Marie (*Ichabod's Mother*); Steven Waddington (*Mr. Killian*); Christopher Walken (*The Hessian Horseman*); Martin Landau (*Van Garrett*).

CREDITS:

Director, Tim Burton; screenplay, Kevin Yagher and Andrew Kevin Walker, inspired by "The Legend of Sleepy Hollow" by Washington Irving; producers, Adam Shroeder, Scott Rudin, and Francis Ford Coppola; original music, Danny Elfman; cinematographer, Emmanuel Lubezki; editors, Chris

Lebenzon and Joel Negron; production design, Rick Heinrichs; art direction, Ken Court, John Dexter, and Andrew Nicholson; special effects, Industrial Light & Magic/Kevin Yagher Productions; visual effects, Shadi Almassizadeh; running time, 105 min.; rating, R.

THE PLOT:

Late in 1799, Constable Ichabod Crane considers himself something of a "modern," practicing detective work in sophisticated New York City with the most scientific approach possible. This cerebral attitude is about to be sorely tested, for Crane is sent upstate, to a village recently plagued by a rash of decapitations. Initially, Crane is sure he can employ his logical strategies—a forerunner of forensic methodologies—to catch the killer. He finds himself in a chilly, dreary hamlet, where simple agricultural people do not accept this boy from the big city. While trying to track down the source of all the murders, Crane is shocked to discover that the victims' heads were never found. He falls in love with the other-worldly local beauty Katrina, daughter of wealthy old Van Tassel. Crane is less than comfortable in the company of her ice-princess of a stepmother Mary. Slender Ichabod must compete with the local bully, Brom, for Katrina's attentions. In time, he wonders if perhaps she is something of a witch, considering her effect on him. This stirs deep, dark memories, for Ichabod's own mother was a Wiccan. In time, his scientific approach gives way to a stiffling sense of superstition as he comes to believe the perpetrator may indeed be the ghost of an ancient Hessian cavalryman. Ultimately, Katrina's magic—if that is indeed what she possesses—is white, i.e. benign. The evil witch is her stepmother, who pays a terrible price for her wickedness. The Hessian Horseman carries her into the terrible tree that serves as gateway to a hell they will share through eternity.

THE FILM:

For historical authenticity, the images of quaint and curious back roads, isolated homes, and small hamlets were modeled on paintings from the Hudson River School. These images were filtered through a cinematographic approach that carefully approximated the drained color of the Hammer films of the late fifties and early sixties, which Burton had loved in his youth. *Sleepy Hollow* might be thought of as a horror film more than a thriller, considering its early revealing of the Horseman. Ultimately, that's not the case, even though Burton liberally partakes of conventions associated with the gothic form. Still, this isn't a film about a man's journey from normalcy and civilization to a strange, eerie land. The opening shot establishes that Crane's Manhattan is not as an American equivalent of Jonathan

Hoofbeats in the Night: Christina Ricci and Johnny Depp recoil from the Hessian Horseman.

Harker's London, the safe place he leaves from and then returns to after a sojourn in Dracula's fairytale kingdom. In Burton's vision, New York is a fetid sty, hardly the symbol of safety. *Sleepy Hollow* is, other than the Horseman's appearances, far more ordinary than the city Crane hails from. In the tradition of the great thrillers, this film concerns a character who finds a ripe nightmare existing just beneath the tranquil surface of what seems to be an ordinary place.

TRIVIA:

The film is filled with references to Burton's favorite movies. The old mill is lifted out of an Oscar-winning Walt Disney short, *The Old Mill* (1937)—until it burns to the ground like the tower in James Whale's *Bride of Frankenstein* (1935). Actors Michael Gough and Christopher Lee were the stars of Hammer's *Horror of Dracula* (1958, #81), and Gough had then played Alfred, the butler in Burton's *Batman* movies. Ichabod's horseback trek over a wobbly covered bridge is a live-action redux of the similar scene in Walt Disney's 1949 animated version. To make it clear that this is a film about films in general, and animated films in particular, Burton has Crane play with a simple toy—a carved circle with a bird on one side, a cage on the other. When an attached string is yanked, the circle spins and the bird appears to enter the cage. This is an anachromism, for that toy was invented by Sir John Herschel in England, circa 1825, then perfected and named the "Thaumatrope" by John Ayton Paris later that same year. By including it in a film set before this predecessor of animated movies existed, and having the hero—Burton's alter-ego—become fascinated with it, the filmmaker references his medium.

Sleepy Hollow won the Oscar for Best Art Decoration/Set Decoration at the 2000 Academy Awards. The Boston Society of Film Critics awarded Emmanuel Lubezki their prize for Best Cinematography. Christopher Walken appeared unbilled as the Horseman. In one of his previous films, *The Dead Zone* (1983), he read aloud from "The Legend of Sleepy Hollow."

ALSO RECOMMENDED:

Anyone interested in catching another great American-heartland ghost story should seek out the fascinating 1972 film, *The Other*, directed by Robert Mulligan, from a classic thriller by actor-turned-author Thomas Tryon. Stage great Uta Hagen has her only major movie role as the distraught lady who tends to a pair of very strange twin boys.

65:

SUDDENLY (1954)

United Artists

> **"I've never killed a president before."**
> —John Baron

CAST:

Frank Sinatra (*John Baron*); Sterling Hayden (*Sheriff Tod Shaw*); James Gleason (*Pop Benson*); Nancy Gates (*Ellen Benson*); Kim Charney (*Pidge*); Willis Bouchey (*Dan Carney*); Paul Frees (*Benny Conklin*); Christopher Dark (*Bart Wheeler*); James Lilburn (*Jud Hobson*); Ken Dibbs (*Wilson*); Paul Wexler (*Deputy Slim Adams*).

CREDITS:

Director, Lewis Allen; screenplay, Richard Sale; producers, Robert Bassler; original music, David Raksin; cinematographer, Charles G. Clarke; editor,

John F. Schreyer; art director, Frank Sylos; special visual effects, Louis DeWitt, Jack Rabin, and Herman Townsley; running time, 77 min.

THE PLOT:

Suddenly, California is ironically named, as nothing ever happens in this small town, particularly on a sleepy Saturday afternoon. Sheriff Tod Shaw has little to do except make sure that no one drives faster than the marked thirty miles per hour speed limit, though he does have a personal problem. Ellen Benson is a beautiful young widow with an eight-year-old boy, Pidge, and a likable father-in-law. The child and Pop like Tod and see him as a candidate for Ellen's second husband. She, however, can't get past the death of her husband during World War II. In addition to idealizing his memory, Ellen has developed an intense hatred of guns, making Tod—who wears one—a difficult man for Ellen to accept.

Everything changes when word reaches town that the President of the United States will arrive on an unscheduled train, disembark in Suddenly, then travel on. Secret Serviceman Dan Carney is dispatched to enlist the sheriff's help—partly as

Blueprint for an Assassination: The house where the killers set up shot is located on a grassy knoll!

a precaution, but also because a stool pidgeon has informed him that an attempt may be made on the president's life. When Carney learns Pop is in town, he heads for the Benson home high on top of a grassy knoll, eager to see his old mentor—for Pop was once with the Secret Service. When Carney and Tod arrive, they are shocked to see three men already there. John Baron, a paid assassin, and several cohorts hold the family at gunpoint, setting up a long-distance rifle at the window. When the lawmen resist, Carney is killed and Tod wounded.

With forty-five minutes left before the train's arrival, the terrified hostages try to figure out ways in which they can prevent the shooting. Quickly, Tod realizes Baron's weaknesses—his desire to brag about the Silver Star he won in combat, whining about his unpleasant childhood, defending his amorality (he's doing this strictly for the money), and protesting far too much when everyone calls him a coward. With the help of a TV repairman who stops by, Tod and Pop use wires and an effectively-placed glass of water to shock one of Baron's associates. As gunfire explodes, the president's train whirs by. Baron is about to turn his wrath on Tod, Pop, and Pidge, when Ellen grabs a gun dropped in the scuffle and uses it. When the smoke clears, she realizes the act was cathartic; now, she will be able to marry Tod.

THE FILM:

Following his Oscar-win as Best Supporting Actor for *From Here to Eternity* (1953), Sinatra—whose career had been on the wane during the decade's early years—was catapulted back into the limelight. He might have played "Terry Malloy" in Elia Kazan's *On The Waterfront* (1954), but turned it down to do this notable "little" film, playing a decidedly unpleasant character. The choice was a wise one, for *Suddenly* provided him with what may be the greatest role of his career. Sinatra brings so much depth to this portrait of a despicable man that one actually feels an inexplicable sense of sorrow when Baron is finally shot, though that is precisely what we have been hoping for all along.

In many ways, *Suddenly* is modeled on *High Noon* (1952, #13). Similarities begin with that moment when the telegraph operator hastily runs to bring a frightening message to the lawman, and continue through the ticking clock countdown to the moment of truth, as well as an ending in which the woman who has previously taken a pacifist stance uses a gun to kill. However inadvertently, the film—though written and produced by a team of "liberal" filmmakers—could be used today as propaganda for the National Rifle Association. This moral fable depicts the manner in which a female who stands for anti-gun position gradually realizes that her overly-idealistic position is wrong. Guns are necessary as a protection against evil.

Director Lewis Allen, mostly known for B-program pictures, created an overpowering sense of suspense within the limited microcosm of a normal, even typical, American household that must "suddenly" come to terms with violence and evil.

TRIVIA:

Paul Frees, who plays Baron's associate, also provided the voice for the unseen television announcer, something he often did in real life to augment his income as an actor. The towns of Newhall and Saugus, both in California, sat in for fictitious "Suddenly." Lee Harvey Oswald screened and studied the film three days before the assassination of President Kennedy in November, 1963. *Suddenly* was then quickly withdrawn from release for theatres and television, ostensibly at the request of Frank Sinatra.

ALSO RECOMMENDED:

The obvious cross-reference is to *The Manchurian Candidate* (1962, #9) in which Sinatra's character attempts to *stop* a presidential assassination. Also recommended is Anthony Mann's little known *The Tall Target* (1951), about a plot to assassinate Abraham Lincoln and the attempts of a railroad detective (Dick Powell) named John Kennedy (I kid you not!) to prevent this.

64:

THE PASSENGER (1975)

Metro-Goldwyn-Mayer

> **"I don't care!"**
> **—David Locke**

CAST:

Jack Nicholson (*David Locke*); Maria Schneider (*The Girl*); Jenny Runacre (*Rachel Locke*); Ian Hendry (*Martin Knight*); Steven Berkoff (*Stephen*);

James Campbell (*Witch Doctor*); Ambroise Bia (*Achebe*); Chuck Mulvehill (*David Robertson the Dead Man*).

CREDITS:

Director, Michelangelo Antonioni; screenplay, Antonioni, Mark Peploe, and Peter Wollen; producer, Carlo Ponti; musical advisor, Ivan Vardor; cinematograher, Luciano Tovoli; editors, Franco Arcalli and Antonioni; running time, 119 min.; rating, R.

THE PLOT:

David Locke is a TV reporter on assignment in Africa, where his job is to procure an interview with a group of elusive guerilla warriors. These are men who actually dare to challenge the status-quo in this trouble-torn country. David, however, feels only like a cipher, stuck in a remote backwater area, removed from anything that is truly important. He cannot make contact with his targets, which causes him to feel impotent, an observer of life rather than a doer. David maintains his sanity only because of the good company provided by an Englishman, David Robertson, staying at the same hotel.

Returning after one particularly gruesome and unsatisfying day, David (Locke) pays David (Robertson) a visit, only to find the man dead of an apparent heart attack, in his room. Impulsively, Locke strips off his shirt and puts on Robertson's, then changes the pictures on their passports. So far as the world knows, David Locke is dead, though, in fact, he is about to try a new life, in the guise of David Robertson. After all, his own existence was so terrible that this can only be an improvement . . . or so he believes for the moment.

With Robertson's plane tickets and travel plans in hand, David flies to Munich, where Robertson was expected. Quickly, though, David realizes that his alter ego was anything but what he appeared to be. No simple "businessman," Robertson was a gunrunner, supplying weapons, ironically enough, to those very rebels whom Locke had been trying to interview. A hippie-ish architectural student attaches herself to David, while his wife, at home in London, senses that something is amiss and sets out in search of David. The real Robertson's enemies, however—government agents who don't want those rebels to get the guns—are now in the process of planning an assassination of what Hitchcock would have called "the wrong man."

THE FILM:

Jack Nicholson had long been intrigued by the idea of working for the greatest of the European directors, and following the impact of *Blowup* (1966, #54), he considered Michelangelo Antonioni just such a person. *The Passenger* (1975) divided critics, who had trouble deciding whether they considered it an intriguingly ambiguous work of existential thinking or a pompous and pretentious attempt to turn a routine thriller plot into an arthouse item. Then again, just such discussion had appeared when *Blowup* premiered nearly a decade earlier. Among the film's defenders were *Newsweek*'s Paul D. Zimmerman, who insisted that "*The Passenger* is Antonioni's most beautiful cinematic canvas and certainly one of the most stunning visual voyages ever filmed."

Prisoner of Love: Jack Nicholson and Maria Schneider.

In *Time*, Jay Cocks applauded the use of "eerie and voluptuous imagery to define a condition of spiritual paralysis." One critic, Bea Rothenbuecher, noted the marvelous combination of Hollywood star and European auteur, pointing out that "Nicholson's natural aura of alienation" makes the Italian director's tale of international intrigue acceptable to American audiences because "he brings a touch of our world to Antonioni's world."

Stanley Kauffmann wanted to know "why does (Nicholson) pass by Schneider in a London park before he later accidentally meets her in Barcelona?" Far from a narrative mistake, this is the key to the drama's meaning. The title refers less to Nicholson's character than Schneider's. The girl's ambiguousness (beginning with her lack of a name) suggests she's the mystery woman all men seek to comprehend but can never know, a passenger who attaches herself to various men. One possible interpretation of the seven-minute, single shot traveling camera finale (the most celebrated set-piece in the movie, and rightly so) is that she's set him up. Thus, she may have been following him early in the film, waiting for the right moment to seemingly meet David "by accident."

Following the shoot, Nicholson said: "Working with (Antonioni) is the outside pole of filmic idiosyncracy. He's fully in control of what he's doing, but he really does it his own way. We'd probably still be shooting if he wasn't locked in by contracts. I mean, he lay down in front of (a) plane to keep Richard Harris from leaving *Red Desert*. The guy just kept shooting and shooting 'cause he loves making movies, and that's why he's great. They tell me I'm the first actor in twenty-five years he got along with, but that was because I really wanted to make an Antonioni movie!"

Trivia:

Less than two years earlier, Maria Schneider had starred opposite Marlon Brando in Bernardo Bertolucci's *Last Tango in Paris* (1973). With *The Passenger*, and star billing alongside Nicholson, it was generally assumed that she would swiftly become a great international star and sex symbol. She never again appeared in a major motion picture.

Also Recommended:

Fans of Antonioni will want to catch *L'Avventura* (1960). At 145 minutes, all of them self-consciously slow-moving, it may be the most purposefully paceless thriller ever made. Nicholson's other top thrillers include a western, *The Shooting* (1966), for Monte Hellman, and *Chinatown* (1974) for Roman Polanski.

63:

KLUTE (1971)

Warner Bros.

> **"I've done terrible things, killed three people. Really, I don't consider myself a terrible man."**
> **—Cable**

Cast:

Jane Fonda (*Bree Daniel*); Donald Sutherland (*John Klute*); Charles Cioffi (*Peter Cable*); Roy Scheider (*Frank Ligourin*); Dorothy Tristan (*Arlyn Page*);

Rita Gam (*Trina*); Nathan George (*Trask*); Vivian Nathan (*Psychiatrist*); Jane White (*Janie*); Shirley Stoler (*Momma Rose*); Robert Milli (*Tom*); Richard Shull (*Sugarman*); Rosalind Cash (*Pat*); Jean Stapleton (*Secretary*); Veronica Hamel (*Model*); Sylvester Stallone (*dancer in club*).

CREDITS:

Director, Alan J. Pakula; screenplay, Andrew and David Lewis; producers, Pakula and David Lange; original music, Michael Small; cinematographer, Gordon Willis; editor, Carl Lerner; art director, George Jenkins; running time, 114 min.; rating, R.

THE PLOT:

The Lonely Crowd: Bree (Jane Fonda) is afraid to open the door to a stranger (Donald Sutherland as Klute).

A businessman friend of John Klute, small town private investigator, disappears without a trace. Klute will not give up trying to learn what happened. From the FBI, he discovers that their only lead is what seems to be a slight connection between the businessman and a high-priced New York City call girl, Bree Daniels. Apparently, the missing man sent her several letters, suggesting some sort of ongoing secret relationship. Klute contacts Bree, but she doesn't want to get involved. Dedicated Klute travels to Manhattan and taps Bree's phone, certain some of her conversations will be so salacious that he can blackmail her into complying. What he fails to realize, at first, is that a mystery man is stalking Bree, perhaps the same person who did away with Klute's friend. Though she initially avoids Klute, then attempts to manipulate him as if he were a non-sexual "John," Bree eventually realizes her own life is in danger, and that only by helping Klute can she save herself.

As this occurs, she realizes Klute is what so many other small-town men, visiting the big city, only pretend to be: ultra-respectable. Though Bree initially laughs at his old-fashioned values, she eventually comes to realize that what she's always hated—to a degree, what drove her to prostitution—was not those values but the phoniness of most people who profess to believe in them. But Klute is "the real thing," and his integrity causes Bree to question her entire lifestyle.

Eventually, we learn that the deceased, Tom Gruneman, inadvertently discovered another "respectable" businessman, Peter Cable, in a hotel room killing call girl Jane McKenna during a kinky sex act. Gruneman had to be eliminated, for he might use this knowledge to have power over, or absolutely ruin, Cable's seemingly clean-cut existence. As a close friend of Jane's, Bree had to be eliminated too, just in case she was, to paraphrase Hitchcock, the "woman who knew too much."

THE FILM:

However pathological Cable may be, he also makes Bree realize that (as in a Hitchcock film) the protagonist is hardly a pure hero, rather linked in subtle ways to the villain, who says, "There are little corners in everyone which were better off left alone; sicknesses, weaknesses, which . . . which should never be exposed. But . . . that's your stock in trade, isn't it—a man's weakness? And I was never really fully aware of mine . . . until *you* brought them out." Thus, Bree is, in a way, responsible for the murders that Cable committed, owing to a universal sense of guilt.

While coming ever closer to solving the case, Bree reveals herself to Klute (and to her psychiatrist, in cutaways) that she harbors a complex attitude toward her work. On the one hand, she can be seen as a retro-woman, utterly uninfluenced by feminism, who allows her body to be used for sizable but ultimately unsatisfying financial profit. Yet Bree also feels that by seemingly submitting to men, she actually assumes control over them. This, it turns out, is why one man was murdered and Bree is currently being stalked: a "suit" with an ultra-respectable reputation said more than he should have and is desperately trying to cover his kinky past.

Under Alan J. Pakula's direction, Jane Fonda created an on-screen female unlike anything presented previously in a commercial film. Pauline Kael called Bree "one of the strongest roles for women ever" written for an American film. Members of the then-burgeoning women's movement complained that it was nonetheless a sad sign of the times that the only strong woman's role in 1971 was that of a prostitute.

TRIVIA:

Foreign distributors believed the film had international potential, but had no idea what to do with the title. In Sweden, *Klute* was distributed as *en smart snut* (a.k.a., "a clever whore"). Though thought of a few years earlier as Henry Fonda's leggy daughter, fit only for projects like *Barbarella* (1968), Fonda was catapulted to the forefront of American movie actresses, winning the National Society of Film Critics Award and New York Film Critics Circle Award for Best Actress, as well as her first Academy Award. When *Klute* was shown on commercial TV, the film was cut down to 108 min. to fit into a two-hour (with commercials) time slot. Incredibly, the one scene that was cut is the episode that allows the audience to understand the key to the mystery, rendering the plot incomprehensible.

ALSO RECOMMENDED:

Pakula's other edge-of-your-seat thrillers include *The Parallax View* (1974), a political suspense thriller that neatly combines Kennedy assassination paranoia with an allegory from the then-current Watergate scandal. Also recommended is *Presumed Innocent* (1990), with Harrison Ford as a prosecutor investigating the murder of a woman he had been involved with, discovering that all the evidence points toward himself.

62:

SE7EN (1995)

Alliance Atlantis Communications

"Only in a world this shitty could you even try to say these were innocent people and keep a straight face."
—John Doe

CAST:

Morgan Freeman (*Detective William Somerset*); Brad Pitt (*Detective David Mills*); Kevin Spacey (*John Doe*); Gwyneth Paltrow (*Tracy Mills*); Richard Roundtree (*Talbot*); R. Lee Ermey (*Police Captain*); Andy Walker (*Corpse*); Daniel Zacapa (*Taylor*); John Cassini (*Davis*); Bob Mack (*Gluttony Victim*); Peter Crombie (*O'Neill*); Cat Mueller (*Lust*).

CREDITS:

>Directer, David Fincher; screenplay, Andrew Kevin Walker; producers, Arnold Kopelson, Stephen Brown, and Phyllis Carlyle; original music, Howard Shore; cinematographer, Darius Khondji and Harris Savides; editor, Richard Francis-Bruce; production designer, Arthur Max; art director, Gary Wissner; special makeup effects, Rob Bottin; running time, 127 min.; rating, R.

THE PLOT:

Gluttony, greed, sloth, envy, wrath, pride, and lust; these are the seven deadly sins, handed down to us through millennia of Judeo-Christian thinking. An unknown serial killer—"John Doe" to the police—is using each in turn as his modus operandi. A pair of mismatched detectives try to bring the criminal to justice before he kills again. Somerset is logical, laid-back, and older, planning to retire soon; Mills is young, more emotional, given to sudden impulsive action, and is at the beginning of what he hopes will be a gratifying career. The first victim, they realize, was guilty of gluttony and, as punishment, forced to eat himself to death. Future victims are likewise murdered according to the deadly sin that he or she is guilty of. Notably horrible is the prideful beauty who became grotesquely disfigured. Then, given the option of killing herself or calling for help, she chooses to end her life rather than continue as a non-beautiful woman.

The policemen realize the killer is trying to "say something," initially believing this twisted moralist wants to preach to the world. As the bodies pile up, and they move closer to a solution of the crime, they come to see he is speaking directly to *them*. When they capture their quarry, "John Doe" reveals he has destroyed Mills's beloved family. The detective goes berserk and kills John Doe in cold blood. At this moment, he realizes he is the ultimate target of John Doe's plan, for he is guilty of the seventh sin: wrath.

THE FILM:

Technically, *Se7en* premiered a new silver retention process called CCE. Key sequences were treated so that they would collect the silver that's ordinarily removed from a celluloid print during filmmaking; this caused those moments to appear notably luminous onscreen, also increasing the density of the image's darker tonal areas. Though *Se7en* was set in the present, director David Fincher chose to recreate the shadow-world of 1940s film-noir thrillers, resulting in yet another modern movie that could not have been made at that time, owing to censorship restrictions, yet are informed by the techniques that defined postwar

Brad Pitt and
Morgan Freeman
close in on the
murderer.

cinema. David Fincher and screenwriter Andrew Kevin Walker decided to bring the killer onscreen some twenty-five minutes before the story concludes, so that we know more than the protagonists and are constantly waiting for them to "catch up" with us, resulting in "suspense" rather "mystery," in which the protagonist is always *last* to learn the killer's identity.

Like many great thrillers from the past, *Se7en* suggests more than it shows, leaving us with the impression that we have seen more graphic violence than was presented onscreen. Rather than diminish the horrific factor, this increases it. As Leonard Maltin noted, "Not much violence per se, but excruciatingly unsettling, almost oppressive at times." Maltin also articulated one criticism that other reviewers echoed, for the dispassionate camera style led to a clammy effect, so "the film seems to wallow in the depths of human depravity that it so passionately decries." Was the film a cool appraisal of our violent world or a heated diatribe about such a situation? Further viewings do not easily resolve this question, which is at the heart of *Se7en*'s unique power to upset.

TRIVIA:

To maintain the surprise of who "John Doe" happens to be, major star Kevin Spacey agreed to take no billing, either in the advertisements or the credits. Mills's fall, during which he injures his arm, was not in the script. This actually happened while Pitt was performing a chase scene and slipped, his arm crashing through a window. Walker hurredly rewrote the script to include this. Somerset occupies office 714; this is an homage to the badge number of Sgt. Joe Friday (Jack Webb) in the *Dragnet* series of the 1960s and 1970s. Like so many postmodernist films, *Se7en* contains endless references to the classic thrillers, including many in this volume: *The Maltese Falcon* (1941, #20), *The Night of the Hunter* (1955, #17), *Klute* (1971, #63), and *Silence of the Lambs* (1991, #10).

At one point, Mills belittles Doe by calling him "a movie of the week, at best." When it came time to show the film on television, executives were uncomfortable with such a dismissive attitude toward their own medium, and changed the line to "book-of-the-month-club selection." The first corpse that the protagonists visit is played the film's screenwriter.

ALSO RECOMMENDED:

Though not an edge-of-your-seat thriller per se, Fincher's *Fight Club* (1999), also starring Pitt, contains most of the director's recurring themes, as well as enough suspense to satisfy. Also, *Panic Room* (2002) with Jodie Foster is a highly engaging if, in comparison to *Se7en* and *Fight Club*, superficial thriller.

61:

THE PIT AND THE PENDULUM (1961)

American-International

> **"No one will ever enter this room again!"**
> **—Francis Bernard (film's final line)**

CAST:

Vincent Price (*Nicholas Medina*); Barbara Steele (*Elizabeth Barnard Medina*); John Kerr (*Francis Barnard*); Luana Anders (*Catherine*); Anthony Carbone (*Dr. Leon*); Patrick Westwood (*Maximillian*); Lynnette Bernay (*Maria*); Larry Turner (*Young Nicholas*); Mary Menzies (*Isabella*).

CREDITS:

Director, Roger Corman; screenplay, Richard Matheson, from a story by Edgar Allan Poe; producers, Corman, James H. Nicholson, and Samuel Z. Arkoff; original music, Les Baxter; cinematographer, Floyd Crosby; editor, Anthony Carras; special effects, Larry Butler and Don Glouner; set designer, David Haller; running Time, 85 min.

THE PLOT:

Francis Barnard travels to the isolated castle where his brother-in-law, Nicholas Medina, lives, to learn how and why Francis's sister, Elizabeth, died under mysterious circumstances. While there, Francis falls in love with pretty young Catherine, Medina's younger sister, who aids him in his efforts. Shortly, they realize Medina is either haunted by the ghost of Elizabeth, or he has gone mad and believes he sees her spectre late at night, when all others are asleep. In fact, Elizabeth is very much alive; she and her illicit lover—Dr. Leon, seemingly Medina's best friend—are plotting to drive Medina mad. They know this will not be difficult, since Medina is plagued by memories of his father, an ordained torturer during the Spanish Inquisiton, who often forced his impressionable son to watch victims writhing in agony.

When beautiful-but-evil Elizabeth thinks she has had her final victory over Medina, he suddenly finds a fresh burst of strength. Totally insane, Medina locks her inside an iron maiden. Then, wrongly believing Francis is his enemy, Medina brings the young man to the torture chamber, places him in the pit, allowing the pendulum—a razor-sharp scythe—to descend. At the last possible moment, Francis is rescued by Catherine, while Medina falls to his death. As the young lovers lock the immense doors behind them, they vow no one will ever enter again. Elizabeth—bound and gagged within the iron maiden—wildly though vainly struggles to alert them to her presence.

THE FILM:

In 1954, twenty-year-old Roger Corman—who had worked as a messenger boy at 20th Century Fox, studied Modern English Literature at Oxford University, and had been employed at the Jules Goldstone literary agency—wrote, produced, and directed his first film, *The Monster From the Ocean Floor* (1954), for $30,000. When the abominably bad horror film scored on the drive-in circuit, Corman quickly set up shop, churning out cheapies with such outlandish titles as *Swamp Women* (1956), *The Wasp Woman* (1959), and *Little Shop of Horrors* (1960), black-and-white exploitation items shot in ten days or less but with such lurid titles that

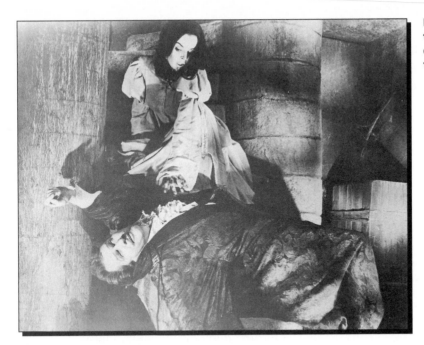

Barbara Steele as the evil wife who drives her husband to madness.

teenagers swarmed in droves to catch them. When the market became saturated with endless imitations, Corman and his sometimes partners, Arkoff and Nicholson of American-International, decided to take a risk and spend a full fifteen days shooting a thriller, at (for them) an unheard of $270,000, in color, with Vincent Price as a nominal name.

House of Usher, inspired by an Edgar Allan Poe story, was written by Richard Matheson, a novelist (*The Shrinking Man, I Am Legend*) and *Twilight Zone* veteran who neatly expanded the Poe concept with a literate script that nicely matched Corman's baroque direction and Price's flamboyant hamming. Positive reviews and strong box-office attendance convinced the producers that they had a franchise on their hands.

Next up was what many observers consider the best in the series, an initially slow-moving story that builds to an incredible crescendo of suspense as the innocent hero finds himself in the hands of the grotesque but strangely sympathetic Price character. "Don't expect Poe," the *New York Times* noted at the time, "but the taste here for poisonous cake with rich, ice-cold frosting, probably would have pleased him." The $200,000 investment of Corman and his cohorts returned a profit of more than two million dollars, insuring that the Poe series would continue. Even in the finest later work, however, there would never again appear any single image so horrifying as the final close-up on Barbara Steele's eyes, as she sinks into madness at the thought of her oncoming slow death within the iron maiden.

TRIVIA:

Roger Corman has said that "the climactic scene is Freud's. . . . On the unconscious level, the pendulum and the pit are male and female [sexual] symbols." The part of young Francis was awarded to John Kerr, a Broadway veteran who had starred in several important studio productions—including *Tea and Sympathy* and *South Pacific*—before being dumped by the majors. For Corman and company, Kerr's name, added to that of Price, was intended to class up the marquee, announcing that Corman's bottom-of-the-barrel production days were over. Yet Kerr's presence is the least convincing thing in the movie. Had he not agreed to do the role, it would have gone to brilliant though then-unknown actor Jack Nicholson (no relation to producer James Nicholson), who would shortly appear in such Corman-directed thrillers as *The Raven* (1963) and *The Terror* (1963).

ALSO RECOMMENDED:

Among the other Poe adaptations, by far the two best are *The Masque of the Red Death* (1964), which contains the most fluid (and Fellini-like) direction of Corman's career, and *The Tomb of Ligeia* (1965), an intelligent, restrained suspense tale written by Robert Towne, who would emerge as a significant talent, winning the Best Original Screenplay Oscar for *Chinatown* (1974), also highly recommended.

60:

THE CONVERSATION (1974)

Paramount Pictures

"Do you feel as if someone is listening to us?"
—Ann

CAST:

Gene Hackman (*Harry Caul*); Teri Garr (*Amy*); Robert Duvall (*The Director*); Cindy Williams (*Ann*); Frederic Forrest (*Mark*); John Cazale (*Stan*); Allen Garfield (*Bernie Moran*); Michael Higgins (*Paul*); Harrison Ford (*Stett*).

CREDITS:

> Director, Francis Ford Coppola; screenplay, Coppola; producers, Coppola and Fred Roos; music, David Shire; cinematographer, Bill Butler; editor, Richard Chew; production designer/art director, Dean Tavoularis; running time, 113 min.; rating, PG.

THE PLOT:

Mark and Ann meet in a park to discuss their adulterous relationship. Neither is aware that their supposedly private conversation is being audio-taped by Harry Caul, a professional eavesdropper. Harry never takes any voyeuristic interest in the people he spies on; he does it for the money and satisfaction of knowing he's the best there is at his amoral job. Nonetheless, this particular discussion proves so unique even Harry can't help but become fascinated by some of the things these lovebirds say to one another.

Harry is supposed to turn the tape over to a man known only as "the Director." When Stett, an emissary, arrives instead, Harry refuses to give his tape to the unknown man. Stett then hurls an unexpected threat at Harry, insisting he has no idea what he's getting himself into. His interest piqued, Harry listens to the tape again, realizing Mark and Ann may have actually been speaking about something other than adultery. But Harry puts the mystery aside when he's seduced by a mysterous woman. However, she steals the tape, and Harry realizes he's been "had," the woman having been hired by Stett.

Then Harry realizes that the Director is married to Ann, and may be planning her murder. Finally, Harry's amorality gives way to an intense interest, even obsession, in this case. Yet, as he pursues what is now a crusade to avoid a killing, he realizes time and time again that just when he believes he's discovered "the truth," that turns out to be nothing more than another incorrect interpretation of "the conversation."

THE FILM:

Francis Ford Coppola had written *The Conversation* six years before it was made, though only after directing *The Godfather* was he allowed to make the more personal film. This delayed timing actually benefited the film, for had *The Conversation* been released in 1968, its serious theme—what Lee Pfeiffer and Michael Lewis described as "the loss of privacy in modern society"—would have been ahead of its time. When the film finally appeared, the bugging of offices by people with power and the existence of critical tapes then-president Richard Nixon secretly made of

Gene Hackman as Harry Caul, wiretapper.

his own conversations were on everyone's minds. *The Conversation* played as a metaphor for the Watergate mentality, rendered in a style that combined elements of Kafka's avant-garde literature with Hitchcock's suspenseful entertainments. Both Judith Crist and Pauline Kael hailed it as "a modern horror film," for an age in which the most terrifying horrors were not bug-eyed monsters but people in expensive suits, who appear at first to be running everything in society for the best interest of all, but may, in fact, be dangerous.

Much of the film's power derives from Hackman's performance, which may be the greatest of his illustrious career, as a man who might be described as a realistically rendered version of the befuddled antihero in *The Trial* (1962). In truth, the film is less perfect than its cult of admirers care to admit. Rather than merely play his story for suspense and let the political implications speak for themselves—as Hitchcock always did—Coppola apparently wanted to make clear, from the opening shot, that this is not just another suspense film, but an important statement as well. To that end, he indulges in a great deal of unnecessary material, apparently intended to give *The Conversation* an allegorical quality. This involves street performers in a New York City setting that appears vaguely futuristic, the film being set the day after tomorrow. The mime performances serve as bookends, a device obviously derived from Michelangelo Antonioni's *Blowup* (1966, #54). There, though, such a quality "worked" in a way that it does not here. Occasionally, the top-notch suspense diffuses slightly, owing to pretentious padding, which stretches the film to its 113 minute length. With this extraneous material cut out, *The Conversation* could have been a minor masterpiece that implied, without flaunting its high seriousness, the same themes in a more entertaining, less insistent manner.

TRIVIA:

Young Harrison Ford, who had been cast by producer Coppola as a yahoo drag-racer in George Lucas's *American Graffiti* (1973), tried to persuade the auteur to let him play the pivotol role of "Mark." At the time though, Frederic Forrest was a far hotter actor. But Coppola did cast Ford as the director's assistant.

ALSO RECOMMENDED:

Dementia 13 (1963), a spooky low-budget chiller that Coppola made for Roger Corman, includes one of the great edge-of-your-seat sequences in B-movie history: a beautiful woman (Luana Anders), swimming underwater in lingerie, brushes up against a dead body. Frightened, she surfaces, only to encounter a male (known to her though his face remains unseen by the audience) about to behead her with an axe. What could have been cheap exploitation was elevated, by Coppola's artistry, even at this early stage, into a remarkable set piece on the order of Hitchcock's *Psycho* shower scene, in which the female lead was also summarily dismissed at mid-movie.

59:

THE SPIRAL STAIRCASE (1946)

RKO Radio Pictures

"Can there be such a thing as a silent scream?"
—Professor Warren

CAST:

Dorothy McGuire (*Helen Capel*); George Brent (*Professor Warren*); Ethel Barrymore; (*Mrs. Warren*); Kent Smith (*Dr. Parry*); Rhonda Fleming (*Blanche*); Gordon Oliver (*Steve Warren*); Elsa Lanchester (*Mrs. Oates*); Sara Allgood (*Nurse Barker*); Rhys Williams (*Mr. Oates*); James Bell (*Constable*); Erville Alderson (*Dr. Harvey*); Ellen Corby (*Next Door Neighbor*); Myrna Dell (*Murder Victim*).

CREDITS:

Director, Robert Siodmak; screenplay, Mel Dinelli, from the novel *Some Must Watch* by Ethel Lina White; producer, Dore Schary; original music, Roy Webb, Constantin Bakaleinkoff, and Dr. Samuel Hoffman (theremin effects only); cinematographer, Nicholas Musuraca; editors, Harry Gerstad and Harry Marker; art directors, Albert S. D'Agostino and Jack Okey; sound effects, John L. Cass and Terry Kellum; visual effects, Vernon L. Walker; running time, 83 min.

THE PLOT:

Set in 1916, elderly Mrs. Warren has been ailing in her mansion for years. Living with her are two sons, serious-minded Albert, a college professor, and selfish Steven, who spends his time wasting the family fortune and running around with loose

Dorothy McGuire on the title object.

women. Realizing both boys are too preoccupied to give her the attention she needs, Mrs. Warren hires a lovely young woman, Helen, to care for her. A mute, Helen can communicate only through hand signs and body language; initially, these suffice as Helen and Mrs. Warren enter into a mother-daughter type relationship. Helen's impediment, however, puts her in a peril, for she cannot scream for help, which she will shortly need.

One by one, attractive young women in the neighborhood—each with a disability— are brutally murdered. Concerned for Helen's safety, Mrs. Warren begs her physician, Dr. Parry, to relocate Helen, though he's surprisingly cool to this idea. Shortly, Helen—who must constantly move up and down the house's central spiral staircase to perform her duties—finds herself confronted with a dark, mysterious figure halfway between the ground floor that hosts visitors to the mansion and the upstairs, where every member of the family hides some dark secret.

THE FILM:

The setting was a key element in the conception, for this story occurs just before America entered the first World War, the event that pulled the nation into the twentieth century. The jazz age and roaring twenties began as soon as the boys came home; although Queen Victoria died in 1901, the early years of the new century had been a carry-over from that period, with its emphasis on old-fashioned values and conservative morality. The work of Sigmund Freud was even then becoming known, particularly his theories that all our actions, however non-sexual they seem, result from repressed urges in the human libido.

At least by implication, *The Spiral Staircase* is a movie about this concept, as a Freudian nightmare of denied sexuality crashes up against the handsome facades of a small town that desperately wants to believe its white-picket fences and stately homes offer respite from the uglier elements of reality. This sets the film clearly in line with such seminal works as Hitchcock's *Shadow of a Doubt* (1943, #27) and David Lynch's *Blue Velvet* (1986, #90). To heighten the suspense, director Robert Siodmak emphasized the killer's eyes, seen in the film's second shot. Anyone watching closely can identify those eyes, viewed in close-up, with the character who is seemingly the most logical and trustworthy of all, Professor Warren. As one of the first psychological thrillers, the film offers a striking combination of conventions from earlier examples of gothic horror with landbreaking use of the surreal shadow-world techniques that would soon dominate thrillers.

As Dragan Antulov has noted, "*The Spiral Staircase* hardly comes to mind when people think about most important genre films in 1940s Hollywood. It may be argued that the great Alfred Hitchcock and his work shadowed the film's reputation, but the real reason probably lies in the fact that the film was at least a few decades ahead of its time. Those who pay attention could see that many thriller directors in later decades have borrowed heavily from *The Spiral Staircase*. The most obvious examples are the use of killer's point of view, strange noises in the dark being mistaken for the killer by its potential victim and sexual activity being equal to death sentence—two clichés almost inseparable from slasher movies." In *Spiral Staircase*, however, the violence is suggested rather than shown. The killer turns out to be the single male inflicted with sexual impotence. Though this gambit had never before been employed, it would become one of the most significant of all thriller themes, reaching its apex in Hitchcock's *Psycho* (1960, #1).

TRIVIA:

At one point, one character attends an early movie show and watches *The John Rice-May Irwin Kiss*, an 1896 featurette sometimes cited (incorrectly) as the first American film ever shown in theatres. This early example of reflexivity is significant. However innocent *The Kiss* seems today, it was damned by Victorian-era censors as a dangerous work that, owing to the larger-than-life depiction of sexuality, might incite members of the public to outrageous acts. The character who commits all the murders is, in fact, the one who was earlier glimpsed obsessively watching that film.

ALSO RECOMMENDED:

The German born Jewish director, who learned the expressionist aesthetic from F.W. Murnau, fled (with his brother Curt) his homeland when the Nazis seized power. Siodmak's acclaimed thrillers include such classics as *Phantom Lady* (1944), *The Strange Case of Uncle Harry* (1945), and *The Dark Mirror* (1946).

58:
PLAY MISTY FOR ME (1971)

Universal

> **"Hi, Dave, it's Evelyn; play 'Misty' for me?"**
> **—Evelyn Draper**

CAST:

Clint Eastwood (*Dave Garver*); Jessica Walter (*Evelyn Draper*); Donna Mills (*Tobie Williams*); John Larch (*Sergeant McCallum*); Jack Ging (*Frank*); Irene Hervey (*Madge Brenner*); Clarice Taylor (*Birdie*); Donald Siegel (*Murphy*); Duke Everts (*Jay Jay*); Brit Lind (*Anjelica*); James McEachin (*Rugged Man*); The Cannonball Adderley Quintet (*jazz group*).

CREDITS:

Director, Clint Eastwood; screenwriters, Dean Riesner and Jo Heims, from a story by Jo Heims; producers, Robert Daley, Jennings Lang, and Bob Larson; original music, Dee Barton, plus "The First Time Ever I saw Your Face" by Roberta Flack and "Misty" by Erroll Garner; cinematographer, Bruce Surtees; editor, Carl Pingitore; art director, Alexander Golitzen; running time, 102 min.; rating, R.

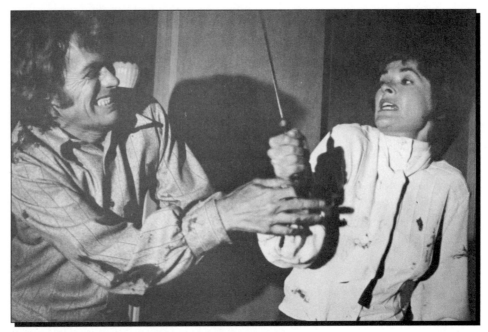

Clint Eastwood and Jessica Walter struggle for dominance.

THE PLOT:

Dave Garver is a popular all-night disc-jockey at a jazz station in Carmel, California. Most evenings, he receives a call from a seductive-sounding woman who requests the Erroll Garner rendition of "Misty." Swinging by a popular pick-up spot, Dave encounters attractive Evelyn Draper, not realizing she's the person who has been calling him. Evelyn made it a point to find out where Dave likes to hang out. They engage in a one-night stand, Dave believing this to have been one more free-sex encounter of the type that have become part of the swinging scene following the sexual revolution of the late 1960s. When Evelyn begins dropping in on him at work and other places, Dave's at first mildly amused, and then concerned that she believes what he considered casual sex is something more serious.

Dave, meanwhile, has rekindled a relationship with Tobie Williams, a former girlfriend. The two realize they may want to get serious. Upon learning this, an out-of-control Evelyn slips into Dave's apartment, uses a large knife to tear apart his possessions, and stabs Dave's cleaning lady when she happens upon the scene. The police arrest Evelyn; in time, she's released and begins calling the station again, requesting "Misty," though assuring Dave there's no longer a problem.

One night, Dave awakens in his apartment, hears "Misty" playing, and realizes Evelyn is there, again wielding a knife. Dave fights off her attack, though she manages to sneak away. It occurs to Dave that Evelyn's wrath may have been redirected to his Tobie. A police officer, McCallum, is sent to protect her, now living with a new roomate—this turns out to be Evelyn—who kills McCallum with scissors, then ties up Tobie to lure Dave into the room. He plays a tape on his show so Evelyn will believe he's still at the station, then hurries over and confronts her in a brutal duel, finally killing Evelyn. As he unties Tobie, the two hear, on the radio, that tape in which Evelyn requests "Misty" and Dave plays it for her.

The Film:

Play Misty for Me marked Clint Eastwood's directorial debut, though he had been growing ever more interested in working behind the camera for some time. While shooting *Two Mules for Sister Sara* (1970) and *Dirty Harry* (1972) for director Don Siegel, Clint persuaded the veteran filmmaker to allow him to work as second-unit director on some of the action sequences. Having emerged as a superstar thanks to Sergio Leone's spaghetti westerns and Siegel's Hollywood films, Clint was in a position to agree to star in *Play Misty for Me* only if he were also allowed to direct. For safety's sake, however, he requested that Siegel be on the set as much as possible.

The film's success allowed Eastwood to embark on a serious career as a director, ultimately winning an Oscar for *Unforgiven* (1992). At the time of its release, *Play Misty for Me* was interpreted as an anti-feminist film by the women's movement, for its inclusion of a seemingly strong, independent woman revealed to be dangerously crazy, whereas the old-fashioned girl is safe and sane. Today, a thematic reading suggests this cautionary fable warns us against the casual sex mentality so prevalent during the early seventies, with Eastwood saying, through this effectively paced and perfectly performed thriller, that a one-night stand can come back to haunt you, a fact that became obvious when the AIDS epidemic struck in the early eighties.

However one interprets the film, Eastwood made clear what Hitchcock had established half a century earlier: the suspense film can be "redeemed" from the realm of superficial escapism if employed to say something about the society from which it derives. Indeed, this is the ingredient that transforms mere entertainment into true art.

TRIVIA:

Eastwood's friend and mentor, Don Siegel, plays the bartender. When the script for *Fatal Attraction* (1987) made the rounds in the early eighties, many directors, including Brian de Palma, turned it down, complaining that the new script too closely resembled *Play Misty for Me*.

ALSO RECOMMENDED:

For purposes of comparison, Adrian Lyne's *Fatal Attraction* (1987) is recommended; the DVD thankfully restores the original conclusion as an "alternative ending." Fans of Eastwood under the direction of Siegel will want to catch *Coogan's Bluff* (1968), a first-rate suspenser about a contemporary western lawman tracking a killer in New York City; *The Beguiled* (1971), in which he plays a yankee held hostage by neurotic Southern women during the Civl War; and *Escape From Alcatraz* (1979), about an actual break from the famous prison. Clint's other top suspense films include Wolfgang Petersen's *In the Line of Fire* (1993), matching his secret service agent against would-be presidential assassin John Malkovich.

57:

THE OLD DARK HOUSE (1932)

Universal Pictures

> **"It was a dark and stormy night."**
> **—J.B. Priestley**

CAST:

Boris Karloff (*Morgan*); Melvyn Douglas (*Roger Penderel*); Charles Laughton (*Sir William Porterhouse*); Lilian Bond (*Gladys DuCane*); Ernest

Thesiger (*Horace Femm*); Eva Moore (*Rebecca Femm*); Raymond Massey (*Philip Waverton*); Gloria Stuart (*Margaret*); John Dudgeon (*Sir Roderick Femm*); Brember Wills (*Saul*).

CREDITS:

Director, James Whale; screenwriters, Benn W. Levy and (uncredited) R.C. Sherriff, from the novel *Benighted* by J.B. Priestly; producer, Carl Laemmle Jr.; music (stock), David Broekman, Bernhard Kaun, and Heinz Roemheld (all uncredited); cinematographer, Arthur Edeson; editor, Clarence Kolster; art director, Charles D. Hall; sound effects, William Hedgcock; running time, 71 min.

THE PLOT:

One dark and stormy night, several sorry travelers find themselves stranded in an unhospitable stretch of English countryside. They take refuge in the home of a family named Femm. First to arrive are Philip and Margaret Waverton, a married couple accompanied by handsome young Roger Penderel. The strange-looking place reflects its occupants, beginning with a hulking butler, Morgan, who eyes the confused, frightened, hungry, soaked people curiously before allowing them to enter. The home's owners are cryptic Horace Femm and his strange sister Rebecca. Clearly not happy to see such intruders, they try to turn them away by claiming there are no beds. Finally, though, they give in.

Horace warns the travelers about Morgan, insisting he is a dangerous brute so they had better keep their distance. Nervous, but not hardy enough to brave the storm, all dress for dinner, only to learn that there are two more visitors, wealthy William Porterhouse and his companion Gladys DuCane, a chorus girl. Gladys talks Roger into going with her to his car to retrieve some liquor, as there's nothing to drink in the house. The two slip off to the barn where they become romantically involved. Shortly, the lights go out and everyone is left stumbling around in the dark. While Margaret is attacked by wild-eyed Morgan, Philip believes he hears a child's voice calling for help. Eventually, the Wavertons come across an elderly fellow, who informs them the reason for Morgan's presence is to control yet another Femm family member, Saul, who is quite mad and kept locked away.

Everyone is terrorized when Saul appears, apparently having escaped. In time they realize that he is not mad, a term that better describes his family members who murdered Saul's sister, then locked him up. Now, though, Saul comes to believe he's his Biblical namesake, and that Roger is "David," so he tries to kill the young man. The house threatens to go up in flames, the Wavertons flee, and Roger and Gladys realize they were meant for one another.

Charles Laughton (left), Raymond Massey (center), Melvyn Douglas (right) and other denizens face "the thing."

THE FILM:

No sooner had they completed *Frankenstein* (1931) than director James Whale and star Boris Karloff were encouraged to begin work on a sequel. But neither wanted to be typecast in the horror genre, so Universal's chief Carl Laemmle was unable to talk either into collaborating on the inevitable sequel for five years. Meanwhile, both wanted to work, and were happy to approach a less fantastical thriller driven by suspense based on the unseen. Both were thrilled to have an opportunity to adapt a literary work by the esteemed John Boynton Priestly, a World War I veteran who made his reputation writing for such free-thinking publications as *The New Statesman*. With 120 books to his credit, Priestley rated as one of the most prolific authors in the English language during the twentieth century. *Benighted* was always a popular favorite, thanks to his ability to take a hoary tale and make the conventional setting and far-fetched situation seem fresh and new owing to a wonderfully ironic tone; with this approach, Priestley invented what would come to be called "tongue-in-cheek."

Despite his great popularity, Priestley's books were seldom filmed during the early sound era for fear that his cleverness and sophistication would not make the transition from page to the screen at a time when expository dialogue had to be spoken loudly and slowly. Whale relished such a challenge, believing that, if skillfully done, the proper combination of scariness and satire could work for the general public. Happily, the experiment worked. Audiences loved the idea of laughing one moment, screaming out in fear the next and, in the movie's most memorable moments, doing both at the same time. Though rarely revived, or even recalled, today, *The Old Dark House* proved that laughs and scares could be mixed together, paving the way for the grand tradition of the comedy thriller.

TRIVIA:

Makeup effects were created by Jack P. Pierce, who did the honors for Karloff as the Frankenstein monster, Bela Lugosi as Dracula, and numerous other Universal horror figures from the thirties to the fifties. In a typical James Whale bit of eccentricity, the role of the family patriarch is played by actress Elspeth Dudgeon. *The Old Dark House* was remade in 1963, shot in England by famed American schlockmeister William Castle (see *Homicidal*, 1961, #98). The 1986 Gene Wilder/Gilda Radner vehicle *Haunted Honeymoon* (1986) was intended as a spoof of *The Old Dark House.*

ALSO RECOMMENDED:

Whale's *Frankenstein* and *Bride of Frankenstein* (1935) rate among the classic horror films, though the presence of oft-seen monsters makes them unacceptable for this volume. Charles Laughton would star in several classic edge-of-your-seat thrillers, including Billy Wilder's superb courtroom drama *Witness For the Prosecution* (1957), with Marlene Dietrich.

56:

HALLOWEEN (1978)

Compass International

"He was the boogeyman."
—Sam Loomis (final line)

CAST:

Jamie Lee Curtis (*Laurie*); Donald Pleasence (*Loomis*); Nancy Loomis (*Annie*); P.J. Soles (*Lynda*); Charles Cypers (*Brackett*); Kyle Richards (*Lindsay*); Brian Andrews (*Tommy*); John Michael Graham (*Bob*); Nancy Stephens (*Marin*); Tony Moran (*Michael at 21*).

CREDITS:

Director, John Carpenter; screenplay, Carpenter and Debra Hill; producer, Hill; music, Carpenter; cinematographer, Dean Dundey; editors, Tommy Wallace and Charles Bornstein; running time, 93 min.; rating, R.

THE PLOT:

Michael Meyers escapes from Smith's Grove, an Illinois mental institution, on October 30, 1978. He heads for Haddonfield, the small town where he grew up. On his trail is Dr. Sam Loomis, who has been caring for Meyers and knows the escapee plans horrible things for the sleepy hamlet where he first turned to murder. In 1963, the six-year-old brutally killed his older sister, who was supposed to baby-sit the little boy but slipped upstairs to make love with her boyfriend. Dr. Loomis fears that Meyers will kill other teenage girls engaged in illicit sex, using a Halloween mask to pass himself off as one more harmless trick-or-treater.

Hiding in his old house, long since abandoned, Meyers spots three girls—Laurie, Annie, and Lindsey—on their way to school. He stalks them, watching to see which are sexually promiscuous. All the while, Dr. Loomis searches desperately, having stopped at the graveyard where he discovered that Judith Meyers's tombstone has been removed from its place. That evening, several girls have baby-sitting jobs. When Meyers discovers Annie is leaving her charge to pick up her boyfriend, he slits her throat. As Lynda and her boyfriend engage in sex, Meyers appears in a sheet and murders them.

The only girl doing her job properly is virginal Laurie, who is serious about taking care of her little brother Tommy. She discovers the bodies of her friends and runs from Michael Meyers, trying to kill him with a knife, though he will not stay down. Dr. Loomis arrives and shoots Meyers several times. He falls out the second-story window. But when Loomis and Laurie peer out, the body is gone.

THE FILM:

Halloween, like its predecessor *Psycho* (1960), has been credited with being "the first slasher film," but such a label is misleading. True, *Halloween* did inspire the low-budget teen-oriented slasher film, with such movies as Sean S. Cunningham's *Friday the 13th* (1980) and Wes Craven's *A Nightmare on Elm Street* (1984), though in fact Tobe Hooper's *The Texas Chain Saw Massacre* (1974) did predate *Halloween*. Significantly, though, John Carpenter's film—like the first entries by Hooper and Craven—was not as violent as people recall. Like Hitchcock's 1960 classic, these movies suggested and implied violence, within a context of intense suspense, more than they actually showed it. In the following years, sequels, spin-offs, and endless imitations did make on-screen violence ever more vivid, graphic, and reprehensible. Still, the initial entries were truly thrillers, and *Halloween* rates as the best of the lot.

Shot on a tight $321,500 budget, the film returned more than fifty million on its initial release. Such success led to a new sub-genre of the thriller, in which teenagers in peril made formulaic situations relevant to

Jamie Lee Curtis as the first "final girl" in modern thrillers, the old-fashioned virgin who survives.

a young audience. All such films had it both ways as to the sexual revolution which came into being during the late sixties and early seventies, along with a new freedom for on-screen sex and violence. Nudity and gore abounds in the later films, something that would not have been possible when the first teen-oriented thrillers—the deplorable *I Was a Teenage Frankenstein*, the excellent *I Was a Teenage Werewolf* (both 1957)—were turned out during the era when a new breed of independent producers first discovered the youth market. On the other hand, *Halloween* and films of its ilk certainly appeared to react against the new sexual promiscuity among teenagers. In every such film, "the last American virgin"—the female who clings to old-fashioned values—is the one who survives as "the final girl." Her free-loving friends are killed, the climaxes of their lives usually occuring during a moment of climax with equally doomed boyfriends.

As Danny Peary put it, "*Halloween* isn't merely an excuse to show people killed off but is foremost a fascinating exercise in style." Carpenter—like Spielberg, Lucas, Scorsese, and other former film students who rose to prominence during the mid-seventies—was well-versed in the old films, employing techniques created by the grand masters, making them relevant to a new generation of movie-goers. *Halloween* is Carpenter's salute to Hitchcock in general, *Psycho* in particular. It's relevant to note that in Hitchcock's film, the adulterous sister was killed in the shower; the implicitly virginal one (Vera Miles) lives at the end and presumably ends up in the arms of the man her sister coveted.

TRIVIA:

Though the film is often compared to Hitchcock, there is a strong Rod Serling influence as well. At one point, Dr. Loomis sadly says, "the evil is gone" from the asylum, into the world. The same words appear in a famed *Twilight Zone* episode, "The Wailing Man," about a seemingly harmless prisoner, held in a castle, who is in fact the devil, hoping to get loose again.

ALSO RECOMMENDED:

Carpenter's early thriller, *Assault on Precinct 13* (1976), took the situation Howard Hawks had developed in *Rio Bravo* (1959)—a motley assortment of lawmen trapped in an isolated building by a mob of outlaws—and successfully transported the concept to our modern mean streets.

55:
DR. JEKYLL AND MR. HYDE (1932)

Paramount Pictures

> **"I'll show you what horror means!"**
> —Mr. Hyde

CAST:

> Fredric March (*Dr. Henry Jekyll/Mr. Hyde*); Miriam Hopkins (*Ivy Pearson*); Rose Hobart (*Muriel*); Holmes Herbert (*Lanyon*); Edgar Morton (*Poole*); Halliwell Hobbes (*Carew*); Arnold Lucy (*Mr. Utterson*); Tempe Pigott (*Mrs. Hawkins*).

CREDITS:

> Director, Rouben Mamoulian; screenplay, Samuel Hoffenstein and Peter Heath, from the novel by Robert Louis Stevenson; producer, Mamoulian; cinematographer, Karl Struss; editor, William Shea; art direction, Hans Dreier; running time, 80 min.

THE PLOT:

Dr. Henry Jekyll, a young idealist, announces to medical students that he hopes to do his part in making Queen Victoria's value system come to full fruition by separating man into two parts, pure brain and absolute beast, and then eliminate the latter. Everyone believes him to be a genius or a madman; fiancée Muriel Carew supports everything Jekyll does and says. His great frustration is that her father won't let them marry at once, for Jekyll wants to share his sexual self with his true love, though other women—including the street slut Ivy—throw themselves at him. When Jekyll takes the potion, the result is the opposite of what he'd hoped for. The beast dominates, as Mr. Hyde runs off to see Ivy and vent his thwarted sexual appetite.

The relationship between Hyde and Ivy grows ever more violent and abusive, until Jekyll realizes he can no longer continue with a double life. Even after he stops taking the potion, he finds himself transforming into Hyde, now wishing he'd listened to the warnings of best friend Lanyon, who insisted, "There are bounds beyond which man should not go!" In his frenzied Hyde state, he strangles Ivy. Realizing he can never have a normal life now, Jekyll determines to break off his enagement. In Muriel's presence, he suddenly turns into Hyde and almost murders her, badly beating General Carew when he intervenes. Hurrying back to his laboratory, Hyde takes the potion and becomes Jekyll again, though Lanyon—knowing the truth—turns him in to the police. As they arrive, Jekyll transforms into Hyde and is shot by a detective, transforming back into Jekyll before everyone's startled eyes.

At the sight of Ivy Pearson's white flesh, Dr. Jekyll turns into Mr. Hyde.

THE FILM:

Robert Louis Stevenson's novel *The Strange Case of Dr. Jekyll and Mr. Hyde* (1888) was a mystery; only on the very last page does the reader discover that Jekyll and Hyde are one and the same. So quickly, though, did word spread of the twist ending that, when the book was adapted as a stage play, that had to be dropped, for it would surprise no one. Instead, the theatre piece by John Balderston offered an exercise in gothic horror, more or less serving as a companion piece to his *Dracula*.

The numerous early screen versions honed to this approach. When Rouben Mamoulian decided to mount the first sound-era film, he emphasized suspense. For the first time, Hyde is not a monster in any supernatural sense (most films have him appear as a combination of vampire and werewolf) but a seeming reversion to an earlier stage on man's evolutionary chain, a paradigm of the missing link. He has absolutely no supernatural powers in this film, but is the dark, hideous, yet strangely charismatic side of an otherwise good man.

Each of us has a touch of the beast somewhere deep down inside, and when Jekyll releases his own, the story serves as a cautionary fable for everyone watching. No wonder, then, when Lanyon screams to the police, "There's your man," he is pointing directly into the camera—at us as much as at Jekyll. Mamoulian created great suspense, while furthering the artistry of the still-emerging sound film, by using the old wipe technique to create split screens that present the audience with moral choices, and slowly-achieved dissolves, the most memorable being that moment when Ivy's shapely leg refuses to disappear from the screen, as the image changes to Jekyll and Lanyon walking and talking about other things. Though on a conscious level, Jekyll has forgotten all about Ivy, on an unconscious one, she haunts him still.

TRIVIA:

Though Ivy may be Miriam Hopkins's best-known screen performance today, she was frustrated at not being allowed to play the less showy part of Muriel. Hopkins had tired of playing street women, and wanted to use the project to prove she could convey class. Mamoulian first conceived of having Hyde appear to be a baboon while listening to radio broadcasts of the Scopes Monkey Trial in 1925, as Darwinism was debated after a young teacher was put on trial for introducing such ideas to his southern high school students. Mamoulian transformed the Victorian-era melodrama into an allegory for evolution.

ALSO RECOMMENDED:

Among the most suspenseful of the other films based on this remarkable literary work is Victor Fleming's 1941 version. At the time, Freud's ideas were hotly debated, so Fleming chose to play the tale as an allegory for psychoanalysis. When Spencer Tracy transforms from Jekyll to Hyde, he barely employs any makeup, suggesting the transformation is essentially mental.

Following the first successful sex-change operation, Hammer produced *Dr. Jekyll and Sister Hyde* (1972) which, despite the comedic-sounding title, is a first-rate thriller. Also recommended: George Cukor's *A Double Life* (1947) in which Ronald Colman (Oscar winner, Best Actor) portrays an actor essaying the role of Othello who succeeds too well in becoming the character and plans the murder of his own actress/wife on opening night.

54:

BLOWUP (1966)

Metro-Goldwyn-Mayer

> **"Seeing may be believing, yet that does not imply it has
> anything to do with the truth."**
> —**Michelangelo Antonioni**

CAST:

David Hemmings (*Thomas*); Vanessa Redgrave (*Jane*); Peter Bowles (*Ron*); Sarah Miles (*Patricia*); John Castle (*Bill*); Jane Birkin, Gillian Hills (*Groupies*); Verushka (*Fashion Model*); Claude Chagrin and Julian Chagrin (*Mimes*); Jeff Beck and The Yardbirds (*Rock Group*). Melanie Hampshire, Jill Kennington, Peggy Moffitt, Rosaleen Murray, and Ann Norman (*Models*); Tsai Chin (*Receptionist*).

CREDITS:

Director, Michelangelo Antonioni; screenplay, Antonioni and Toninio Guerra, from a short story by Julio Cortázar, with additional English dialogue by Edward Bond; producers, Carlo Ponti and Pierre Rouve; original music, Herbert Hancock; cinematographer, Carlo Di Palma; editor, Frank Clarke; art director, Assheton Gorton; running time, 111 min.

THE PLOT:

Swingin' London in the mid-sixties: The Beatles and Rolling Stones are at the height of their international appeal, Carnaby Street dictates the fashions of America and the western world, casual drug use has become widespread, and the sexual revolution is in full swing. At the epicenter of all such action stands Thomas, an ultra-mod young photographer who looks like a rock star and is treated much like one by the beautiful models he immortalizes in photo sessions that grow orgasmic, as Thomas symbolically rapes them with his camera. Yet none of this gives Thomas true pleasure; he has become blasé to the wild life of excess lived for immediate gratification.

The Camera as Phallus: David Hemmings and Verushka.

Bored with glamour, he begins shooting pictures of London's worst slums. While strolling through a park, Thomas notices two people, apparently kissing, and snaps a few photos, then wanders off. Momentarily, the woman comes rushing after Thomas, demanding he give her the film. Assuming she must be a married woman who was having an adulterous affair, Thomas slips her another roll of film, insists it's the one containing the pictures he took, and leaves. Back in his studio, Thomas develops the film, thinking it reveals a sexual tryst. Then, he becomes uncomfortable, realizing that something else is there—lost and/or hidden in the image—beyond what he apparently witnessed.

Obsessively, Thomas blows up small sections of the image to several dozen times lifesize, studying them intensely, searching for whatever continues to elude him. Then, he he spies what he's looking for, a small detail that suggests the woman may not have been kissing the man but killing him. Frightened, Thomas drives back to the park that night. In a space behind several trees he finds the dead body of the man.

Thomas heads back to his studio to pick up the blowups and share them with someone, perhaps friends, maybe the police. But when he arrives, the studio has been ransacked, and the pictures and negatives are gone. Heading back to where he's just seen the body, Thomas discovers nothing, realizing he has no way to prove any of this actually happened. Besides, he no longer trusts his own eyes; without proof on paper of what goes on around him, he is no longer sure what constitutes reality as opposed to fantasy. Shortly, Thomas begins to wonder whether it in fact did happen, or if he imagined it all. Finally, Thomas watches as several mimes pretend to play tennis; as he comes to believe in their game, Thomas realizes he can hear the sound of the ball being hit back and forth.

The Film:

Blowup might be described as a cross between Hitchcock's *Vertigo* (1958, #11) and Richard Lester's *Help!* (1964), at once a mod romp through swinging London and an erotically-charged thriller about a man who comes to believe he's been lured into a deadly trap by a beautiful, mysterious woman. Here is one more case of a genius-level filmmaker "redeeming" the thriller form by shooting what might have been a humble genre exercise so originally, endowing the material with such unexpected depth that what we see transcends any conventions of the form. No matter how much suspense we may experience along the way, the final impact is of having watched a film of major social significance, in this case an existential view of the world that, in its final moments, lures us into a solipsistic state in which we doubt the validity of everything we've seen. We are, therefore, left wondering if objective reality can ever be known, or if anything and everything we experience finally exists only in the mind's eye. The character of Thomas becomes Hamlet for the hippie era.

Trivia:

This was the first British feature to be released in which full frontal female nudity, including pubic hair, was shown onscreen. "Thomas" was modelled on two then-popular photographers, David Bailey and Terence Donovan. Terence Stamp was in the running with David Hemmings for the role. The part of the rock band that breaks its own guitars was written specifically for The Who. When they could not adjust their concert schedule to appear, The Yardbirds were cast instead. Though the film appears to have been shot on realistic London settings for total accuracy of detail in the scene, Antonioni repainted many buildings so as to create a subtle surrealism in which the "real world" is transformed into an expressive movie set.

ALSO RECOMMENDED:

Brian De Palma's *Blow Out* (1981) is an unofficial remake, with sound substituted for sight. Similar themes can be found in Alejandro Amenábar's *Open Your Eyes* (1998). See also *The Passenger* (1975, #64).

53:
SAFETY LAST (1923)

The Sam Goldwyn Company

> **"The sky really *is* the limit!"**
> **—Harold Lloyd**

CAST:

Harold Lloyd (*Harold Lloyd*); Mildred Davis (*Mildred*); Bill Strothers (*Limpy Bill*); Noah Young (*The Policeman*); Westcott Clarke (*Mr. Stubbs, the floorwalker*); Mickey Daniels (*Newsboy*); Anna Townsend (*Grandma*); Helen Gilmore (*Outraged Customer*); Roy Brooks, Gus Leonard (*Worker*); Charles A. Stevenson (*Ambulance Attendant*).

CREDITS:

Directors, Fred C. Newmeyer, Sam Taylor and (uncredited) Harold Lloyd; screenplay, Jean C. Havez, Sam Taylor, H.M. Walker, Tim Whelan and (uncredited) Lloyd; producer, Hal Roach; cinematographer, Walter Lundin; editor, Thomas J. Crizer; art director, Fred Guiol; running time, 78 min.

THE PLOT:

Like other young men during the post-WWI era, Harold Lloyd leaves his small town (Great Bend) behind to seek fame and fortune in the big city. All he finds is a clerk's job at De Vore's Department Store. When his fiancée Mildred unexpectedly comes to visit (he has written her, claiming to be the manager), Harold tries

Harold Lloyd: the stunt as gag, the comedy as thriller.

to complete his humble tasks while appearing to be a big shot. Finally, Harold comes up with a scheme to win publicity for the store: have a friend, an excellent climber, scale the twelve-story building's side, floor by floor. This will win him a vice-presidency. But when the big day comes, his friend cannot perform as planned. Harold himself must scale the building, and at each juncture, the ever more desperate climber—social as well as literal—must confront some new threat: a flock of pigeons, a piece of netting, a pair of painters with a protruding plat-form, an opening window, an unattached piece of rope, a snarling dog, a gigantic clock, a loose flagpole, and a revolving weather-vane among them.

THE FILM:

During the early days of screen comedy, Hal Roach, who teamed Laurel with Hardy and put together the original Little Rascals/Our Gang ensemble, also pro-duced this, the best known film of Harold Lloyd. Nicknamed "The Third Genius"—after Charlie Chaplin and Buster Keaton—Lloyd could be as funny as his contemporaries. His lower status may derive from his films' comparative lack

of emotional pathos and intellectual substance as well as the way his films celebrated the American Dream ideal of the twenties, rather than comically condemn-
ing that concept as leftish thinkers like Chaplin and Keaton did. Still, Lloyd has his
place in film history. To this day, stunts are known, by the people who perform
them, as "gags," a reference to Lloyd's career. In comparison to Chaplin's sentimen-
tal ballet and Keaton's stoic mime, Lloyd developed complicated stunt work. Lloyd
elevated stunts, until then thought of as crude and broad, to the defined level of an
art form, if always rendered in humorous terms. Behind his horn-rimmed glasses
and under the ever-present straw hat, Lloyd's on-screen persona (a variation of his
own personality) was a meek-mannered, self-serving bumbler who hungered for
fame and fortune. In the end, he won both through a Horatio Algerish combination
of luck, pluck, and sheer accicent—being in the right place at the right time and
having the forsight to cash in on any situation he found himself in.

Richard Schickel has noted that Lloyd's ever more elaborate and death-defying
climbs up the sides of recently completed skyscrapers served—beyond the level of
comedy-thriller entertainment—as a succession of effective symbols for the mainstream attitude at a time when everything from the stock-market to ladies' hem-
lines was going up. The image of Harold, hanging precariously in mid-air, caught
something essential in the spirit of the times, when everyone believed that in the
rugged world of modern big business, an earnest individualist could achieve pretty
much anything he set his mind to.

Adding greatly to the thriller element in Lloyd's comedy was camera-
placement, for he clearly did not rely on stunt-doubles (though Bill Strothers does
sit in for Harold for one particularly precarous shot) or back-projection. Indeed,
Harold lost his left thumb and two fingers performing stunts while performing in
Haunted Spooks (1920), and had to wear specially created leather gloves to keep the
audience from seeing the sorry condition of his actual hands.

When the 1930s arrived, the Great Depression hit America. Lloyd's movies
were never again quite as popular, despite his immense likeability; his greatness
had been in providing endless variations on the theme of upward mobility during
a decade when most everyone really did believe that the sky was the limit.

TRIVIA:

Lloyd's leading lady was Mildred Davis, his real-life wife. The idea for *Safety Last*
came to Lloyd when he witnessed a man named William Strothers performing a
human fly act at an actual downtown department store in Los Angeles. Strothers
appears as Lloyd's friend in *Safety Last*. To break any fall that might have killed
their star, the crew placed a safety device just below camera-range. When filming

was completed, a crew member took a sack containing scrap materials identical in weight to Lloyd's body weight and dropped it to see what would happen. The safety device broke apart and the sack fell to the sidewalk eleven stories below.

ALSO RECOMMENDED:

Lloyd took his daredevil brand of comedy to the gridiron for *The Freshman* (1925), the greatest single comedy ever made about the rough sport of football. *The Kid Brother* (1927), his last great silent comedy, also contains several thrilling sequences. Harold had earlier made similar, if less spectacular, climbs in *Look Out Below* (1919), *High and Dizzy* (1920), and *Never Weaken* (1921); he would do so again in *Feet First* (1930).

52:
WAIT UNTIL DARK (1967)

Warner Bros.

> **"Mr. Roat, are you looking at me?"**
> **—Suzy Hendrix**

CAST:

Audrey Hepburn (*Suzy Hendrix*); Alan Arkin (*Roat/Harry Roat Jr./Roat Sr.*); Richard Crenna (*Mike Talman*); Efrem Zimbalist Jr. (*Sam Hendrix*); Jack Weston (*Carlino*); Samantha Jones (*Lisa*); Julie Herrod (*Gloria*); Jean Del Val (*Elderly Man*); Frank O'Brien (*Shatner*).

CREDITS:

Director, Terence Young; screenplay, Robert Howard-Carrington and Jane Howard-Carrington, from the stage play by Frederick Knott; producer, Mel Ferrer; original music, Henry Mancini; cinematographer, Charles Lang; editor, Gene Milford; art director, George Jenkins; running time, 108 min.

THE PLOT:

A young beauty named Lisa supports her swinging lifestyle by carrying heroin into the United States from Canada inside the doll she carries. While landing at a New York airport, she realizes that dangerous men are closing in on her. In a state of panic, Lisa hands the doll to the nearest man, likable Sam Hendrix, insisting it's a present for her daughter. When Lisa darts away, Sam doesn't know what to do with the doll other than carry it to the Manhattan apartment he shares with Suzy, his wife. Suzy has recently survived an autmobile accident that left her blind, and is in the process of learning how to make her way around the apartment. Gloria, a little girl from next door, regularly stops by to help out whenever Sam has to be out of town on business.

Criminal mastermind Harry Roat wants the heroin back, and knows he must find the doll. He forces Lisa to tell him who she gave it to, then brutally murders her. Knowing that it's somewhere in the Hendrix apartment, Roat draws two con-men—tall, handsome Mike Talman and his roly-poly sidekick, Carlino, neither of whom wants anything to do with violence—into his convoluted plot. Mike is to arrive at the apartment while Sam is off on business, introduce himself as an old army friend of Sam's, and ingratiate himself with Suzy. While in the blind woman's apartment, "visiting" with her, Mike can try to discover the doll's whereabouts. Roat, meanwhile, will augment this "life-as-theatre" routine, showing up in various guises—an elderly lunatic and an outraged husband—to draw away Suzy's attention, leaving Mike more time to find the doll. Carlino will play the part of a police officer who arrives on the scene. Suzy, however, is too smart for them, gradually figuring out that this is a scheme. In time, Roat kills both of his easygoing colleagues, then comes after Suzy.

THE FILM:

Thanks to Terence Young's careful pacing and cautious build-up, the tension—escalating all along—suddenly roars into high gear. Realizing that she's in mortal danger, Suzy refuses to panic and makes her own blindness work in her favor by smashing all the lights, thereby reducing Roat to her own level of sightlessness. Since she has been learning how to negotiate around the rooms, Suzy is actually in a far better position than he. Unfortunately, she has forgotten one single light—the small one in the refrigerator. When Roat opens its door, the audience shrieks with true terror born of suspense, for we see more than she does, of course, and know that Suzy is in grave peril even when she believes herself to be safe. Until that moment when Roat figures out how to regain the upper hand, followed by Suzy's

Life as theatre: Richard Crenna, Jack Weston, and Alan Arkin perform an elaborate scenario for blind-girl Audrey Hepburn.

incredible but believable victory over her adversary, the movie had momentarily become what Val Lewton always called for as the ultimate in realistic horror: a black screen onto which the audience projects its own worst fears, as strange sounds appear on the track.

As James Kendrick has written, the plot is, upon close examination, "contrived, but (the movie itself) is a perfect example of how mood, atmosphere, music, and direction can overcome plot weakness." Frederick Knott had always hoped that Alfred Hitchcock might direct the film version of his hit play, as Hitchcock had an earlier film based on Knott's first great success, *Dial M for Murder* (1954). The doll containing the heroin serves as a perfect MacGuffin, that seemingly insignificant object for which all the characters will risk their lives. Though the initial premise—Lisa handing the valuable item to the nearest person and then leaving—struck many as far-fetched, it is a variation on another Hitchcock theme: any ordinary person can be drawn into a mire of the macabre just by being in the wrong place at the wrong time. Having characters play roles within the film is a life-as-theatre theme that Hitchcock often returned to, most obviously in *Stage Fright* (1950).

TRIVIA:

The little boy playing with a ball in the opening airport sequence is Robby Benson. Set in New York, some of the exterior footage was actually shot there, though most of the movie was done in Montreal. The original Broadway play had starred Lee Remick, with Robert Duvall as the wicked Roat. One ploy appeared borrowed from William Castle rather than Alfred Hitchcock. At the point when all the lights are dimmed onscreen, theatre managers were informed that they ought to dim the lights in the theatre so that total darkness would prevail, a technique that had succeded in scaring the wits out of Broadway theatregoers and worked again in the movie.

ALSO RECOMMENDED:

The Hitchcock version of Knott's play *Dial M for Murder* (1954) works excellently as a film. Another fine thriller about a blind girl attempting to ward off killers is *Blind Terror* (a.k.a. *See No Evil*, 1971) with Mia Farrow.

51:

AND THEN THERE WERE NONE (1945)

20th Century Fox

> **"Very stupid to kill the only servant in the house.**
> **Now we don't even know where to find the marmalade."**
> —**Judge Quinncannon**

CAST:

Barry Fitzgerald (*Judge Francis J. Quinncannon*); Walter Huston (*Dr. Edward G. Armstrong*); Louis Hayward (*Philip Lombard*); Roland Young (*Detective William Blore*); June Duprez (*Vera Claythorne*); Mischa Auer (*Prince Nikita Starloff*); C. Aubrey Smith (*General Mandrake*); Judith Anderson (*Emily Brent*); Richard Haydn (*Thomas the Butler*); Queenie Leonard (*Ethel the Maid*); Harry Thurston (*Boatman*).

CREDITS:

Director, René Clair; screenplay, Clair (uncredited) and Dudley Nichols, from the story and play by Agatha Christie; producers, Clair, Harry M. Popkin and Leo C. Popkin; original music, Mario Castelnuovo-Tedesco and (uncredited) Charles Previn; cinematographer, Lucien N. Andriot; editor, Harvey Manger; art direction, Ernst Fegté; running time, 98 min.

THE PLOT:

Late one Friday afternoon, a small boat carries an odd assortment of people to an isolated island, crowned with a mansion upon the crest of its largest hill. All have been invited to attend a celebration, but no sooner do they arrive than the awful truth becomes clear: their host is nowhere to be found, and they are to be killed, one by one, for crimes real or imagined in each person's past. On a great table in the parlor is a decoration featuring replicas of the ten little Indians from the old nursery rhyme. The visitors can't escape, as the boat is gone and will not return until Monday. As they die off, each is killed in the manner of the next line in that

Ten little Indians . . .

old ditty. Despite the dangers, guests do strike up relationships, including a friend-ship between equally cynical and self-serving Judge Quinncannon and Dr. Arm-strong, as well as a romance between the youngest and most attractive among the visitors, handsome Philip and pretty Vera.

The seemingly final twist is that Quinncannon, apparently killed two-thirds of the way through, faked his death and reveals himself to be the killer after Vera shoots Philip, he being the only other survivor, therefore certain to kill her next. No sooner does the judge take poison (he is near death anyway) than Philip steps up beside him, revealing to the doomed man that young love has, as always, con-quered all.

THE FILM:

Though Agatha Christie's original narrative and eventual play was essentially a thriller, laced with characteristic touches of wry comedy, René Clair—the great Gallic director of such film classics as *À nous la liberté* (1931)—wisely chose to play the piece as black humor without ever diminishing the scream quotient. By keeping the murders offscreen, in the darkness and shadows, he created a tangible mood of constant menace that would have been shattered if we actually ever saw anyone die.

Clair breaks with both the narrative and stage origins, transforming what could have been canned theatre into pure cinema by making his camera a virtual character rather than a mere recording device. He offers a close-up of a doomed guest, who stares directly into the camera as he figures out the murderer's identity, then gasps, "I've got it!", just before a huge stone crushes him. The camera wanders through the spooky mansion, slithering up and down the spiral staircase. Clair returns again and again to the sea, pounding in on the island's rough shore, word-lessly reminding us of the isolation.

Voyeuristic shots are featured, in which characters peep through keyholes at one another, the camera assuming the Peeping Tom's point of view, forcing us to share in the lurid act of secretly looking. The single set offered a difficult but provocative challenge ("making a film in a telephone booth," as Hitchcock once described it) that the greatest filmmakers have always relished, including Hitchcock himself in *Lifeboat* (1944), *Rope* (1948), and *Rear Window* (1954, #6).

TRIVIA:

The story has been filmed a total of four times (officially), though its essential premise—a group of people who are murdered one by one by an unknown assassin—has been imitated more often than any other plot in the suspense genre. As incredible as it seems today, the original title of Christie's book was *Ten Little Niggers*. However politically incorrect this may appear, she meant no slight, since the term—for Brits of her age—was then no more intended as an insult than for an Anglo American of that time to refer to Native Americans as Indians. When the book was printed in America, the title was changed to *Ten Little Indians*, which served as the title of the eventual 1966 remake.

The classic 1945 film, however, carried the title of the original book when it was produced and then released in England. However, the distributors instead chose to take the final verse of the nursery rhyme which serves as a recurring device, and it is this title that now blesses the book, both in England and America. Incidentally, the premise—combined with that of another of Ms. Christie's stories, *The Mousetrap*—were blended to create the popular board game, Clue.

Also Recommended:

The 1966 remake, though not up to the original, does create considerable suspense, and features bravura performances by Stanley Holloway, Leo Genn, and Wilfrid Hyde-White, as well as glamorous Shirley Eaton, best known as the gilded lady in *Goldfinger* (1963). Among the best spin-offs is William Castle's *The House on Haunted Hill* (1958), an inspired if tacky B-movie that, like its superior antecedent, combines macabre humor with intense thriller moments.

50:

CARRIE (1976)

United Artists

"Pimples are the Lord's way of chastising you."
—Margaret White

Cast:

Sissy Spacek (*Carrie White*); Piper Laurie (*Margaret White*); Amy Irving (*Sue Snell*); William Katt (*Tommy Ross*); Betty Buckley (*Miss Collins*);

Nancy Allen (*Chris Hargensen*); John Travolta (*Billy Nolan*); P.J. Soles (*Norma Watson*); Priscilla Pointer (*Mrs. Snell*); Sydney Lassick (*Mr. Fromm*); Stefan Gierasch (*Mr. Morton*); Michael Talbott (*Freddy*); Edie McClurg (*Helen*); Doug Cox (*"The Beak"*).

CREDITS:

Director, Brian De Palma; screenplay, Lawrence D. Cohen, from the novel by Stephen King; producers, De Palma, Paul Monash, and Louis A. Stroller; original music, Pino Donaggio; cinematographer, Mario Tosi; editor, Paul Hirsch; art directors, Jack Fisk and William Kenney; special effects, Kenneth Pepiot and Gregory M. Auer; running time, 87 min.; rating, R.

THE PLOT:

All her life, Carrie White has felt like an outcast among the "normal" kids at her school. When her first menstruation appears, later than for the other girls, she's rudely abused by them. Desperate, Carrie returns home, but finds little solace with her mother, a member of the right-wing Christian fringe. Margaret shouts at Carrie, warning Carrie that if she isn't careful, her soul will belong to the devil. Quietly suppressing her rage, Carrie nurtures a secret gift: she has been blessed—perhaps cursed—with telekinetic powers that allow her to move and explode objects via extreme concentration.

The only person who tries to reach Carrie in a positive way is Miss Collins, a sympathetic teacher. Even her sincere efforts can't counter the powerful odds that force Carrie into a corner, leaving the soft-spoken teenager with no alternative but to unleash her rage. This occurs at the high school prom; Carrie, who did not expect to be invited at all, is asked for a date by Tommy Ross, the most attractive boy of the "in" crowd. This is a set-up. At the moment when Carrie is crowned queen of the prom, the other girls arrange for a bucket of blood to fall on Carrie's head. While everyone laughs, Carrie focuses on death and destruction, causing all there to perish horribly.

THE FILM:

Carrie's phenomenal success led to a tide of teen-oriented thrillers beginning in the late seventies and running strong ever since. Most are far more violent than *Carrie*; viewers discovering it for the first time will perhaps be surprised, even disappointed, that the only horrific acts of bloodletting occur during the final act. Director Brian De Palma was not aware that he was inventing a new type of

The Moment of Truth: Carrie (Sissy Spacek) is mad as hell and isn't going to take it anymore.

scarefest; rather, he was hoping to reinvent the suspense film, which takes its time setting up characters. The situation gradually escalates until a burst of violence at the climax works as a catharsis, as in ancient tragedy, releasing the viewer from pent-up emotions we have shared with the characters.

"The man who would be Hitchcock" is the way several film historians have described De Palma, though he was willing to incorporate some decidedly seventies stylistic developments—most notably split screen—into the thriller form. Ironically, these technical approaches—which made the film seem hip and modern then—date it today. What doesn't suffer is the concept that Stephen King hit upon in his slim but notable first novel. Virtually every high school student harbors feelings of resentment for the way in which he or she was treated: at best ignored, at worst maligned. Truth be told, each harbored fantasies of revenge.

In its vividly-rendered story, *Carrie* touched what King has called a "pressure point" in viewers by daring to realize, first in print and then on film, those shared secret fantasies. This makes the film of particular interest today, in light of the Columbine shootings and other incidents of high school violence in which some face-in-the-crowd student unleashes such anger at both likely targets and innocent bystanders. The real tragedy is that the vision of *Carrie* is, today, no longer merely a fantasy.

Despite the film's power, it's limited by what would become the major flaw in De Palma's later films. His movies are weighed down by a self-conscious application of stylistic devices—slow-motion, languid camera-movement, etc.—that too often appear to be nothing more than flamboyant techniques offered for their own sake, rather than as a means of telling a story. Even such self-indugence can't spoil *Carrie*, which neatly demolishes the hippie-era myth from a few years earlier—

that a new generation of flower-power youth suffered none of the smallness of attitude that characterized previous generations. Consciously or not, King and/or de Palma told a story that belied such naive if sweet notions.

TRIVIA:

Stephen King was so unknown at the time that his name was incorrectly spelled "Steven King" in the opening credits of the initial release print. The high school seen in the film is Pier Avenue Junior High in Hermosa Beach, California. In the film, it's rechristened Bates High, one of the filmmaker's many homages to Hitchcock in general, *Psycho* in particular. Director De Palma married actress Nancy Allen shortly after working with her in this, their first film together. Budgeted at $1,800,000, the film returned $12,500,000 (then a hefty sum) in its initial U.S. release. Priscilla Pointer, who plays the mother of Amy Irving's character, is Irving's mother in real-life.

ALSO RECOMMENDED:

De Palma's other recommended films are his early thriller, *Sisters* (1973) with Margot Kidder, and *Obsession* (1976), with Genevieve Bujold; both are unoffical remakes of his favorite Hitchcock movie, *Vertigo* (1958, #11).

49:

HUSH . . . HUSH, SWEET CHARLOTTE (1964)

20th Century Fox

> **"Let me tell you, right here on the public street, in the light of day, that murder starts in the heart, and its first weapon is a vicious tongue."**
> **—Jewell Mayhew**

CAST:

Bette Davis (*Charlotte Hollis*); Olivia de Havilland (*Miriam Deering*); Joseph Cotten (*Dr. Drew Bayliss*); Agnes Moorehead (*Velma Cruther*); Cecil

Kellaway (*Harry Willis*); Victor Buono (*Big Sam*); Mary Astor (*Jewel Mayhew*); Wesley Addy (*Sheriff Standish*); William Campbell (*Marchand*); Bruce Dern (*John Mayhew*); Frank Ferguson (*Editor*); George Kennedy (*Foreman*); Dave Willock (*Taxi Driver*); John Megna, Kelly Flynn (*Boys*); Ellen Corby (*Lily*); Percy Helton (*Funeral Director*).

CREDITS:

Director, Robert Aldrich; screenplay, Lukas Heller, from Henry Farrell's novel *Whatever Happened to Cousin Charlotte*?; producers, Aldrich and Walter Blake; original music, Mack David (title song) and Frank De Vol; cinematographer, Joseph F. Biroc; editor, Michael Luciano; art director, William Glasgow; running time, 133 min.

THE PLOT:

For four decades, Charlotte Hollis has been a spinster, shut up in her decaying Southern mansion, rumored to be mad. The locals believe Charlotte killed her fiancé moments before their wedding; Charlotte herself can no longer recall whether or not she killed handsome John Mayhew. She was found standing over the body, her wedding dress bloodied, the murder weapon—a knife—in her hand. Only Velma, the old family servant, remains loyal, tending to Charlotte. Now, though, the state plans on running a highway through the property. Obstinate as ever, Charlotte fires an old gun at men in bulldozers, so they send for her cousin Miriam to help Charlotte make the difficult adjustment.

Then again, Miriam will inherit the land and money should Charlotte have to be committed to an asylum. Miriam asks Dr. Drew Bayliss, a family friend, to try and determine Charlotte's mental state. Charlotte soon sees and hears the ghosts of her deceased lover and father. Panicky, Charlotte mistakes Drew for a spirit. Terrified as to what will happen if the body is discovered, Miriam helps her cousin to dispose of it. Then, Drew comes back from the dead; at the sight, Charlotte goes completely mad. Drew then removes the makeup; he and his lover Miriam have successfully driven Charlotte over the edge. Hearing their conversation, Charlotte pushes over an old statue, killing them both. Meanwhile, elderly Jewell Mayhew confesses to the age-old murder, allowing Charlotte to step into the light of day and live what is left of her life.

THE FILM:

In 1962, Robert Aldrich revived the long-faded careers of Bette Davis and Joan Crawford, queens of Warner Bros. and MGM respectively, with *Whatever Hap-*

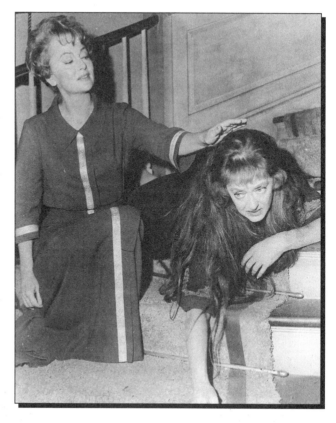

Reunion: Onetime Warner Brothers stars Olivia de Havilland and Bette Davis, together again.

pened to Baby Jane? (1962). Davis played a onetime star, reduced to a cruel caretaker for her invalid sister, Crawford. The film was played as an over the top black comedy, one of the first Grand Guignol films of the sixties in which the Old Hollywood was mocked by the newcomers. The film proved to be hugely popular. And while it didn't lend itself to a sequel, there was no reason why Aldrich couldn't mount a spin-off—an entirely new story that repaired the onetime antagonists for the title "Queen of Hollywood."

There was a major stumbling block. Davis had always despised Crawford, and bellowed at the thought of working with her. In fact, after the first few days of shooting on *Whatever Happened to Baby Jane?*, the two rarely did a scene together. Aldrich would shoot Davis's lines over the shoulder of a stand-in, then do the same with Crawford, splicing the film together in the editing room. But the very different concept of *Hush . . . Hush Sweet Charlotte*—the two women would have to appear onscreen together for lengthy scenes—made this impossible. As shooting was about to begin, Davis threw a temper tantrum, demanding that Crawford withdraw from the project. Out of politeness, word went out that Crawford was ill and couldn't work.

Davis then suggested Olivia de Havilland, with whom she often co-starred with at Warner Bros. In fact, *Hush . . . Hush Sweet Charlotte* would not work nearly so well with Crawford, owing to the career baggage a star always brings to the latest project. Despite the fact that Miriam has plentiful reasons to want Charlotte out of the way, we must never suspect her, or the film's great twist wouldn't work. Crawford had played so many villainous women in the past that it would be hard *not* to suspect her at once. De Havilland, however, was best known for sweet, strong, loyal best friends—most notably in *Gone With the Wind* (1939)—so her canon of portrayals actually assisted in keeping anyone from suspecting she might be the villain.

TRIVIA:

Agnes Moorehead won the Best Supporting Actress Oscar for her bravura performance as a maid. The film was shot in and around Baton Rouge, Louisiana, with the Houmas House Plantation serving as Charlotte's home. The role of Jewel Mayhew was created with Barbara Stanwyck in mind. She turned the part down, not wanting to play fourth fiddle to Davis, De Havilland, and Moorehead. The role went to Mary Astor (see *The Maltese Falcon*, 1941, #20), who had long since retired from films but agreed to return for this choice role.

ALSO RECOMMENDED:

For films of this sub-genre, the aforementioned *Whatever Happened to Baby Jane?* (1962) is a must. Davis shines in *The Nanny* (1965), while Crawford finally got to play in her own geriatric horror item, *Strait-Jacket* (1964). Another top teaming of grand dames: Geraldine Page and Ruth Gordon in *Whatever Happened to Aunt Alice?* (1969).

48:

THE CONTENDER (2000)

DreamWorks

"Sometimes you can assassinate a leader without firing a shot."
> **—advertising tag line**

CAST:

Gary Oldman (*Rep. Sheldon "Shelly" Runyon*); Joan Allen (*Laine Hanson*); Jeff Bridges (*President Evans*); Christian Slater (*Webster*); Sam Elliott (*Newman*); William L. Petersen (*Hathaway*); Saul Rubinek (*Jerry Tolliver*);

Philip Baker Hall (*Billings*); Mike Binder (*Hollis*); Robin Thomas (*William Hanson*); Mariel Hemingway (*Cynthia*); Kathryn Morris (*Agent Willomina*); Kristen Shaw (*Fiona Hathaway*); Douglas Urbanski (*Makerowitz*); Noah Fryrear (*Timmy*); Angelica Torn (*Dierdra*).

CREDITS:

Director, Rod Lurie; screenplay, Lurie; producers, Marc Frydman, Douglas Urbanski, Will Bär, James Spies, and Gary Oldman; original music, Larry Group; cinematographer, Denis Maloney; editor, Michael Jablow; production design, Alexander Hammond; running time, 127 min.; rating, R.

THE PLOT:

Governor Jack Hathaway fishes by an out-of-the-way bridge while giving an interview to a journalist. Their session is interrupted when a vehicle rolls off the bridge, into the water. Without hesitation, Hathaway dives in and attempts to rescue the trapped girl. Though she drowns, he becomes a national celebrity, so it's assumed President Evans will pick Hathaway to replace his recently deceased vice-president. However, Evans picks a woman. Things will not go easy for Senator Laine Hanson.

Mike Binder as the communications director and Joan Allen as Senator Laine Hanson observe the hearings that will determine whether she becomes the first female vice-president; the thriller form, redeemed through social content.

Conservative Representative Shelley Runyon digs up an old rumor that Laine may, while in college, have participated in group sex. When the president asks if there's any truth to this, Laine refuses to defend herself.

Runyon becomes so desperate to deny Laine the position that he throws his support behind Democrat Hathaway. When the president's detectives discover Hathaway had paid the doomed girl to crash the car so he could save her (the drowning was the only accidental part), the governor is destroyed and Runyon's credibility questioned. Laine finally admits to Evans that she did not engage in the reputed incident. She had refused to answer because she believed the question (which never would have been asked of a man) should not have been asked of her, as a woman—or as a person.

The Film:

While working as a Los Angeles film critic, Rod Lurie presented an award to actress Joan Allen. Inspired by her talent, Lurie sat down before his word processor and, with no idea where he was going, knocked out in seventy-two hours the first draft of *The Contender*. Allen agreed to play Laine, but when Lurie visited various studios with the package, he was told he could have a thirty-five-million-dollar budget if a superstar like Michelle Pfeiffer played the part. Lurie refused, then raised nine-million dollars and shot the movie independently. When Steven Spielberg saw the results, he picked up the film for distribution by DreamWorks, allowing the high-quality work to receive the national exposure it deserved.

The Contender created such excitement—in the age of special-effects cinema, someone dared make a thought-provoking political thriller—that ABC dedicated an entire session of *Politically Incorrect* to discussing its themes. One brilliant stroke was having President Evans nominate Laine not for the expected idealistic purposes, i.e., it's the right thing to do, since he believes Laine is the perfect person for the job, but for issues involving self-interest—he wants to insure his personal legacy and believes nominating a woman will insure him a positive place in history, even if she isn't the most qualified contender. Even the villain, Runyon, conveys remarkable dimensions, since Lurie directed Gary Oldman to play the character as the most idealistic person onscreen (however much we may hate the senator's right-wing but clearly sincere values).

As Carlo Cavagna noted, "Lurie builds the suspense without calling on political-thriller clichés. There are no black helicopters, no chase scenes, no government agents in unmarked cars following people around, and no sneaking into private offices to copy computer files frantically before being discovered. . . . Lurie confounds our expectations. Because the writing is so sharp, Lurie has no need to resort to slick editing. The drama is in the words, and Lurie relies on the audience to pay attention."

The thriller element is so subtle (though always present) that one almost forgets this is in any way, shape, or form a genre piece. We accept it as a realistic drama while watching, only on later consideration realizing it obeyed all the ground rules of a top-notch thriller. This includes the carefully set-up ending—a true Hitchcockian "twist" rather than a double-dealing "trick" owing to one shot. Moments before the car careens off the bridge, Hathaway glances at his watch. Initially, this seems only an inconsequential detail. In retrospect, it visually clues the viewer that Hathaway expected the "accident," wondering why his ill-fated confederate had not yet arrived.

TRIVIA:

Though Allen was nominated for Best Actress, Lurie did not receive nominations for Best Writer or Best Director, though the nation's film critics unanimously agreed he should have received nominations in both and won for the former. Lurie did win the Alan J. Pakula award (honoring the memory of the late director who gave us *All the President's Men*) as Best Screenwriter "for artistic excellence by illuminating issues of great social and political importance." Gary Oldman agreed to co-produce as well as play Runyon under the strangest of circumstances. Apparently, he misread the script as a conservative diatribe, wrongly believing his character was the hero, and Joan Allen the villain!

ALSO RECOMMENDED:

Lurie's first film as writer-director, *Deterrence* (1999), is also a striking example of political suspense, with Kevin Pollak as a president dealing with a nuclear crisis. For another fine political thriller, see *Seven Days in May* (1964).

47:

SEVEN DAYS TO NOON (1950)

London Films/British Lion

"There is a term for such a man: He is a terrorist!"
—Superintendent Folland

CAST:

Barry Jones (*Prof. John Malcolm Francis Willingdon*); André Morell (*Superintendent Folland*); Hugh Cross (*Stephen Lane*); Sheila Manahan (*Ann Willingdon*); Olive Sloane (*Miss Goldie Phillips*); Joan Hickson (*Mrs. Emily Georgina Peckett*); Ronald Adam (*Prime Minister Hon. Arthur Lytton*); Marie Ney (*Mrs. Willingdon*); Wyndham Goldie (*Vicar*); Russell Waters (*Detective Davis*); Martin Boddey (*General Willoughby*); Victor Maddern (*Jackson*); Geoffrey Keen (*Loudmouth*); Merrill Mueller (*News Commentator*); Joss Ackland (*Station policeman*).

CREDITS:

Directors, John and Roy Boulting; screenplay, Roy Boulting, James Bernard, and Frank Harvey, from a story by Paul Dehn; producers, the Boulting Brothers, with Peter De Sarigny; original music, John Addison; cinematographer, Gilbert Taylor; editors, the Boulting Brothers; art director, John Elphick; running time, 93 min.

THE PLOT:

No one could be more unassuming than quiet Professor Willingdon (Barry Jones), soft-spoken head of research at England's Wallingford lab, where all key nuclear research in the United Kingdom takes place. One day, the little man fails to show up for work. When the other scientists check, they realize materials for an atomic bomb have been taken from the premises. Shortly, the prime minister receives a note, written in the prose everyone has always associated with this dogged and reliable (or so they believed) Willingdon. The government has seven days to meet all his demands, or he will explode a nuclear device in the middle of London. This is no simple case of blackmail for profit, for Willingdon is not after money. A dedicated family man, he has no ambitions in life other than to contribute to society while providing for wife and children. Yet he has come to believe, during the past few years, that nuclear weapons will spell the end of mankind. Therefore, he has chosen to fight fire with fire. His only demand is that the government completely abandon their nuclear weapons policy.

The government cannot comply, so they assign Superintendent Folland to track down the fugitive. Shortly, the investigator learns Willingdon has slipped into London. Law enforcement groups employ every means possible to locate his precise whereabouts. A key—and controversial—decision is

Nowhere Man: The idealist as terrorist.

to keep the threat from the public, so the news media is not advised as to what's happening, in hopes of avoiding a panic. All around London, posters are put in place, offering rewards for anyone who can lead the police to this dangerous fugitive, though the precise nature of his "crimes" are not yet announced.

Incredibly, Willingdon walks around in full view, one of those face-in-the-crowd type people who other citizens pass on the street without noticing, even if they have just glanced at one of the wanted posters. Willingdon is the anonymous person, a nowhere man. Is he quite mad, or, as even Folland comes to believe, the only sane person in a world gone mad? As the days turn to hours, the hours to minutes, the government finally admits to the public what has been going on. As citizens panic, Folland finally comes across potent leads, even as Willingdon prepares to go through with his threat.

THE FILM:

The Boultings would earn their place in movie history with their marvelous series of gentle satires and smart spoofs, including *Lucky Jim* (1957), *I'm All Right Jack* (1959), and *Heaven's Above* (1963), the latter two starring Peter Sellers. How fascinating, then, to happen across this brilliant thriller and realize it was made by those same geniuses who had such a talent to make England—and the world—chuckle. As Damian Cannon has written, "*Seven Days to Noon* is a classic character-driven film with an extremely realistic atmosphere. The motivation of Willingdon and the subtle ways in which his breakdown manifests itself are beautifully played. Performances of equal depth are abundant in this movie as each character behaves in exactly the way that you would expect, given their individual backgrounds. The power that one man can have over millions is seen in the daily newspapers, heard in the street-level rumors and felt by everyone."

Seven Days to Noon was the first film to feature a portrait of a modern terrorist, the type that came into existence when the postwar world entered the nuclear age. Part of the film's remarkable power is the manner in which it balances sympathy between the "little guy," as even the investigator refers to Willingdon with a modicum of sympathy, with a greater concern for the ordinary English people hurrying to evacuate a great city. We can agree with the rightness of Willingdon's values while objecting to his frightful approach, making the character—and the film—incredibly complex to watch.

TRIVIA:

When released in the United states, *Seven Days to Noon* received (in 1952) the Academy Award for Best Adapted Screenplay. It was shot in a style called "the dramatized documentary," in which filmmakers strove to make fictional films look, sound, and feel as if they were true stories being captured on the fly; this style was as dominant in Britain during the postwar years as neorealism was in Italy and film noir in America. Despite its lofty reputation as a clasic thriller, the film unaccountably remains (as of this writing) unavailable on either home video or DVD.

ALSO RECOMMENDED:

For a film that combines the plot of *Seven Days to Noon* with the concept of an American military officer gone mad, as featured in *Dr. Strangelove* (1964), catch Robert Aldrich's *Twilight's Last Gleaming* (1977) with Burt Lancaster.

46:

BLOOD SIMPLE (1984)

Foxton Entertainment

> "In Russia, they got it all mapped out so everyone pulls for
> everyone else. But down here in Texas, you're on your own."
> —Loren Visser

CAST:

John Getz (*Ray*); Frances McDormand (*Abby*); Dan Hedaya (*Julian Marty*); M. Emmet Walsh (*Detective Loren Visser*); Samm-Art Williams (*Meurice*); Deborah Neumann (*Debra*); Raquel Gavia (*Landlady*); Van Brooks (*Lubbock Man*); William Creamer (*Old Cracker*); Loren Bivens (*Strip Bar Exhorter*); Shannon Sedwick (*Stripper*); Nancy Finger (*Overlook Girl*); Holly Hunter (*Helene Trend*).

CREDITS:

Director(s), Joel Coen and (uncredited) Ethan Coen; screenplay, Coen and Coen; producers, Ethan Coen and Mark Silverman; original music, Carter Burwell and Jim Roberge; cinematographer, Barry Sonnenfeld; editor, Roderick Jaynes and Don Wiegmann; production designer, Jane Musky; running time, 97 min.; rating, R.

THE PLOT:

Julian Marty grows ever less satisfied with his life. His time is divided between attempting to eke out a living in the bar he owns and dealing with Abby, his unfaithful wife, who's hardly been trying to cover up her affair with rugged bartender Ray. So Marty hires a sleazy, unkempt private eye, Loren Visser, to kill Abby. Visser agrees, then kills Marty instead, figuring that if he knocked off Abby, he'd have to silence Marty to eliminate a possible witness. The problem is that Marty isn't dead, and when Visser left Marty for dead at the bar, the envelope Marty had handed him didn't contain the papers Visser needed to keep himself clear of murder—though Marty *hasn't* been murdered. At least, not yet.

The characters grow ever more self-serving, until no loyalty—not even the sexual bond between Abby and Ray—matters. All anyone cares about is his or her own survival. As the shabby, sleazy Visser puts it, "The world is full of complainers. But the fact is, nothing comes with a guarantee. I don't care if you're the Pope of Rome, President of the United States or Man of the Year, something can all go wrong. But go ahead, complain, tell your problems to your neighbor, ask for help, and watch him fly!"

The birth of neo-noir: Dan Hedaya and Frances McDormand.

THE FILM:

By the mid-eighties, fans of serious cinema had grown disenchanted with most of the product coming out of Hollywood. The success of such franchises as *Star Wars* and *Indiana Jones*—however fine individual installments might have been—led to a blockbuster mentality. Every studio concentrated on its big Christmas and summer releases, movies so immense and so committee-driven that a fifty-million-dollar budget, unthinkable a few years earlier, now seemed economical. Happily, a backlash appeared: the early independent films of Steven Soderbergh, Spike Lee, Sam Raimi, and the Coen Brothers proved the most inventive and innovative films were those shot on a shoestring budget, with a postmodernist script—at once involving and self-satirizing—replacing special effects.

During this period, the noir sensibility—out of favor for a quarter-century—experienced a comeback as the public responded to films that offered lone wolf heroes wandering down the mean streets of a big city. Lawrence Kasdan's *Body Heat* (1981) was the tip of the iceberg. Though a box-office success, some observers felt that the film was too clinical in its approach to the revived technique, as well as too indebted to a single past work—*Double Indemnity* (1944, #22)—to fully satisfy.

Three years later, the edgier but more impressive *Blood Simple* appeared. Everything was done on locations in and around Austin and Houston, Texas. Devoid of *Body Heat*'s appealing though derivative story, *Blood Simple* presented its more original yarn (more like a left-over script from the late-forties that had never been filmed than a knockoff of one that had) in a no-nonsense style. Roger Ebert put it this way, "*Blood Simple* is comic in its dark way, and obviously wants to go over the top. But it doesn't call attention to its contrivance. It is easy to do a parody of film noir, but hard to do good film noir, and almost impossible to make a film that works as suspense and exaggeration at the same time. *Blood Simple* is clever in the way it makes its incredulities seem necessary."

TRIVIA:

The film's cinematographer, Barry Sonnenfeld, provided the voice for Marty's vomiting sequence. Ethan Coen graduated from Princeton, while Joel did grad-work at N.Y.U. Joel Coen had never directed a film before. *Blood Simple* won The Sundance Film Festival's Grand Jury Prize in 1985, the Edgar Allan Poe award for Best Motion Picture in 1986, and the Independent Spirit Award for Best Director, Joel Coen, that same year. The fifteenth anniversary reissue print includes a faux presentation by a film scholar who lauds the use of state-of-the-art special effects to enhance the movie. This, of course, was something of a dig at those Speilberg/Lucas extravaganzas that were in fact visually enhanced for their re-releases. *Blood Simple* never had any special effects, nor does it contain them now.

ALSO RECOMMENDED:

Second only to *Blood Simple*, Lawrence Kasdan's aforementioned *Body Heat* (1981) rates as the best nouveau-noir of the eighties. Coen fans will want to catch *Fargo* (1996). Though less a generic thriller than *Blood Simple*, the film is, if anything, an even more remarkable movie, and it does contain a considerable amount of suspense, along with Frances McDormand's Oscar-winning performance, as well as Best Screenplay honors for the brothers. Some might argue that *Fargo* ought to be included here. Yet its brilliance derives from its status as a one-of-a-kind film—part comedy and part thriller—which helps explain why it can't be categorized as *anything*, other than great.

45:

THE KILLING (1956)

United Artists

"This is a bad joke without a punch line."
—Sherry's dying words after George does her in

CAST:

Sterling Hayden (*Johnny Clay*); Coleen Gray (*Fay*); Vince Edwards (*Val Cannon*); Jay C. Flippen (*Marvin Unger*); Marie Windsor (*Sherry Peatty*); Ted DeCorsia (*Randy Kennan*); Elisha Cook, Jr. (*George Peatty*); Joe Sawyer (*Mike O'Reilly*); James Edwards (*Parking Attendant*); Jay Adler (*Leo*); Tim Carey (*Nikki Arcane*); Joseph Turkel (*Tiny*); Kola Kwariani (*Maurice Oboukhoff*); Tito Vuolo (*Joe*); Dorothy Adams (*Ruthie*); James Griffith (*Grimes*).

CREDITS:

Director, Stanley Kubrick; screenplay, Kubrick (plot) and Jim Thompson (dialogue), from the novel *Clean Break* by Lionel White; producers, James B. Harris and Alexander Singer; original music, Gerald Fried; cinematographer, Lucien Ballard; editor, Betty Steinberg; art director, Ruth Sobotka Kubrick; special effects, Dave Koehler; running time, 83 min.

THE PLOT:

All his life, small-time con man Johnny Clay has hoped to make his "killing"—the jackpot that would allow him to leave his sleazy life behind and hurry away to live in luxury. Johnny hopes to form a team to pull off a racetrack heist, so he rounds up a group of assorted low-lifes, none with a notable reputation as a criminal. Johnny must have a cashier at the track serve as his inside man; this role goes to George Peatty, a timid man who wants to score in hopes that money may keep his sexy wife from cheating on him. A bartender at the track will be Johnny's "eye"; this will be gruff O'Reilly, who needs cash to care for his convalescing wife. A corrupt cop will allow them to get away at the right moment; Randy is made to order. There must be a moneyman to finance this operation; Marvin Unger can handle that, if his profit margin is large enough.

Sterling Hayden, the perfect postwar hero, attempts to finally score his "killing."

Unger comes up with the $2,500 necessary to hire a crack shot to bring down a racehorse as he makes a key turn; Nikki Arane will serve that purpose. Finally, a decoy must start a fight that will distract guards at the track; this is Kola. Johnny's not-so-magnificent seven set out to perform a ruse that must be played like a game of precision chess. Nothing can go wrong; in fact, absolutely everything does.

Most of the problems are due to Sherry, engaged in an adulterous affair with nickel-and-dime criminal Val Cannon. She has informed her lover about the coming heist, so he sends men to kill all the participants and grab the stolen money. But George survives and returns to the apartment where he murders her. Johnny and his girlfriend grab the suitcase full of money and get to the airport, where their escape seems certain. As the suitcase moves along the conveyer belt toward the plane, a freak accident causes it to fall off. The suitcase opens and the money flies away like confetti. As the cops close in, Johnny could easily escape, but what has transpired has made him so cynical that, with a humorless grin, he gives up without flight or fight.

THE FILM:

When Stanley Kubrick's *The Killing* came out of 1956, it was dismissed as a minor-league redux of John Huston's *The Asphalt Jungle* (1950), which had featured the same leading man. Some observers at the time insisted that noir had run its course. But *The Killing*, though shot on a tight-budget of $230,000, belied such claims, even if its status as a crime-thriller classic had to wait for rediscovery following the enshrinement of Kubrick as a world-class filmmaker. Though few noirs would be made after *The Killing*, until its revival in the eighties (see *Blood Simple*, 1984, #46), the film serves as perfect bookend with *The Asphalt Jungle* (1950), a fact Quentin Tarantino attested to when *Reservoir Dogs* (1992) offered an unofficial remake of both.

The Killing sets the pace for post-modernist movies that defy logical narrative structure, leaping back and forth in time, repeating a single incident in a series of multiple flashbacks from varied characters which then, *Rashomon*-like, reveal the different ways in which diverse people perceive the same event. The voice-over narration, wrongly criticized by Leonard Maltin for being too "Dragnet"-ish, provides the key to this film's power, as well as its uniqueness when compared to *Asphalt Jungle*. Here, the filmmaker reveals his fatalistic bent: even as the characters desperately plot and plan, we know from the world-weary tone that they cannot succeed. Watching the film has nothing to do with any traditional sense of suspense, in which we wait to learn what will happen, but a redefined alternative, in which we sense early on that the plan is doomed, and wait to see how that will happen. That has to do with the one thing that cannot be thought out in advance: The element of human emotion.

TRIVIA:

The working title of *The Killing* was *Bed of Fear*. Cinematographer Lucien Ballard employed the widest camera lens then available, a twenty-five mm adjustment, to employ the full possibility of deep focus. Kubrick originally planned to shoot in Manhattan environs, where the novel is set. When no racetrack in the area would give permission to film on the premises, the setting was changed to the West Coast.

ALSO RECOMMENDED:

Reservoir Dogs should be viewed in tandem with both *The Killing* and *Asphalt Jungle* to catch the key influences on Tarantino. Kubrick fans will want to see *Killer's Kiss* (1955), an intriguing earlier attempt to reinvent the noir thriller.

44:

THE CHINA SYNDROME (1979)

Columbia Pictures

"It's the right thing to do."
—Ted Spindler

CAST:

Jane Fonda (*Kimberly Wells*); Jack Lemmon (*Jack Godell*); Michael Douglas (*Richard Adams*); Scott Brady (*Herman De Young*); James Hampton (*Bill Gibson*); Peter Donat (*Don Jacovich*); Wilford Brimley (*Ted Spindler*); Richard Herd (*McCormack*); Daniel Valdez (*Hector Salas*); Stan Bohrman (*Pete*); James Karen (*Churchill*); Rita Taggert (*Rita*).

CREDITS:

Director, James Bridges; screenplay, Bridges, Mike Gray and T.S. Cook; producers, Michael Douglas and Bruce Gilbert; original music, Stephen Bishop; cinematographer, James Crabe; editor, David Rawlins; production designer, George Jenkins; special effects, James F. Liles and Henry Millar; special visual effects, Richard Edlund; running time, 123 min.; rating, PG.

THE PLOT:

Kimberly Wells is a typical TV newswoman of her time—that is, more concerned about her hairstyle and ratings clout than the substance of what she covers. That all changes suddenly when she's sent to a nuclear power plant to videotape a fluff piece (the type of story to which female broadcast journalists were then assigned) about its daily operations. An emergency occurs, which she and cameraman Richard Adams record. A worker had misread levels as reported by a faulty gauge, and added too much water to the plant's core, setting off a reaction that might have turned into a cataclysmic chain reaction were it not for fast work by controller Jack Godell. Back at the TV station, Kimberly and Jack set to work on what they believe will be a striking and substantial piece of journalism. Until, that is, their executives decide that it's necessary to bow to the powers that be, giving in to those people from the plant who insist the story must be killed or they will face a major lawsuit.

With this event, the radicalization of Kimberly begins. As she and Richard pursue the truth, they realize that in a few seconds, the acccident would have resulted in what's secretively referred to as the "China Syndrome." Had the core superheated to the point of exploding, it would have melted through the ground in the direction of the other side of the world, spun about by gravity, resulting in the potential death of millions of people. Stunned, Kimberly and Richard want to share this with the public, though their station—however hungry for ratings—is too timid to take on the nuclear power industry. Until, that is, Jack Godell realizes all the security seals in the plant are fake. He turns against the people he works for, joining Kimberly and Richard in their crusade to expose the supposedly safe industry for what it is: a clear and present danger to all.

Director James Bridges sets up a shot with Jane Fonda as a TV newscaster whose life and career are shattered following a nuclear meltdown.

THE FILM:

When the film opened—late February, 1979—audience reaction was mild and mixed. Then, an accident at the Three Mile Island nuclear site in Harrisburg, Pennsylvania had newscasters talking about a real-life "China Syndrome." The following weekend, the film sold out across the country, as people hurried to theatres in hopes of better understanding what was going on around them.

Another film on the same subject, Mike Nichols's *Silkwood* (1983), took its title from a real-life nuclear plant worker who was exposed during an accident to potentially deadly radioactivity. When she began to crusade for greater safety measures, Karen Silkwood was—like *China Syndrome*'s fictional Godell—chastized by fellow workers, the very people she hoped to win protection for, owing to their concern about paychecks. However well-intentioned, *Silkwood* suffered because telling a real-life story was not necessarily the most effective means to bring the problem to light. Nichols could not dramatize anything that he couldn't prove to be true, since he was dealing with a specific nuclear power plant. If he showed (as many people believed) that the executives hired people to kill Karen Silkwood (Meryl Streep) to silence her, the filmmakers would have been brought to court; perhaps an injunction would bar the film's release on the grounds that it conveyed extravagant and unprovable claims. So the *Silkwood* script was diluted, focusing on a fictional lesbian affair between Silkwood and a girlfriend (Cher) to kill time that might better have been spent creating a fact-based thriller.

Here, director James Bridges had no such problem. Though Lemmon's Godell is clearly intended as a stand-in for Silkwood, no one could sue since the film was presented as a work of fiction. The nuclear power company is given a fictional name; any real-life nuclear plant that sued would inadvertantly suggest that their "shop" was as incompetently run as the one in the movie. By presenting fact-based material as fiction, with the names changed, *China Syndrome* proved it *was* possible to make a film that went way beyond a specific story about one accident. By creating their own specificity, the filmmakers provided a symbolic warning with far more depth and dimension than any single case study ever could, while masking this in a work that satisfied as suspenseful entertainment.

TRIVIA:

Michael Mann, who would shortly emerge as a major director, plays the cameo role of a TV consultant. In addition to Fonda and Douglas, there is another second-generation actor in the cast: Peter Donat, son of Oscar-winning actor Robert Donat, who had starred in Hitchcock's *The 39 Steps* (1935). There is no actual musical score, though Stephen Bishop's recording of "Somewhere in Between" is heard in a natural situation.

ALSO RECOMMENDED:

For a striking example of liberal filmmaking that fictionalizes reality in a combination of suspense thriller and message movie, catch Costa-Gavras's *Z* (1969), about a political assassination. *Z* was the winner of the Oscar for Best Foreign Language Film.

43:

PEEPING TOM (1960)

Astor

"I'd just love to take your picture."
—Mark, to his first victim

CAST:

Carl Boehm (*Mark Lewis*); Moira Shearer (*Vivian*); Anna Massey (*Helen*)
Maxine Audley (*Mrs. Stephens*); Esmond Knight (*Arthur*); Bartlett Mullins
(*Peters*); Brenda Bruce (*Dora*); Martin Miller (*Dr. Rosen*); Pamela Green
(*Milly*); Michael Powell (*Prof. Lewis*); Shirley Anne Field (*Diane Ashley*).

CREDITS:

Director, Michael Powell; screenplay, Leon Marks; producer, Powell; music,
Brian Easdale; cinematographer, Otto Heller; editor, Noreen Ackland; running time, 103 min. (director's cut).

THE PLOT:

Mark Lewis has a technician's job at a British film studio. An aspiring director,
Mark picks up prostitutes and loose women, becoming sexually involved with
them, capturing the trysts on film, then killing each new victim at the height of
sexual passion. Mark does this with a mirror in place so the woman will witness
her demise even as he immortalizes it on celluloid. Though the police attempt to
discover the murderer's identity, they remain stalled until Mark turns his attentions
away from street women, toward more normal girls. These include Vivian, murdered at the studio when Mark persuades her to stick around after hours for a
screen test. He then becomes interested in Helen, who inhabits a flat in his rooming house.

The two date. As he feels ever more comfortable with her, Mark wavers:
would he like to have a normal relationship for the first time, or make Helen his
next victim? At a vulnerable moment, Mark shows Helen a collection of films from
his boyhood, made by Mark's father, who literally turned the child's youth into a
filmed experience. Ever since, Mark has not been able to fully experience anything

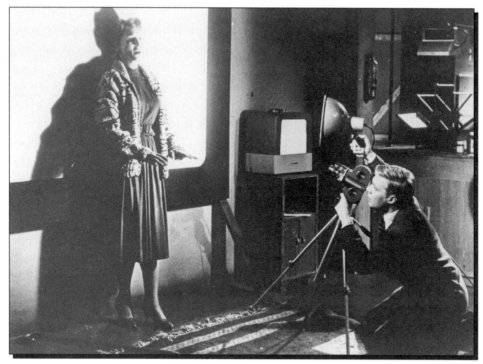

Sex as Death: Carl Boehm as the serial killer who photographs women as he kills them.

unless he captures it with a camera. Helen's mother, blind yet able to intuit things other people miss, alerts the police. When they arrive, Mark films his arrest and, as he commits suicide, his death. The last thing Mark sees is the reflection of himself in the mirror as his life ends.

THE FILM:

Peeping Tom was released in Britain in 1960, the same year *Psycho* hit American screens. Though *Psycho* generated controversy, Hitchcock managed to push the on-screen sex-and-violence envelope without shoving it over the edge. Hitchcock had made clear that he would, in the upcoming decade, veer into darker material. This is what *Peeping Tom* proposed in England.

Michael Powell was one of England's most highly regarded directors, having helmed the beloved entertainment *The Thief of Baghdad* (1940), the wartime propaganda feature *One of Our Aircraft is Missing* (1942), and a legendary ballet film, *The Red Shoes* (1948). Unlike Hitchcock, he made the mistake of going too far, too fast. *Peeping Tom* was damned by the press and largely suppressed as pornographic. Powell's career was all but destroyed by the damnation of this work.

A highly edited version eventually played on the American grindhouse circuit a few years later. In time, the notion of dealing openly with sexual perversity in the context of a suspense film would become acceptable. As Danny Peary points out, Mark has much in common with Peter Lorre in *M* (1931, #2)—both are initially perceived as despicable villains and both become strangely sympathetic during the course of the story by directors Powell and Fritz Lang. We gradually see them less as the "others" of the typical thriller than as victims of terrible childhood experiences that left them unable to operate in any other ways. They are, therefore, not responsible for their actions, which is also true of Norman Bates in *Psycho* (1960, #1). Three great filmmakers force their audiences into an awareness, however vague, that there is not necessarily a simple line of demarcation between the "normal" and the "abnormal." It's more a case of "there but for the grace of God go I."

This has an impact on the way in which the suspense works in each film. Early on, we totally sympathize with victims of the serial killers, perched on the edges of our seats as they are menaced because we believe we could, if we happened to be in the wrong place at the wrong time, be in that dangerous position. During each film's second half, the audience begins to emphathize with the killer, hoping he will somehow avoid capture. A viewer leaves having been put in touch with something deep and dark within his own being, an element that may never have been stirred into consciousness without contact vis-a-vis the film. This explains the upsetting quality of *Peeping Tom* and other such films; what the viewer is most upset about is not what occured onscreen but what he has been forced to recognize in himself.

In *Peeping Tom*, that's made all the more horrific because it is, in essence, a movie about movies. We have come to see this, as with every film we approach, as a voyeuristic experience; every moviegoer is, in essence, a Peeping Tom. So the public tends to recoil from a film that puts us in touch, in no uncertain terms, with this terrible truth.

TRIVIA:

Powell loved redheads as much as Hitchcock did his blondes. Moira Shearer, one of the female leads, previously starred for Powell in *The Red Shoes*. Powell plays the disturbed antihero's psychotic father in *Peeping Tom*.

ALSO RECOMMENDED:

Though the suspense is far tamer, don't miss Powell's subtly erotic *Black Narcissus* (1948), about a group of nuns (including Deborah Kerr) who become sexually crazed when a masculine figure enters their enclave.

42:

DEAD OF NIGHT (1945)

Ealing Studios

"Why do I feel that I've been here before?"
—Walter

CAST:

Mervyn Johns (*Walter*); Roland Culver (*Eliot*); Mary Merrall (*Mrs. Foley*); Frederick Valk (*van Straaten*); Antony Baird (*Hugh*); Judy Kelly (*Joyce*); Sally Ann Howes (*Sally*); Michael Allen (*Jimmy*); Googie Withers (*Joan*); Ralph Michael (*Peter*); Michael Redgrave (*Max*); Hartley Power (*Kee*); Basil Radford (*George*); Naunton Wayne (*Larry*); Peggy Bryan (*Mary*).

CREDITS:

Directors, Basil Deardon (primary), Alberto Cavalcanti, Robert Hamer, Charles Crichton; screenwriters, John Baines, Angus MacPhail, and T.E.B. Clarke, from stories by H.G. Wells, E.F. Benson, and Baines and MacPhail; producer, Michael Balcon; music, Georges Auric; cinematographers, Jack Parker and H. Julius; editor, Charles Hasse; running time, 104 min.

THE PLOT:

Walter Craig is awakened by a phone call, requesting he drive to Pilgrim's Farm, far out in the country. But as Walter arrives, he's seized by a sense of déjà vu and feels as if he's been here before. When Walter enters, he senses that he knows Eliot Foley, the owner, and has met the other people gathered there. Dr. Van Straaten suggests Walter may have encountered them in a dream, and requests they identify themselves through poignant stories from their individual pasts.

Hugh tells about the time he had a bizarre dream in which a hearse pulled up and the driver told him, "Room for one more." Frightened, Hugh turned and ran. Later, he was about to board a bus when the driver seemed to be the horrific figure from his dream and said the same thing. Hugh didn't get on board, and so wasn't killed when the bus shortly exploded.

Sally relates the time she attended a Christmas party and everyone played

Michael Redgrave and "friend."

hide-and-seek. She found a little boy crying, and was surprised not to have seen him earlier at the festivities. When she returned to the main group and told them, everyone went silent, as a boy of just such description had been killed in the house years earlier.

Joan remembers an incident in which she was given a lovely mirror by her husband. When she set it in their bedroom, it reflected a Victorian-era period and the murder of a wife by her husband. Joan's husband fell under the spell and almost killed her.

George and Larry competed for the affections of the same woman, Mary Lee, until one tricked the other into commiting suicide. The ghost had his revenge, however, by visiting the couple on their wedding night.

A brilliant ventriloquist, Max Frere, endowed his dummy with such vivid personality that it took over his identity, becoming the dominant personality.

When Walter and the doctor are left alone, the traveler finally realizes why he's so disturbed: he cannot control the urge to murder Van Straaten. But before he can complete the strangulation, he's woken by his wife, who tells him he'd been screaming, owing to a nightmare. Then, the phone rings, and he's summoned to Pilgrim's Farm, sensing as he drives up that he's been here before.

THE FILM:

Dead of Night was produced by Michael Balcon who in the early 1930s gave a young director named Alfred Hitchcock his first important job. After Hitchcock left for America, Balcon carried on the tradition. This is where the cinematic anthology thriller was born. Never before had there been any major attempt to collect a series of suspense tales, all linked by a single theme (in this case, the presence of a ghost) in stories that differ drastically in tone, held together by a framing device that in the end ties them neatly, though unexpectedly, together.

Ultimately, the greatest impact occured some ten years later, when TV's legendary suspense shows *Alfred Hitchcock Presents* and *The Twilight Zone* (and, later still, *Rod Serling's Night Gallery*) brought the form to a medium even more appropriate for such storytelling. At least two of the original *Dead of Night* stories showed up on *The Twilight Zone*, "Room For One More" (in which a more modern plane was substituted for the bus) and "The Ventriloquist" (Cliff Robertson played the part that Redgrave had created.) That story, the greatest and most memorable in the film, would be unofficially remade as *Magic* (1978), with Anthony Hopkins playing the ventriloquist.

TRIVIA:

When Universal studios distributed the film in America, their executives decided to eliminate "The Golfing Story" because of its offbeat comedy. Their feeling was that this jarred too much with the otherwise spooky sense of the other episodes. This created an unforeseen difficulty, for the Naunton and Wayne characters were essential in the framing story, though their reason for being at Pilgrim's Farm now made no sense at all. And it's worth mentioning that both Alfred Hitchcock and Rod Serling chose to include a dark comedy every so often on their television series.

ALSO RECOMMENDED:

Catch Hitchcock's *The Lady Vanishes* (1937), the film in which comic players Naunton and Wayne were first coupled. Michael Redgrave, seen as the ventriloquist here, plays the offbeat lead in that comedy thriller. Hammer studios would, when it finally depleted all the possibilities in *Dracula*, *Frankenstein*, and *The Mummy*, turn to the anthology *Dr. Terror's House of Horrors*, their most appealing venture in this form. In time, horror comic books would be turned into films, including *Tales From the Crypt* (1972) and *Vault of Horror* (1973). Stephen King got into the act with *Creepshow* (1982), directed by George Romero.

41:

SLEUTH (1972)

20th Century Fox

"I understand you want to marry my wife."
—Andrew

CAST:

Laurence Olivier (*Andrew Wyke*); Michael Caine (*Milo Tindle*).

CREDITS:

Director, Joseph L. Mankiewicz; screenplay, Anthony Shaffer, from his play; producers, Morton Gottlieb, David Middlemas, and Edgar J. Scherick; original music, John Addison; cinematographer, Oswald Morris; editor, Richard Marden; production Designer, Ken Adam; art directors, Peter Lamont; special visual effects, Leslie Hillman; running time, 138 min.

Michael Caine and Laurence Olivier shine in Sleuth, a perfect two-character thriller.

THE PLOT:

Ambitious cockney Milo Tindle attempts to work his way up the British social ladder by serving as hairdresser to pampered wives of important people. He had the good luck (or so it would seem) to enter into a tempestuous affair wth Mrs. Marguerite Wyke, wedded to a wealthy mystery writer. With apparent magnanimity, Andrew invites Milo to his estate, where the two will discuss a possible divorce and remarriage. No sooner are the two together—and isolated—then it becomes clear the lower-class climber and the upper-class wag have something in common: both love to play games. For Milo, who has had to fight for everything in life, games provide release and escape. For Andrew, who has had everything served to him on a silver platter, games are the essence of his existence; playing them is the one thing that provides his life with a sense of meaning.

Andrew spots Milo's weak point, a self-consciousness about his humble origins. Class, Andrew insists, is character; those of the lower-classes possess base traits as people. Andrew suggests he and the deeply-insulted Milo might involve themselves in a little bit of harmless sleuthing to determine who actually is "superior." Milo realizes the invitation was in itself the opening move of a chess-like game in which he's inextricably involved. The game begins when Andrew suggests he'd like to help Milo find a sufficient source of income so Marguerite will not in time desert Milo for a wealthier man. Andrew invites Milo to steal some of Andrew's precious jewels, then "fence" them while Andrew makes an insurance claim, a perfect plan to improve each man's financial status. When Milo goes through with the theft, Andrew faces him with a gun, sardonically announcing this was all a ploy to have an excuse to shoot Milo as a petty thief—killing him for stealing the jewels to compensate for Milo's stealing Andrew's wife—and get away with the perfect crime.

Andrew pulls the trigger and Milo falls down—dead to the world but not actually dead. Humiliation, not murder, was Andrew's "game." Milo acts as if he's thankful to be alive, but inwardly experiences rage, and wants to get even, which he then proceeds to do.

THE FILM:

In 1963, Joseph Mankiewicz was one of the most revered writer-director-producer talents in the industry, with such film classics as the Oscar-winning *All About Eve* (1950) to his credit. Then 20th Century Fox invited him to take over the troubled *Cleopatra* film from Rouben Mamoulian (see *Dr. Jekyll and Mr. Hyde*, 1932, #55). Shortly, delight turned to terror as the shoot became a disaster, owing in part to the open romance between the then married (to other people) leads, Elizabeth Taylor and Richard Burton. Its considerable qualities aside, *Cleopatra* went down in film history as a legendary bomb, almost taking its studio down with it. The director's reputation did not escape unscathed either. Mankiewicz, however, refused to accept that *Cleopatra* would be his final legacy and searched for a project that would redeem his reputation. He found it in *Sleuth*, Peter Shaffer's masterful play that had dazzled audiences in London and on Broadway.

A mere recording of a stage success, however well-scripted, would not do the trick. Mankiewicz knew he had to create visual suspense that would equal the verbal brilliance, and began working out a series of images that would effectively convey the ideas. The labyrinthian maze of a garden Milo must make his way through in the opening serves as a fitting metaphor for the film to follow. Throughout, Mankiewicz and cinematographer Oswald Morris employ their frame to tell us what we need to know about what's actually going on rather than what seems to be happening. When Milo and Andrew appear to be growing emotionally closer, they are kept at far ends of the screen, allowing a close observer to grasp that the friendship is only an illusion. When their dialogue suggests they are at extreme odds, a camera angle is carefully chosen to indicate, by making them appear to be closer to each other even as they stand apart, that they have actually forged a relationship.

Like Hitchcock's *Rear Window* (1954, #6), *Sleuth* reveals that an essentially one-set film can be totally cinematic. It's not how many set-ups the director has to shoot, but how the director shoots the set-up that counts.

Trivia:

The film's opening credits announced four additional characters and actors who play them: Alec Cawthorne as "Inspector Doppler," John Matthews as "Detective Sergeant Tarrant," Eve Channing as "Marguerite Wyke," and Teddy Martin as "Police Constable Higgs." That's part of the film's game; there are ultimately no characters, and no actors, other than Olivier and Caine.

Also Recommended:

Anthony Shaffer provided the script for *The Wicker Man* (1973, #72). Caine starred in a similar play-to-film project, *Deathtrap* (1982), for director Sidney Lumet. The central metaphor of game-playing provided the premise for David Fincher's *The Game* (1997), as well as Curtis Harrington's *Games* (1967), with Simone Signoret.

40:

ISLAND OF LOST SOULS (1933)

Paramount Pictures

> **"Don't look back!"**
> **—Montgomery (film's final line)**

CAST:

Charles Laughton (*Dr. Moreau*); Richard Arlen (*Edward Parker*); Leila Hyams (*Ruth Thomas*); Bela Lugosi (*Sayer of the Law*); Kathleen Burke (*Lota the Panther Woman*); Arthur Hohl (*Montgomery*); Stanley Fields (*Captain Davies*); Paul Hurst (*Captain Donahue*); Hans Steinke (*Ouran*); Tetsu Komai (*M'ling*); George Irving (*American Consul*); Joe Bonomo, Buster Crabbe, and Alan Ladd (*Beasts*); Harry Ekezian (*Gola*); Rosemary Grimes (*Samoan Girl*); Bob Kortman (*Hogan*).

CREDITS:

Director, Erle C. Kenton; screenplay, Waldemar Young and Philip Wylie, from the novel *The Island of Dr. Moreau* by H.G. Wells; original music, Arthur Johnston and Sigmund Krumgold; cinematographer, Karl Struss; art director, Hans Dreier; special makeup effects, Wally Westmore and Gordon Jennings; special sound effects, M.M. Poggi; running time, 70 min.

THE PLOT:

While traveling in a remote area of the south seas, young Edward Parker becomes lost and almost drowns before he's picked up by a passing ship, the Covena. On board, he notices a number of exotic animals, all caged, that Captain Davies is transporting to the isolated island of Dr. Moreau. More disturbing still is a man covered with fur. When Parker attempts to confront the drunken captain about this being, he's deposited along with the creatures and left on the island. Once inside Moreau's fantastical villa, Parker becomes infatuated with a beautiful young woman, Lota, despite his being engaged to a Victorian gentlewoman, Ruth, back home in England. Gradually, Parker realizes that Lota is, in fact, a panther that Dr. Moreau has transformed into something resembling a human. The hideous half-man, half-beast creatures that crawl about the grounds are the result of the doctor's less successful experiments in his "house of pain."

Worried about her husband-to-be, Ruth convinces a likable curmudgeon, Captain Donohoe, to help her track down Parker. They arrive at the island where the only thing standing between Ruth and the rampaging beasts is the whip-wielding Moreau, who reminds them of the "law": not to walk on all fours, not to spill blood. "Are we not men?" Speaker of the Law asks. When Moreau orders one of his man-beasts to kill the interlopers after his assistant, Montgomery, helps the others plan an escape, the creatures turn on the "creator" who has broken his own law about spilling blood. Their speaker—a virtual Choragos among the creature-chorus—chants, "We are not men; we are not beasts. Half-man; half-beast. *Things!*" They carry Moreau into the house of pain and vivisect Moreau as the others escape, except only Lota, who gives her life to buy the others time to reach a boat.

Charles Laughton faces Bela Lugosi and the pack: "Not men . . . not beasts . . . *things!*"

THE FILM:

In the Hollywood of the 1930s, every studio presented a new "slate" of films each year, a program consisting of works in various genres ranging from the musical to the western to the thriller to more ambitious dramatic and comedic works. Within this context, each studio did become known for one specific genre—horror at Universal, westerns at Republic, dance-musicals at MGM, crime movies at Warner Bros. Yet each dutifully rounded out their offerings with at least one film that would have seemed more likely to have derived from another studio.

With this concept in mind, it makes a bit more sense that a studio like Paramount (known in the 1930s for its glib comedies and urbane dramas) would release a film like *Island of Lost Souls*, however much it resembled one of Universal's famed monster movies (including the iconographic presence of Bela Lugosi). Still, in the final analysis, this is a thriller, not a traditional horror movie. As in the H.G. Wells novel, Moreau is a scientist, attempting to experiment with what we would now refer to as DNA components, dedicating himself to discovering the Darwinian connection between man and beast. Though the film is considered a classic, H.G. Wells did not approve. In his book, Moreau had been presented as a well-intentioned fellow—a twentieth century tragic hero who, in attempting to perfect mankind, inadvertantly threatens to destroy it—on the order of Mary Shelley's Dr. Victor Frankenstein or Robert Louis Stevenson's Dr. Henry Jekyll.

"Oh, how like a god I feel!" Moreau mutters at one point, speaking words that appear in Frankenstein and Jekyll/Hyde films. This is about the fall from grace of a great man whose overwhelming hubris causes his great ideals to turn to dust, though only after impacting the world in an unintentionally negative way. Wells was offended by Laughton's flamboyant performance, which transformed Moreau into a cackling fiend. Had he still been alive, Wells would doubtless have much preferred Burt Lancaster's portrayal in the 1977 film version, though that film is considerably less frightening.

TRIVIA:

On its initial release, the film was banned in England owing to horrific implications and grotesque imagery. In addition to the presence of future stars Buster Crabbe and Alan Ladd as beasts, Randolph Scott is also on view in one brief shot. Joe Bonomo, who plays another beast, had previously served as Lon Chaney's stunt-double in *The Hunchback of Notre Dame* (1923). The film was shot entirely on Catalina Island, California, employing the then-revolutionary Western Electric Sound System.

ALSO RECOMMENDED:

Charles Laughton's rare ventures into the thriller genre include the title character in William Dieterle's lavish remake of *The Hunchback of Notre Dame* (1939) and the crafty lawyer in Billy Wilder's remarkable court-room thriller *Witness For the*

Prosecution (1957). He performed for Hitchcock in *Jamaica Inn* (1939) and learned enough from the master of suspense to later direct one of the greatest thrillers of all time, *The Night of the Hunter* (1955, #17).

39:

FRENZY (1972)

Universal Pictures

"This time, maybe we *did* get the wrong man!"
—Inspector Oxford

CAST:

Jon Finch (*Richard Blaney*); Barry Foster (*Bob Rusk*); Alec McCowen (*Inspector Oxford*); Barbara Leigh-Hunt (*Brenda Blaney*); Anna Massey (*Babs Milligan*); Vivien Merchant (*Mrs. Oxford*); Billie Whitelaw (*Hetty Porter*); Bernard Cribbins (*Forsythe*); Clive Swift (*Johnny*); Michael Bates (*Sgt. Spearman*).

CREDITS:

Director, Alfred Hitchcock; screenplay, Anthony Shaffer, from the novel *Goodbye Picadilly, Farewell Leicester Square* by Arthur La Bern; producers, Hitchcock and William Hill; original music, Ron Goodwin; cinematographer, Gil Taylor; special photographic effects, Arthur Whitlock; editor, John Jympson; production design, Sydney Cain; art direction, Robert Laing; running time, 116 min.; rating, R.

THE PLOT:

Modern London is terrorized by Jack-the-Ripper type murders, and Inspector Oxford is assigned to stop the killer. One chief suspect is Richard Blaney, a sullen ne'er-do-well who was seen entering his ex-wife's office shortly before she was murdered. No one suspects Blaney's friend, the redheaded, mother-dominated Bob Rusk, who owns a popular vegetable store and is considered a jolly good fellow by all. Rusk, however, is the killer. When Blaney—realizing the authorities are after him—goes to Rusk for help, the "friend" sets him up for a quick arrest. Rusk has also killed Blaney's girlfriend, Babs, and must dispose of the body, dumping it in a truckful of potatoes. Owing to the constant proddings of his gourmet wife, Inspector Oxford wonders, following Blaney's conviction, if in fact Rusk was actually guilty. Oxford closes in on Rusk even as Blaney escapes from prison and sets out to wreak vengeance.

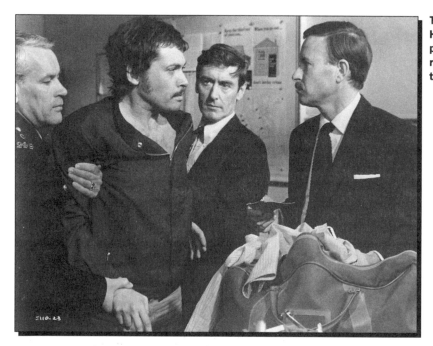

The Wrong Man: Hitchcock's penultimate film returned the director to his former glory.

THE FILM:

By the time he made *Frenzy*, many observers of the thriller had counted Alfred Hitchcock down and out. Following the remarkable success of *Psycho*, his films made during the sixties—*The Birds* (1963, #23), *Marnie* (1964), *Torn Curtain* (1966), and *Topaz* (1969)—had grown progressively less satisfying for audiences and critics. Meanwhile, other filmmakers turned out a series of much admired genre masterpieces, *Charade* (1963, #83), *The Manchurian Candidate* (1962, #9), and *Rosemary's Baby* (1968, #19) among them. Knowing his reputation would be dimmed if he didn't provide one final classic, Hitchcock decided to go back to where he had begun—London—and, with his penultimate film, offered a winner, combining his old-fashioned techniques with the most contemporary concepts of sex and violence in cinema.

Almost all of the great Hitchcock themes are here. The initials of hero and villain suggest they are doppelgangers, the evil and good side of the same coin. The heavy, as is so often the case with Hitchcock, is likable while the protagonist is not pleasant. Hinted at in earlier Hitchcock films, eating becomes the dominant metaphor for sexuality and murder. There are two MacGuffins—the club tie and the diamond stickpin. The police are well-meaning but incompetent. What we watch rates as suspense rather than mystery because the filmmaker allows us to grasp the identity of the villain long before the protagonist does. And there is the "wrong man" theme, more vivid here than even in Hitchcock's film of that name.

The film contains some of the finest sequences Hitchcock ever executed. Though some viewers consider the devastating rape and murder of Mrs. Blaney offensive to women—dismissing it as a caricature of Hitchcock's earlier violent assaults on females—the scene is actually presented from the woman's point of view. This allows everyone in the audience—including men—to suffer with her. In no way is the sequence sexually arousing. When Babs is murdered, Hitchcock refuses to show us what we expect to see. To go through the horrors again would indeed be exploitation. Instead, his camera slowly descends one of those legendary spiral staircases, bringing us out to the street, where we stare at the building in which a horrific act is taking place, unable to do anything. Nothing quite matches the remarkable sequence in which Rusk leaps into the back of the truck to extract his jeweled stickpin from the hardened grip of his latest victim. The scene is both suspenseful and darkly comic. We are put in the unpleasant situation of rooting for Rusk to get the job done. No wonder that, when talking about this character and other killers in his films, Hitchcock said, "It's a movie about the audience, really!" Always, he deeply involves us with characters who represent the potential for darkness in each of us.

TRIVIA:

Anthony Shaffer also wrote *The Wicker Man* (1972, #72) and *Sleuth* (1972, #41). Hitchcock makes one of his famous cameo appearances in the opening sequence, appearing in a bowler hat by the River Thames. Contrary to public belief, Hitchcock did not insist on doing a walk-on in every film, nor does he appear in each of the movies he directed. Hitchcock began the practice while working in England, where budgets were so tight that all directors had to appear in crowd scenes because producers couldn't afford extras. When he arrived in Hollywood, Hitchcock did not plan to do any more cameo appearances, but felt he had to relent after realizing that American audiences had come to expect to see this most uniquely proportioned celebrity-director.

ALSO RECOMMENDED:

Hitchcock's first great thriller, *The Lodger* (1926), is also a modernized variation of the Jack the Ripper myth. Two of the other best Ripper movies are John Brahm's 1944 remake of *The Lodger*, and that director's follow-up, *Hangover Square* (1945), both starring Laird Cregar as the obsessive murderer.

38:

INVASION OF THE BODY SNATCHERS (1956)

Allied Artists

> **"They're here—and *you're next!*"**
> **—Miles Bennell**

CAST:

Kevin McCarthy (*Miles Bennell*); Dana Wynter (*Becky Driscoll*); King Donovan (*Jack*); Carolyn Jones (*Theodora*); Larry Gates (*Dan Kaufman*); Jean Willes (*Sally*); Virginia Christie (*Wilma*); Ralph Dumke (*Sheriff*); Whit Bissell, Richard Deacon (*L.A. Doctors*); Dabbs Greer (*Gas Station Guy*); Sam Peckinpah (*Meter Man*).

CREDITS:

Director, Don Siegel; screenplay, Daniel Mainwaring, from the story by Jack Finney; producer, Walter Wanger; music, Carmen Dragon; cinematographer, Ellsworth Fredericks; editor, Robert S. Eisen; running time, 80 min.

THE PLOT:

In a Los Angeles emergency room, an hysterical patient tells two disbelieving doctors a bizarre story. Miles Bennett is a doctor himself, from the small town of Santa Mira. His strange adventure began when he returned home following a medical conference and became concerned that his patients had begun to act strangely. Many people insist their relatives are not who they claim to be, though everyone looks normal. Then, the accusers suddenly recant, now looking as distant and emotionless as those they previously denounced. Miles attempts to balance this bizarre phenomenom with his revived romantic interest in Becky Driscoll.

Shortly, their friends Jack and Wilma find a half-formed body in their basement, encased in a pod. This is the manner in which unseen invaders from space have duplicated humans, then taking their places. With the entire town turning into such replicants, trucking additional pods to nearby communities, Miles and Becky attempt to escape and warn the world. When she makes the mistake of falling asleep, Becky becomes one of the pod people. Miles manages to get away but, screaming out warnings on the highway to passing cars and trucks, he is mistaken for a madman. The L.A. doctors are about to institutionalize Miles when they receive a report that a truck has crashed and strange pods are spread over the highway. As they rush to warn the government about the very real problem, Miles finally relaxes, knowing that he has saved humankind.

The Film:

Originally, the movie was to have been a tight seventy-five minutes, without the prologue and epilogue. Executives at the nominal Allied Artists company were concerned that it would be too negative to end with an image of the crazed hero standing in the middle of a highway and hurredly filmed the wraparound segments. To a degree, this lessens the impact of what otherwise stood as a neat halfway point between *Tales From the Crypt* comics and TV's *The Twilight Zone*. Any damage, however, was minimal. A project that began as something of a joke in Hollywood—a 1950s monster movie made on such a tight budget that they couldn't afford a monster—turned out to be a low-budget thriller classic.

This was due to Don Siegel's low-key direction, emphasizing the fear factor rather than the kind of cut rate special effects which make many other science fiction flicks of the fifties appear silly today. Other than the pods, which appear to be oversized watermelons, there is nothing on screeen that is fantastical, not even a single flying saucer hovering over the earth. Like Hitchcock's *The Birds*, shot six years later on a considerably larger budget, *Invasion of the Body Snatchers* is a movie about our complacency, and the dangers this opens us up to. It is also and about paranoia, neatly transferred to the audience. The calm, everyday settings of Santa Mira only add to the notion of a nighmarish undercurrent to American society in general, and the 1950s in particular.

Invasion of the Body Snatchers has often been taken as an allegory on the McCarthy era, though it isn't at all easy to determine the film's precise politics. Some see it as an attack on the witch-hunting mentality, here disguised as sci-fi.

**The last embrace:
Kevin McCarthy
and Dana Wynter.**

The "pod people" can be viewed as the "silent majority" that only wants to make it through the day. Others see the film differently. When Miles sneaks up on a group of pod people, piling more pods on a truck for exportation, he's devastated by their total conformity to a single purpose. Though it may be possible to read the movie as a liberal attack on McCarthyism, it is also possible to see it as a conservative statement about the dangers of communism.

Perhaps that's what makes the film so effective, nearly fifty years after it initially appeared and despite the presence of two remakes, both of which had larger budgets. Fortunately, Siegel was able to lure two actors not associated with sci-fi thrillers to his project. Known for more upscale non-genre films, Kevin McCarthy and Dana Wynter play their roles as if appearing in a *Peyton Place*-type tale about middle-American relationships. This neatly transforms into effective suspense because, as film historian Carlos Clarens has written, "The ultimate horror in science fiction is neither death nor destruction but dehumanization."

TRIVIA:

The small part of a man who arrives to check the gas meter, and is mistakenly assumed to be an alien, is played by Sam Peckinpah, shortly to emerge as a major writer-director (see *Straw Dogs*, 1971, #33).

ALSO RECOMMENDED:

The most effective variation on this theme was, in fact, provided by George A. Romero in *Night of the Living Dead* (1968), adding graphic violence to the mix but keeping the essential notion of normal, everyday people terrorized not by big bugs or lobster men but the most terrifying thing of all: their neighbors, who have finally transformed into the monsters we always secretly suspected they were.

37:

THE COLLECTOR (1965)

Columbia Pictures

> **"Don't worry; I'll respect your every privacy."**
> **—Freddie Clegg**

CAST:

> Terence Stamp (*Freddie Clegg*); Samantha Eggar (*Miranda Grey*); Mona Washbourne (*Aunt Annie*); Maurice Dallimore (*Neighbor*); Allyson Ames (*Potential Victim*); Gordon Barclay, David Haviland (*Clerks*); William Bickley (*Crutchley*); Kenneth More (*Man on Street*).

CREDITS:

> Director, William Wyler; screenplay, John Kohn and Stanley Mann, from the novel by John Fowles; producers, Kohn and Jud Kinberg; original music, Maurice Jarre; cinematographers, Robert Krasker and Robert Surtees; editors, David Hawkins and Robert Swink; art director, John Stoll; running time, 119 min.

THE PLOT:

Freddie Clegg is an obscure bank clerk who has, all his life, collected things. His favorite boyhood collection was butterflies. He would catch them, then carefully preserve their once-ethereal beauty for all time under glass. After Freddie inherits an isolated home, a new idea occurs to him: he will collect young women in the same way. Freddie stalks Miranda Grey, whom he notices going to and from her job. He carefully plans a strategy, then abducts Miranda. Initially, she's afraid Freddie will molest her, though he has no plans to do so. A twisted romantic, Freddie promises to treat her as befits a lady if only Miranda will remain with him for four weeks. During that time, Miranda is drawn into an eerie relationship with her captor, humoring him while always attempting to come up with some means of escape. When the time is up, Freddie will not let her go; he believed that, if exposed to him, Miranda would fall in love and want to remain there. During a fierce rainstorm, she almost escapes, though he recaptures her. Owing to exposure, Miranda contracts pneumonia and, despite Freddie's sincere efforts to nurse her to health, dies. At first, Freddie mourns her; then, he snaps back, deciding it's time to start stalking some new young woman.

THE FILM:

Few movies are significant as *The Collector* in signifying the changeover from the old studio-bound Hollywood to a new mentality that emerged in the sixties. A well-respected professional, William Wyler—the man who had presented audiences with such classy items as *Wuthering Heights* (1939) and *Ben-Hur* (1959)—brought his reknown as a superb technician and inspired director of actors to what, in lesser hands, would have been summarily dismissed as outrageous exploitation. With Wyler's elegant touch in place, *The Collector* emerged as a surprisingly restrained, high-quality film about what would seem the least likely subject for such treatment:

Terence Stamp and Samantha Eggar.

a tale of sexual obsession and intense bondage. But this superbly mounted work could not be dismissed, even at Academy Awards time, when it was nominated for (but did not win) an Oscar in almost every category for which it was eligible. Elliott Stern has noted, "*The Collector* is every bit as perverse as the times would permit," pushing limits of that era. Its unlikely success with mainstream moviegoers helped to necessitate the creation of a ratings system two-and-a-half years later. Essentially, Wyler redeemed what is essentially salacious material by demonstrating that it could be mounted with great style, altering the audience's previously dichotomized notion of sleazy entertainment and classy art.

Perhaps the film's most remarkable quality is its ability to allow a viewer to enter into the psyches of both Freddie and Miranda. She is the more sympathetic of the two, an ordinary woman (except for her extreme beauty) who has been unceremoniously yanked from everyday life. Virtually any member of the audience can imagine him- or herself becoming, in one's worst nightmares, such a victim. Yet the story is told not from her point of view but, as had been the case with John Fowles's novel, Freddie's, setting the pace for such literary works as Bret Easton Ellis's *American Psycho* and varied suspense thrillers of the 1970s that allowed audiences to view female victims through the male predator's eyes.

This creates a double sense of suspense, which had never before been attempted in motion pictures, and would never be fully equalled since. Because we, as viewers, have been forced to divide our empathies, we experience an unexpected emotional reaction when, during a rainstorm, Miranda slugs Freddie with a shovel. Part of us roots for Miranda to escape, while on some level, we want Freddie to hold her back so the bizarre relationship can continue, and we, in turn, can continue to voyeuristically peek in on it. If there's a flaw, it's that on several occasions Miranda could clearly escape, but does not take advantage of the situation; even audiences captivated by the film groaned, on its initial release, at such lapses in believability.

TRIVIA:

Fascinated by the concept of making a movie that essentially featured only two characters, Wyler hired two writers, two producers, two cinematographers, and two film editors. His films are characterized by an effective use of the deep-focus shot, though many film historians now credit this technique not to Wyler but his regular cinematographer, Greg Toland, who had developed this approach while working with Orson Welles on *Citizen Kane* (1941). This technique successfully kept numerous characters in a single frame, all on the same level of interest, thereby eliminating the use of editing.

ALSO RECOMMENDED:

For an intriguing variation on this theme, locate a copy of René Clement's *Joy House* (1964). A fugitive (Alain Delon) is similarly captured and held hostage by a pair of beautiful women (Lola Albright and Jane Fonda); here, though, the victim is sexually exploited by his captors.

36:

LAURA (1944)

20th Century Fox

"Has it occured to you that you're in love with a corpse?"
—Waldo to Mark

CAST:

Gene Tierney (*Laura*); Clifton Webb (*Waldo Lydecker*); Dana Andrews (*Mark McPherson*); Judith Anderson (*Ann Treadwell*); Vincent Price (*Shelby Carpenter*); Dorothy Adams (*Bessie Clary*); James Flavin (*McAvity*).

CREDITS:

Director, Otto Preminger; screenplay, Jay Dratier, Samuel Hoffenstein, and Betty Reinhardt, from the novel by Vera Caspary; producer, Preminger; music, David Raksin and Johnny Mercer; cinematographer, Joseph La Shelle; editor, Louis Loeffler; running time, 88 min.

THE PLOT:

New York detective Mark McPherson shows up at the plush apartment of a socialite/celebrity after she's brutally murdered with a shotgun one Friday night. He sets about interviewing various people who knew her intimately, and are most likely to have been involved in the killing. These include Laura's superficially charming fiancé Shelby, her haughty friend Ann, and her cynical, sophisticated

The portrait of Laura: Gene Tierney and a notably obsessed Dana Andrews.

mentor Waldo. All are suspects and, while they apparently loved Laura, each had reason to want her dead.

In flashback, we see how a small-town girl born with remarkable natural beauty became a member of Manhattan's elite set. She dared approach the epicene Waldo at the Algonquin and, after initially rejecting her, he fell under her spell. Alone in Laura's apartment on Saturday night, Mark silently consumes alcohol, while listening to the piece of music most associated with Laura. As he becomes ever more inebriated, his growing obsession runs wild. Then, the bell rings. When Mark opens the door, Laura stands before him, looking confused. The woman who took the shotgun blast in the face was, it turns out, not Laura but a flighty model who'd been staying in the apartment and mistaken for Laura by whoever killed her. Shortly, suspicion turns on Laura herself, who had a motive to kill the girl: she was the lover of Laura's fiancé Shelby. Then again, Shelby may have done it to cover up his indiscretion. Or Ann, herself in love with Shelby. In time, Mark comes to realize the killer must be Waldo, whose relationship with Laura was platonic. Fearing Laura would eventually leave him for one of the more rugged men she found herself attracted to, Waldo planned to kill Laura rather than lose her, shooting the wrong woman by mistake. Though he returns to finish the job, Waldo is stopped—and killed—by Mark.

THE FILM:

Laura is often cited as one of the prime examples of film noir, a shadowy style of grim mystery combined with psychological complexity. The film's demi-monde is a night-world in which self-serving characters eagerly betray one another in their pursuit of personal indulgence. The fish out of water—the sardonic working-class anti-hero thrust into a high-class setting—is Mark. Today, in the post-Tarantino film world, he may seem typical of tough guy heroes (indeed, even ordinary). Yet this was a breakthrough presentation, for the traditional cinematic gumshoe may have been laconic on the surface, though turns out to be a sentimentalist down under; this is true for both Humphrey Bogart as Sam Spade in John Huston's *The Maltese Falcon* (1941, #20), or Bogie as Philip Marlowe in Howard Hawks's *The Big Sleep* (1946).

But the eras of Dashiell Hammett and Raymond Chandler were waning; in the 1950s, a new kind of detective hero would emerge, as embodied by Mike Hammer in the novels of Mickey Spillane, most notably *I, The Jury* (1953). This character is a mean-spirited bully, not a crusader hiding under a wise-guy demeanor. He can be perversely cruel, and that well describes Mark in this film, whose obsession is, when analyzed, grotesque. Along with *Vertigo* (1958, #11), *Laura* is one of the few mainstream movies made on the subject of necrophilia. There are other ways in which the film dared to tread on ground that Hollywood had, up until that point, cautiously avoided. Though the script never makes this explicit, there are numerous hints in dialogue and *mise-en-scène* that suggest Waldo is homosexual. Likewise, Laura is, by implication, something of a slut.

There is a dark implication to the conclusion, in which Laura ends up on the arm of Mark. A superficial viewing of the film might lead one to believe that this is a conventional happy ending: the killer is dead, the hero gets the girl. Yet we can't forget the brutality (much of it unnecessary) Mark has displayed toward various people. He loved Laura because he could not have her, she being dead. As it turns out, she is very much alive, and the real Laura is—other than her surface beauty—nothing like the woman he imagined her to be. Similarly, there is no indication that he has arced, and is now in any way purged of his violent tendencies. What occurs at film's end is not the incarnation of a dream but the beginning of a nightmare.

TRIVIA:

Laura was remade for television twice, first in 1956, the second in 1968. The roles of McPherson and Lydecker were played by the same two actors—Robert Stack and George Sanders—in both productions. Dana Wynter played Laura in the first, Lee Radziwell (sister of Jacqueline Kennedy) in the second.

ALSO RECOMMENDED:

For another other great Otto Preminger film noir featuring Dana Andrews as a tough cop and Gene Tierney as the object of his fascination, catch *Where the Sidewalk Ends* (1950). Intriguingly, that film features a cameo appearance by the famed costume designer Oleg Cassini, who was, at the time, married to Tierney.

35:

THE IPCRESS FILE (1965)

Rank Film Organization

"You're supposed to be at work!"
—Courtney to Palmer when he discovers her
snooping in his home

CAST:

Michael Caine (*Harry Palmer*); Nigel Green (*Major Dalby*); Guy Doleman (*Colonel H.L. Ross, Defense Ministry*); Sue Lloyd (*Agent Jean Courtney*); Gordon Jackson (*Agent Jock Carswell*); Aubrey Richards (*Dr. Radcliffe*); Frank Gatliff (*"Bluejay," aka Grantby*); Thomas Baptiste (*Barney*); Oliver MacGreevy (*Housemartin*); Freda Bamford (*Alice*); Pauline Winter (*Charlady*); Anthony Blackshaw (*Edwards*); Barry Raymond (*Gray*).

CREDITS:

Director, Sidney J. Furie; screenplay, Bill Canaway and James Doran, from the novel by Len Deighton; producers, Harry Saltzman and Ronald Kinnoch; original music, John Barry; cinematographer, Otto Heller; editor, Peter Hunt; production design, Ken Adam; art director, Peter Murton; running time, 108 min.

THE PLOT:

Harry Palmer served as a sergeant in the British army until his individualistic attitudes and con-man sensibility landed him in the brig. His former officer secures Palmer's release from detention, arranging for him to work for security. At first, the job is incredibly boring, for all Palmer does is file papers like a clerk. Finally, he receives an actual spy mission. The bureau has undertaken the investigation of several top-level scientists who briefly disappeared, apparently kidnapped. But the men showed up several days later, seemingly no less the worse for wear. In fact, each had been brainwashed during his absence by an enemy power. Palmer must discover who is doing this and why.

As he embarks on the escapade, Palmer realizes he has been picked for the job not because he's the most qualified but the most expendable—the agent sent

To make his spy more realistic than James Bond, Michael Caine decided to play the role in glasses; the babe is Sue Lloyd.

on this mission is not expected to come back alive. As one more scientist is spirited away, Palmer follows the trail, at last coming in contact with Grantby, alias "Bluejay," the mastermind. At first, Palmer's plan to escape with the prisoner backfires, for the scientist can no longer talk about his specialty, "proto-proton scattering," as a result of tampering with his mind. When Palmer persists, he's captured and subjected to the very sort of brainwashing the scientists have undergone. Yet he manages to cling to his values, however tested they have been by circumtances that turned him cynical. The key to a successful resolution, Palmer realizes, is a small piece of recording tape labelled "Ipcress." In due time, he and the scientist make it back to headquarters.

THE FILM:

The 1960s craze for spy films officially began with the release of *Dr. No* (1962), first of the James Bond films adapted from the novels of Ian Fleming by Harry Saltzman and Albert "Cubby" Broccoli. The Bond films were planned and executed as fantasies, as were most of the imitative series spawned by 007's success: James Coburn as Derek Flint, Dean Martin as Matt Helm, et. al. There were anti-Bond spy films, however, which attempted to remind audiences that spying was, in the real world, a sordid and unglamorous profession. Among the best of these were Martin Ritt's *The Spy Who Came In from the Cold* (1965) with Richard Burton, adapted from a realistic novel by John Le Carré. In between romanticized fantasies and turgid dramas existed a surprisingly happy compromise: Len Deighton's series about a reluctant spy whose misadventures tread a delicate balance between the believably grim and the glamorously diverting.

Surprisingly, the Harry Palmer films were produced by Saltzman and Broccoli, the same team that was turning out the 007 escapist epics. Though people now refer to to Deighton's spy stories as "The Harry Palmer Novels," one of the interesting elements of the books is that the hero is never named. This endowed him with a mysterious quality and, at the same time, an existential aspect, both basic to the appeal of each installment. Though the choice of "Palmer" as a last name has never been explained, the character was named "Harry" at Michael Caine's suggestion, after one of the producers.

The brainwashing sequences are as upsetting as those that had appeared in a more serious film, *The Manchurian Candidate* (1962, #9). Sidney J. Furie's surreal filming of them—oblique angles, eccentric lighting, and odd camera movements, abetted by John Barry's evocative music—created a unbearable tension. Furie objected when Saltzman insisted a fight scene be added to make the movie more commercial, though he relented when he realized he could stylize this, shooting the entire event from inside a phone booth to transform what might have been overly conventional into yet another surreal set-piece. Michael Caine's romance with pretty Sue Lloyd countered the harsher aspects with a sensual aspect that helped to make this a popular success.

TRIVIA:

The role of Harry Palmer was originally offered to Christopher Plummer, who would have taken the part had he not been paid more money to star opposite Julie Andrews in *The Sound of Music* (1965). Once Caine assumed the role, he asked if the character might wear glasses, since he himself needed them to see properly. The director and producers loved the idea, for this furthered anchored Palmer in reality.

ALSO RECOMMENDED:

Both sequels are well worth catching. *Funeral in Berlin* (1966), directed by Guy Hamilton (who also did the honors on several Bond films), offers a spellbinding cat-and-mouse yarn about Palmer's uneasy relationship with a defecting Russian officer (Oskar Homolka). *Billion Dollar Brain* (1967), directed by Ken Russell, is more surreal than its predecessors, but no less engaging.

34:
IN THE HEAT OF THE NIGHT (1967)

United Artists

> **"They call me *Mister* Tibbs!"**
> **—Virgil Tibbs**

CAST:

Sidney Poitier (*Detective Virgil Tibbs*); Rod Steiger (*Police Chief Bill Gillespie*); Warren Oates (*Officer Sam Wood*); Lee Grant (*Leslie Colbert*); Larry Gates (*Eric Endicott*); James Patterson (*Purdy*); William Schallert (*Mayor*

Schubert); Beah Richards (*Mama Caleba*); Quentin Dean (*Delores*); Scott Wilson (*Harvey*); Peter Whitney (*Officer George Courtney*); Larry D. Mann (*Watkins*); Matt Clark (*Packy*); Peter Masterson (*Fryer*); Jester Hairston (*Henry*).

CREDITS:

Director, Norman Jewison; screenplay, John Ball and Stirling Silliphant, from a novel by John Ball; producer, Walter Mirisch; original music, Quincy Jones; cinematographer, Haskell Wexler; editor, Hal Ashby; art director, Paul Groesse; running time, 109 min.

THE PLOT:

On a hot summer night in the small town of Sparta, Mississippi, a wealthy, powerful Northern industrialist is murdered. When various redneck police officers set out on a search for the killer, one comes across a well-dressed black man at the train station. The assumption is that any black man discovered near the sight can be assumed to be guilty, so the man is arrested and brought to the jail where he is treated with contempt by pompous and burly police Chief Bill Gillespie. To this good ol' boy's surprise, the black man turns out to be a law officer from Philadelphia, Detective Virgil Tibbs, in town to visit a relative. Reluctantly, Gillespie agrees to allow Tibbs to help him on the investigation, which leads them through various strata of deep South society, from redneck whites in their shanty cabins to the upper-crust Anglos in mansions, as well as through the mostly destitute black community.

THE FILM:

In the spring of 1968, *In the Heat of the Night* won five Academy Awards, including Best Actor (Rod Steiger) and Best Picture. In retrospect, this may seem out of proportion for what is, essentially, a genre piece, if done with splendid attention to detail, wonderful pacing, and a marvelous set of characters, all performed by excellent actors. Still, the film was in competition with Mike Nichols's *The Graduate* and Arthur Penn's *Bonnie and Clyde*, a pair of films remembered today as tips of the iceberg for a new American cinema, innovative in a way *In the Heat of the Night* was not. Yet the importance—indeed, necessity—of the Oscar tribute becomes clear when one grasps the importance of this film to the late-sixties, the implications and subtexts of which might be lost on modern-day viewers who are unaware of the tense situation in America at that moment in time.

The redemption of the thriller: Civil Rights themes were presented in the context of a suspenseful entertainment.

Lest we forget, the Deep South was then so ripe with bigotry, director Norman Jewison dared not film his movie on actual locations. Most of *Heat of the Night* was shot in Illinois to avoid attacks by the Ku Klux Klan, then supported by an overwhelmingly large portion of the white southern population. This slickly produced genre piece, in which a bigoted Southern redneck police chief learns to accept a black man who is his superior in intellect, morality, and pretty much everything else, was taken not only as a murder mystery, but as a Civil Rights statement. When Steiger—who, as a liberal, was the moral opposite of the character he plays—received his statuette, he employed the moment to emotionally express his political values by echoing a key phrase of that era, "We *shall* overcome!"

TRIVIA:

This was one of the first detective dramas to employ forensics, Virgil's forte, in solving a murder. Both cinematographer Haskell Wexler and editor Hal Ashby had aspirations to direct. Wexler's initial effort at becoming an auteur, *Medium Cool* (1969), about journalism and politics in the tense social climate of 1968, was met with mostly positive reviews and was a modest hit at the box office. Yet he returned to cinematography, on occasion working for Ashby, who became a major director; perhaps their most reknown collaboration was *Coming Home* (1978), about women on the home front during the Vietnam war. *In the Heat of the Night*'s Oscar sweep was not complete, in part because Norman Jewison was not awarded the statuette. That went to Mike Nichols, whom many people felt had deserved the award a year earlier for *Who's Afraid of Virginia Woolf?* Sidney Poitier was overlooked in the Best Actor category—he wasn't even nominated—largely because he had won five years earlier for *Lillies of the Field*. Steiger's role was a supporting one, though he too had been passed over, when in 1965 Lee Marvin won Best Actor for *Cat Ballou*, despite the widespread belief that it would go to Steiger for *The Pawnbroker*. Poitier revived his role as Virgil for two follow-ups, *They Call Me MISTER Tibbs!* (1970) and *The Organization* (1971)—both conventional potboilers.

ALSO RECOMMENDED:

Director Jewison also made *A Soldier's Story* (1984), yet another tense murder mystery set in the South, featuring a Civil Rights theme. It features Denzel Washington in one of his earliest roles. The lead is played by Howard E. Rollins, who shortly portrayed Virgil Tibbs on the TV version of *In the Heat of the Night*, with Carroll O'Connor taking over the Rod Steiger role. For a far lighter but no less successful suspense thriller by Jewison, check out *The Thomas Crown Affair* (1968) with Steve McQueen and Faye Dunaway, a charming romantic caper about a high-class jewel thief and the lovely lady investigator sent to stop his next non-violent crime—if, that is, she doesn't fall in love first.

33:

STRAW DOGS (1971)

Cinerama

> **"I will not tolerate violence against this *house*!"**
> **—David Sumner**

CAST:

Dustin Hoffman (*David Sumner*); Susan George (*Amy*); Peter Vaughan (*Tom Hedden*); T.P. McKenna (*Major Scott*); Del Henney (*Venner*); David

Warner (*Henry Niles*); Ken Hutchinson (*Scott*); Colin Wellannd (*Rev. Hood*); Jim Norton (*Cawsey*); Sally Thomsett (*Janice*).

CREDITS:

Director, Sam Peckinpah; screenplay, Peckinpah and David Zelag Goodman, from the novel *The Siege at Trencher's Farm*, by Gordon Williams; producer, Daniel Melnick; original music, Jerry Fielding; cinematographer, John Coquillon; editors, Paul Davies, Roger Spottiswoode, and Tony Lawson; running time, 113 min.; rating, R.

THE PLOT:

David Sumner, an American scientist and mathematician, and his English-born wife, Amy, travel to the isolated village in Cornwall where she grew up. Amy is a woman of the senses, half-Lolita, half-Constance Chatterley. David is a man of the mind, cerebral about all things. David will spend the next several months working on his book, though Amy grows bored, and often interrupts him. David suggests she spend more time outside of the house. She does, flirting with the working men who are repairing the downtrodden farm. Shortly, the village toughs hate them both, hungrily desiring the woman, nastily dismissing the man who works with his brain rather than, like them, brawn.

Though the couple attempts to live out a hippie vision—going "back to nature" to get close to the earth and rekindle their fading love—what occurs is anything but a romantic rebirth. Nature, and men who live close to it, are not benign, but malevolent. They rape David's wife (though it's difficult to tell whether she's victim or instigator) and hang his cat. When they track and plan to kill a mentally-challenged man named Niles (who had molested and accidentally killed a schoolchild), David will stand no more. He grabs a gun and, in one of the extended exercises in slow-motion violence Peckinpah became famous for, shoots them as they attempt to enter his house. Husband and wife are at last reunited, joining together to exact violence on the frightening elements—yet another instance of "the other"—that would break in and do violence to them.

The final sequence, a dazzling combination of action and suspense, is rendered with a moral ambiguousness that makes it unique. The toughs attack the house late at night, and David is clearly not defending the "honor" of his wife, which he seems vaguely aware was lost long ago. He is, to a degree, defending the life of Niles; the toughs initially intend, at this pont, no direct threat to David and Amy, and would gladly leave the couple alone if only David would turn over Niles. What keeps the bloodletting from becoming a simplistic case of good protecting from evil is that Niles is in fact guilty of the twin crimes he's been accused of, so there is nothing particularly glorious about what David does. It is not the courageous defense of a wronged innocent but of a child abuser and killer. What Niles brings out in David is not the best, but the worst, within him.

"I got all of 'em," David smiles at the end. But there is no easy way back from the violence into which he has been drawn. When, after the interlopers are all dead, Henry Niles sadly says, "I don't know my way home," David replies, "Neither do I."

"I got 'em all!" Dustin Hoffman as David Sumner.

THE FILM:

Pauline Kael hailed *Straw Dogs* as "a fascist masterpiece," at once admiring the remarkable artistry of the world-class director and, at the same time, criticizing the reactionary vision he so brilliantly put onscreen. Peckinpah was out of touch with the attitudes of his times—the antiviolent, profeminist positions of the post-Woodstock era—and proves even more controversial today, in the age of political correctness. Like D.H. Lawrence, Peckinpah presupposes that it is not only a man's right but his duty to dominate his woman, despite her strong need to offer mighty resistance which she hopes he will be man enough to overcome. Like Ernest Hemingway, Peckinpah proceeds from the concept that to be a man, one must sooner or later test oneself in violent combat and, like Hemingway's bullfighters and soldiers, know the moment-of-truth exhilaration of bloody victory. From Robert Ardrey, Peckinpah borrowed the notion of territorial imperatives, a belief that what we fight for is the sanctitiy of our corner of the universe, the property—most often a house—that becomes an expression of the essence of ourselves. However offensive that vision may seem, it is the manner in which this vision shapes every aspect of *Straw Dogs* that qualfies the film as an organically-organized work of art, however disturbing—or even offensive—to a viewer's sensibilities.

TRIVIA:

Some three hundred years before the birth of Christ, "straw dogs" were oriental artifacts meant to be first worshipped, then afterwards put to the torch. For Sam Peckinpah, that notion applies equally to the totems and taboos of civilized society, which the filmmaker viewed not as a monolithic, far-reaching positive force on our lives, but as a flimsy, unsubstantial illusion. While we pay homage to society on a daily basis through the economic, religious, and social institutions, the structure of society—for Peckinpah—was only an elaborate game, a kind of hoax. Finally, we—like David Sumner—must put our civilized order aside and act as the Neanderthals which, in essence, we still really are.

ALSO RECOMMENDED:

Peckinpah's other exercise in thriller genre is the little appreciated Steve McQueen/ Ali MacGraw teaming, *The Getaway* (1972).

32:

THE BLACK CAT (1934)

Universal Pictures

> **"Even the phone is dead!"**
> **—Hjalmar Poezlig**

CAST:

Boris Karloff (*Hjalmar Poelzig*); Bela Lugosi (*Dr. Vitus Werdegast*); David Manners (*Peter*); Jacqueline Wells (*Joan Alison*); Lucille Lund (*Karen Werdegast Poelzig*); Egon Brecher (*The Majordomo*); Harry Cording (*Thamal, Werdegast's "Servant"*); Henry Armetta, Albert Conti (*Policemen*); John Carradine (*Organist*); Symona Boniface (*Cult Member*).

CREDITS:

> Director, Edgar G. Ulmer; screenplay, Ulmer, Peter Ruric, and (uncredited) Tom Kilpatrick, inspired by Edgar Allan Poe's story; producer, Carl Laemmle Jr.; original music, James Huntley and Heinz Roemheld, cinematographer, John J. Mescall; editor, Ray Curtiss; art director, Charles D. Hall; make up, Jack P. Pierce; set designer, Ulmer; special photographic processes, John P. Fulton; special matte effects, Russell Lawson; running time, 65 min.

THE PLOT:

The legendary Orient Express passes through Budapest. On board are a pair of honeymooners, mystery writer Peter Alison and his bride Joan. Sharing their coach is Dr. Vitus Werdegast, a softspoken Hungarian who is also headed for Vizhegrad, if for considerably less pleasant reasons. He's going to visit an architect named Hjalmar Poelzig, though Werdegast's insistence that the man is "an old friend" is undercut by the doctor's cryptic tone. Werdegast's wife was taken away from him by Poelzig eighteen years earlier, before Werdegast was sent to Russia's Kurgaal Prison, from which he's recently been released. Arriving at Vizhegrad, they disembark—along with Werdegast's frightful servant Thamal—and board a bus that whisks them past ruined earth and endless graves, the result of The Great War.

When the coach rolls over in a torrent of rain and the driver is killed, the couple can't proceed to their hotel, but must accompany Werdegast to the eerie house atop the hill, where the Majordomo meets them. The mountaintop home of Poelzig was built on the base of Fort Marmorus, a site of violence and despair. Polelzig sleeps, in his bedchamber, behind elegant veils, alongside a beautiful young eighteen-year-old girl. He does not sexually molest the virgin bride, Karen, daughter of Werdegast and his late wife, whom Poelzig seduced, murdered, then mounted as a perpetually beautiful ornament. In glass cases lining the basement, Poelzig keeps bodies of beautiful women—Karen's mother included—in suspensed animation, floating forever for his sinister delight. Like Werdegast, Poelzig is attracted to Joan, only for a far more hideous reason: he plans to keep the young couple, who have apparently not had the opportunity to consummate their marriage, in the castle until the night of the next full moon, when Joan will serve as the virgin sacrifice he and other devil worshippers regularly perform.

Realizing this, Werdegast temporarily sets his plans for vengeance aside to try and win freedom for the young people in a bizarre game of chess. But Poelzig's mania for evil knows no bounds; he kills Karen rather than allowing her to be reunited with her father. Poelzig is about to do the same with Joan when Werdegast binds and skins Poelzig alive, even as Peter rescues Joan from the satanic cult.

THE FILM:

The Black Cat was "suggested" by Poe's story. Such a creature appears briefly, shocking superstitious Werdegast. Carl Laemmle (Jr.) had discovered that the stories of Poe, in public domain and therefore had for nothing, were known to the public; by employing the titles for his horror films, he could "pre-sell" movies. If *The Black Cat* has little to do with its literary antecedent, it does capture the sensibililty of Poe himself, who—like Poelzig—slept beside an underage virgin bride until she died, at which point he immortalized her untouched beauty—in verse rather than behind glass.

Edgar G. Ulmer might have become a legendary director of thrillers, worthy of comparison with James Whale and Todd Browning, but his penchant for sleeping with wives of important people in Hollywood led to termination of his Universal contract, at which point he had to

Strange obsession: The "floating woman" comes between old friends Bela Lugosi and Boris Karloff.

accept jobs with studios on Poverty Row. Before that happened, he directed this, his minor masterpiece. *The Black Cat* featured the first teaming of Boris Karloff and Bela Lugosi. As has been noted, the film contains "dark sexual repression, twisted relationships, and aberrant behavior, Satanism, devil worship, black mass orgies, necrophilia, pedophilia, sadistic revenge, murder and incest." Ulmer got away with his grotesquerie because he implied, rather than graphically portrayed, the hideous doings; even the final pièce de résistance, in which Lugosi skins a bound Karloff, is done as shadow play, through terrible suggestions rather than vivid depictions. It was difficult to censor what was not shown, qualifying the film as a thriller rather than a horror movie.

TRIVIA:

In the original credits, Boris Karloff was listed as, simply, "Karloff"—the name, or so Universal believed—now synonymous with terror; in fact, his name had not been listed at all in credits for *Frankenstein*, the actor playing the monster originally identified only by a question mark. Lucille Lund played both the daughter Karen and, in the glass case, Karen's mother. John Carradine, who would shortly assume the role of Dracula in Universal's ongoing series, appears unbilled as the organist at the Black Mass. The script was partly inspired by the real-life trial of Aleister Crowley, a Satanist on whom Ulmer based Karloff's character.

ALSO RECOMMENDED:

Ulmer's other recommended film is *Bluebeard* (1944), starring John Carradine as the man who married and murdered seven women. Among Universal's other teamings of Karloff and Lugosi, the best by far is Lew Landers's *The Raven* (1935), released jointly with *The Black Cat* on home video.

31:

IN COLD BLOOD (1967)

Columbia Pictures

> **"I thought Mr. Clutter was a real gentleman . . . right up**
> **to the moment I cut his throat."**
> **—Perry Smith**

CAST:

Robert Blake (*Perry Smith*); Scott Wilson (*Dick Hickock*); John Forsythe (*Alvin Dewey*); Paul Stewart (*Reporter Jenson*); Gerald S. O'Loughlin (*Harold Nye*); Jeff Corey (*Mr. Hickock*); John Gallaudet (*Roy Church*); James Flavin (*Clarence Duntz*); John Collins (*Judge Roland Tate*); Charles McGraw (*Mr. Smith*); Will Geer (*Prosecutor*); James Lantz (*Officer Rohleder*); John McLiam (*Herbert Clutter*); Brenda Currin (*Nancy Clutter*); Ruth Storey (*Bonnie Clutter*); Paul Hough (*Kenyon Clutter*).

CREDITS:

Director, Richard Brooks; screenplay, Brooks, from the book by Truman
Capote; producer, Brooks; original music, Quincy Jones; cinematographer,
Conrad (L.) Hall; editor, Peter Zinner; production design/art direction,
Robert F. Boyle; special effects, Chuck Gaspar; running time, 134 min.

**Before the
atrocity.**

THE PLOT:

In Holcomb, Kansas, 1959, two itinerant losers, Perry Smith and Dick Hickock,
decide to rob a family named Clutter by slipping into their isolated house late at
night, tying everyone up, then making off with ten thousand dollars. The two have
convinced themselves that the money, which does not exist, is kept in a safe. As
their tawdry plan evolves, something horrific develops: they will murder the Clut-
ters. During the gruesome incident, they become so obsessed with the oncoming
massacre they almost forget to look for items to steal. Their subconscious need to
murder overtakes any conscious desire for monetary gain, and the police who
investigate this crime realize that at once.

The two are quickly apprehended. A well-known writer (called "Jensen")
finds himself obsessed with the case. Journeying to Kansas, he follows the trial,
then interviews the condemned men while they await execution on death row. He
comes to realize that these pathetic people represent a darkness that has been fes-

tering in society during the postwar years, and was about to explode into the mainstream. If only he can come to understand precisely what it was that drove them to do this deed, perhaps he can write a book that will allow people to understand what has been going wrong in our society.

THE FILM:

During the sixties, the issue of escalating violence would become a key issue in our national debate and an ongoing theme in motion pictures, from *Psycho* (1960) through *Bonnie and Clyde* (1967) to *The Wild Bunch* (1969). Such films, whatever the ostensible period in which they were set, were informed by and reflected a decade filled with political assassinations, ghetto burnings, racially-motivated murders, and the ever more controversial Vietnam War. One key piece of literature was Truman Capote's analytical study of two men who had brutally murdered a family. In addition to addressing the issue of violence in society—redeeming what might have been exploitive material through intelligent analysis of the motives of the killers—Capote's book also redefined writing by breaking down the barriers between fiction and fact, resulting in a new term—"the non-fiction novel."

The challenge for filmmaker Richard Brooks was not only to tell the story effectively but to visually approximate Capote's verbal approach. With that aim in mind, Brooks insisted on shooting on actual locations in Edgarton and Emporia, Kansas, as well as Kansas City, Missouri. All the scenes in the Clutter house were filmed there, and the courtroom scene was likewise shot in that very place, with half the jurors agreeing to portray themselves. Even the hangman who executes the condemned killers was played by the actual person. The photos in the house are not pictures of the actors playing the Clutter family but of the real family.

One reason the movie so terrified audiences was the fact that relative unknowns played all the parts. But if the executives at Columbia Pictures had had their way, things would have been very different; they lobbied to have Paul Newman and Steve McQueen in the roles of the killers and Henry Fonda as the chief investigator. Despite his admiration of all three, Brooks held firm, insisting that by having beloved stars play the parts—in particular, the murderers—this would have taken the edge off the intensity that he hoped to create, for, on some level, viewers could escape the tale's terrible implications by reminding themselves this was only a re-enactment, the familiar faces of stars diminishing the heightened sense of realism.

The most brilliant decision was to jump over the murders as they occur during the story, moving on to the investigation and trial. Viewers believed they had been spared the experience of watching the crimes re-enacted. At the last moment, Brooks includes the crimes in a flashback, devastatingly photographed by Conrad Hall in a widescreen process. Brooks's worst choice was to include Capote's conclusions about the death penalty (featured as a voice-over) that contradicted the reaction of many moviegoers who were relieved when the killers were finally hanged.

TRIVIA:

At one point, Dick and Perry pick up a pair of hitchhikers. Robert Blake mentions a motion picture, John Huston's *The Treasure of Sierra Madre* (1948). Blake played a Mexican child in that film. When Blake was accused of murdering his wife in 2000, observers noticed that a lifelong rage directly paralleled the actor with the role he perfectly embodied here.

ALSO RECOMMENDED:

For a similar example of an actual arrest and trial of violent criminals employed as an anti-capital punishment statement, catch Richard Fleischer's *Compulsion* (1959), about the Leopold and Loeb case. Also, John McNaughton's *Henry: Portrait of a Serial Killer* (1990).

30:
THE THING FROM ANOTHER WORLD (1951)

RKO Radio Pictures

> **"Tell the world, tell this to everyone wherever they are:**
> **keep looking—watch the skies!"**
> **—Scotty (film's final line)**

CAST:

Margaret Sheridan (*"Nikki" Nicholson*); Kenneth Tobey (*Capt. Patrick Hendry*); Robert Cornthwaite (*Dr. Arthur Carrington*); Douglas Spencer (*Ned "Scotty" Scott*); James R. Young (*Lt. Dykes*); Dewey Martin (*Crew*

Chief Bob); Robert Nichols (*Lt. McPherson*); William Self (*Corp. Barnes*); Eduard Franz (*Dr. Stern*); Sally Creighton (*Mrs. Chapman*); John Dierkes (*Chapman*); Robert Bray (*Captain*); James Arness (*The Thing*).

CREDITS:

Directors, Christian Nyby and (uncredited) Howard Hawks; screenplay, Hawks and Ben Hecht (both uncredited) and Charles Lederer, from the short story "Who Goes There?" by John W. Campbell Jr.; producer, Hawks and Edward Lasker; original music, Dimitri Tiomkin; cinematographer, Russell Harlan; editor, Roland Gross; art directors, Albert S. D'Agostino and John J. Hughes; running time, 87 min.

THE PLOT:

Near the U.S. Air Force's North Pole base, something crashes from out of the sky. A team of servicemen dig it out, realizing they have come in contact with one of the flying saucers everyone has been buzzing about. Inside they find a frozen but still living creature and bring it back to their base. When the alien thaws out, it requires the men's blood to survive. The servicemen search for a way to kill the thing before it kills them, though the scientists who share the outpost want to bring it back alive to learn. "There are no enemies in science," Carrington insists, "only phenomena to study." The issue breaks down to the old conflict between the Army's brawn and the scientist's brains, until they come together as a group and, by combining the best of both worlds, defeat the thing. A human vegetable, it can regrow arms when they are cut off, but like all vegetables, may be killed by boiling. The men trick the thing into entering their domain while they use heating facilities to reduce it to rubble.

THE FILM:

The first flying saucer sightings took place in the American Midwest in 1947 and 1948, creating an immediate fascination with the concept of invaders from Mars or some other planet. Not surprisingly, Hollywood was quick to get into the act, though most films were cheaply made B-pictures boasting little beyond exploitation values. Producer Howard Hawks offered something else with *The Thing*, telling his story in a low-key documentary fashion, with a well-developed ensemble of characters—ordinary, believable human beings all—which increased audience involvement. As *Boxoffice* noted at the time, "this is by far the most fanciful—and in many respects the most engrossing" of all entries in the then-new genre, noting that while "it assumes a pseudo-scientific approach, the film is geared for chills."

Kenneth Tobey (Center) leads a team of soldiers and scientists against the thing.

The problem with most films of this era is that they show too much, too soon. By revealing the monster (and, more often than not, what Stephen King calls "the zipper up the back" of the costume,) movies allowed audiences to adjust to whatever big bug filmmakers placed onscreen; to again borrow from King, however horrible it might be, the vision was not as bad as the individual imagined. What the films quickly become, then, is an update of the old horror films. Hawks and Nyby wisely opted for suspense by keeping the title creature offscreen for as long as possible. Audiences—then and now—squirmed in their seats for nearly ninety minutes, even as the filmmakers appeared ready to reveal their full hand only to, again and again, slide their ace before our eyes so quickly we couldn't get a good look.

Though at first glance a far cry from what one typically thinks of as a Howard Hawks film—this is the only science-fiction film he ever made—*The Thing* incorporates genre conventions into his personal vision. As in films as diverse as *Scarface* (1933), *Air Force* (1943), *Red River* (1948), and *Hatari!* (1962), the focus is on a diverse group of men, becoming a true community only when a strong, indepedently-minded woman serves as the necessary catalyst to transform rugged indidivudalists into a male group. Also characeristic of Hawks is the overlapping dialogue to insure an ongoing sense of realism.

Trivia:

Like so many other major-league filmmakers during the postwar era, Hawks moved into independent production with his own company, Winchester Films. This allowed him to develop ideas in-house, then offer them to studios like RKO Pictures, which co-produced and distributed *The Thing*. For the difficult stunt work, Hawks hired no less than thirteen professional stunt people, including three who became legendary in the business: Leslie Charles, Dick Crockett, and Billy Curtis. Though Christian Nyby is listed as the director, almost all of the film was made by Hawks. Nyby, Hawks's trusted editor, had pleaded with his boss for a chance to break out and direct a film himself. Once given the opportunity, he was unable to complete the task, so Hawks stepped in. Knowing that the film's score had to be unique, Dimitri Tiomkin created it on a theremin, an electronic invention that sends off odd sounds. As a result, this became de rigueur for 1950s sci-fi films.

ALSO RECOMMENDED:

William Cameron Menzies's *Invaders From Mars* (1953) provides considerable thrills, viewing the deadly visitors from the point of view of a small boy. Second only to the Hawks film is Byron Haskins's *War of the Worlds* (1953), adapted from the H.G. Wells classic. Worth catching too is John Carpenter's unfairly maligned remake (1982).

29:

REPULSION (1965)

Royal Films/Compton

> **"The nightmare world of a virgin's dreams."**
> —advertising tag line

CAST:

Catherine Deneuve (*Carol Ledoux*); Ian Hendry (*Michael*); John Fraser (*Colin*); Yvonne Furneaux (*Hélène Ledoux*); Patrick Wymark (*Landlord*); Renee Houston (*Miss Balch*); Valerie Taylor (*Madame Denise*); James Villiers (*John*); Helen Fraser (*Bridget*); Hugh Futcher (*Reggie*); Monica Merlin (*Mrs. Rendlesham*); Imogen Graham (*Manicurist*); Mike Pratt (*Workman*); Roman Polanski (*Spoon Player*).

CREDITS:

Director, Roman Polanski; screenplay, Polanski and Gérard Brach, with additional dialogue (adaptation) by David Stone; producer, Gene Gutowski and Michael Klinger; original music, Chico Hamilton; cinematographer, Gilbert Taylor; editor, Alastair McIntyre; art director, Seamus Flannery; special sound effects, Stephen Dalby, Leslie Hammond, and Tom Priestley; running time, 105 min.

THE PLOT:

Carol and Helen, sisters from Belgium, live in swinging London of the mid-sixties. Though Helen is every inch the mod girl, enjoying a wild fling with her latest (married) boyfriend, Carol remains aloof, distanced, quiet, timid. She barely speaks to the customers while working at a beauty salon, then hurries home to her apartment, ignoring all the men who whistle at her. A virgin—unless, that is, she was molested while young by her father—Carol is repulsed by the presence of men, even Colin, an engaging young fellow who pays her great respect and would like to strike up a serious relationship. But when her sister takes off for a week's vacation, Carol—alone in her apartment—gradually descends into abject madness. She imagines that monstrous men are hiding in the shadows and that they rape her nightly.

In time, she stops going to work and wanders around her apartment all day in her lingerie. Eventually, she loses any touch with reality. When the landlord shows up for his money, and makes a pass, she brutally murders him. Worried about Carol, Colin shows up, and she kills him, too. When her sister returns, she and her boyfriend find Carol in a comatose state, wandering the apartment as if in search of some part of her soul that was stolen away, many years ago now, by the man who damaged her—psychically and physically—during a seemingly sweet family sojourn.

THE FILM:

"A wicked tale of madness and female paranoia," Edward Guthmann calls it. "Polanski's direction is tight and controlled and manages to place us inside Deneuve's head as she comes to see any man as a potential assailant. Haunted by nightmares of rape and violation, she hallucinates arms coming out of the two walls of her hallway (a steal from Cocteau's *Beauty and the Beast*)." The term *steal* seems unfair, though. While there is an element drawn from the Cocteau classic, that's but one of many elements Polanski incorporates into his singular work. Informed by many influences, this emerges as a unique motion picture thriller,

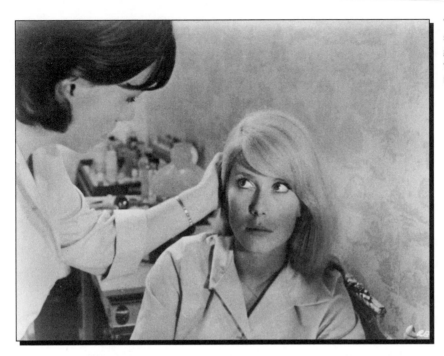

The seemingly sweet and normal girl cannot respond to "the touch" of man or woman.

aesthetically daring, emotionally riveting, and intellectually daring, particularly for its time.

The idea of creating an ever-changing, ever more distorted mis-en-scène that mirrors the central character's altering mental states was the essence of the first great thriller, *The Cabinet of Dr. Caligari* (1919, #100). Carol recalls such diverse Hitchcock characters as Norman Bates in *Psycho* (1960, #1) and the title character in *Marnie* (1964): a combination of the seemingly normal person who is quite mad under the surface, and the elegant blond, as deadly as she is alluring. Hitchcock's love of "shooting a movie in a goldfish bowl or telephone booth"—*Lifeboat* (1944), *Rope* (1948), and *Rear Window* (1954, #6) all taking place in a confined space—is the basis of *Repulsion*. Still, whenever the character of Carol leaves her room, the sounds of the street are not presented realistically (though that's the initial impression) but surrealistically, subjectively, as we hear them in the distorted manner a paranoid like Carol would—all noises being magnified and oppressive.

Following the success of his Polish art films, Polanski had headed for London to be part of the city's exciting arts-and-entertainment scene that had engendered everything from The Beatles to Carnaby Street fashions. Though the producers at Compton would have been satisfied with a traditional thriller, Polanski gave them something more: a film that could compete with anything Hitchcock himself was doing at the time. Apparently, the violence we see onscreen in Polanski films is not entirely artificial. Barbara Leaming wrote in her biography of the filmmaker that Deneuve was initially uncomfortable with wielding the candlestick with which she kills gentle Colin. Polanski endlessly baited her, purposefully making Deneuve grow angry with him. Leming writes, "She tried to control her rage, but Polanski continued. Then she exploded. He gave her the candlestick and she swung at him. The camera had been rolling, and now Polanski had the performance he wanted. The Deneuve the spectator sees on screen is not acting—the violence is real, directed at Polanski."

TRIVIA:

One year after *Repulsion,* Polanski directed *Cul-De-Sac,* an appealingly oddball comedy-thriller in which Donald Pleasence plays a wealthy man with a much younger wife. The latter was portrayed by Françoise Dorléac, redheaded sister of Deneuve. Shortly thereafter, Dorléac was killed in a car accident.

ALSO RECOMMENDED:

Polanski's classic thrillers include *Rosemary's Baby* (1968) and the exquisite detective thriller *Chinatown* (1974). His lesser known but equally stimulating thrillers include *Knife in the Water* (1962), a Polish production (and Polanski's feature-film directing debut) about the escalating sexual tension between two men and a woman on an isolated boat. That film was unofficially remade as an Australian thriller, *Dead Calm* (1989) by Phillip Noyce, with Nicole Kidman, Sam Neill, and Billy Zane.

28:
THE FUGITIVE (1993)

Warner Bros.

> **"Your fugitive's name is Dr. Richard Kimble; go get him."**
> **—Sam Gerard**

CAST:

Harrison Ford (*Dr. Richard Kimble*); Tommy Lee Jones (*Deputy Marshal Samuel Gerard*); Jeroen Krabbé (*Dr. Charles Nichols*); Joe Pantoliano (*Mar-*

shal *Cosmo Renfro*); Daniel Roebuck (*Marshal Biggs*); Tom Wood (*Marshal Newman*); Sela Ward (*Helen Kimble*); Julianne Moore (*Dr. Anne Eastman*); L. Scott Caldwell (*Marshal Poole*); Andreas Katsulas (*Sykes, a.k.a. "The One-Armed Man"*) Ron Dean (*Detective Kelly*).

CREDITS:

Director, Andrew Davis; screenplay, Jeb Stuart and David Twohy, from a story by Twohy, based on characters created by Roy Huggins; producers, Arnold Kopelson and Nana Greenwald; original music, James Newton Howard; cinematographer, Michael Chapman; editors, Don Brochu, David Finfer, Dean Goodhill, Dov Hoenig, Richard Nord, Dennis Virkler; production design, Dennis Washington; art director, Maher Ahmad; special effects coordinator, Roy Arbogast; stunt coordinator, Terry J. Leonard; running time, 127 min.; rating, PG-13.

THE PLOT:

Chicago surgeon Richard Kimble returns home late one night to find his wife Helen dead as a one-armed man flees the scene. But the nightmare is just beginning. Police arrest him for murder and a jury convicts him. Shortly, Kimble is on his way to prison and eventual execution, though he escapes during a train wreck. The government brings in Gerard, a U.S. Marshal, to track Kimble down. Shortly, the hunt becomes an obsession. Kimble, meanwhile, is lost in a wintry scene, knowing he must locate and wring a confession from the one-armed man before the police find him. Here, the film makes a major departure from the TV series. The one-armed man, who in this version *did* kill Kimble's wife, turns out to be the pawn of a vast conspiracy of doctors who wanted Kimble out of the way so he would not be able to expose their fraudulence in a drug case.

THE FILM:

Like its TV predecessor, *The Fugitive* offers a pop-culture incarnation of Victor Hugo's tortured antihero Jean Valjean from *Les Miserables*, hounded by a relentless policeman, plunged into a Kafka-esque nightmare world of surreal shadows. Quite impossible here was a duplication of the series' epic quality, taking Kimble on a four-year tour of duty, criss-crossing the country during his odyssey through America's big cities and half-forgotten byways. And owing to the low-budgets of TV drama at that time, *The Fugitive* was played as a psychologically-oriented suspense drama rather than as action-thriller.

Harrison Ford as the pursued . . .

. . . and Tommy Lee Jones as the pursuer.

But this movie belonged to the early nineties, and was a Harrison Ford vehicle to boot. Producer Kopelson wisely decided to retain only the basic premise of desperate fugitive, relentless detective, and elusive one-armed man. Andrew Davis was then set free to make a pluperfect example of the kind of action/suspense that plays best to today's audiences, explaining why a film that might have been a pale imitation of a beloved show—like so many movies based on old series—is anything but that. One wonders if Hitchcock himself might have been tempted to direct, were he still alive and working at the time, for *The Fugitive* plays as an exquisite rendering of one of his favorite suspense themes, "the wrong man."

As the chase continues, Gerard wonders if his prey may be innocent, though, wisely, this is suggested not in anything he says, but rather in the looks that cross his eyes, as a stoney man feels some long-dormant sensitivity stirring deep within. Jones's is the showier role, but it plays a neat yin to Ford's yang, as the inwardly suffering Kimble grows ever more desperate. As Harrison Ford explained, "the character is not unique, but his circumstances are," allowing him to portray a modern American Everyman who finds himself in a situation that the average guy will, fortunately, never know. In the film's most memorable moment, high atop a dam, we are treated to the stunning special effects and stunt work that made this an instant classic.

TRIVIA:

The film, like its TV predecessor, was vaguely suggested by the real-life case of Sam Sheppard, a respected man who was convicted of killing his wife but never retracted his insistence of absolute innocence. Initially, Ford turned down producer Kopelson, at which point he tried and failed to put together a package with actor Alec Baldwin and director Walter Hill. Richard Jordan was scheduled to play Dr. Charles Nichols. When he became ill as filming began, Jeroen Krabbe was brought in to play the part. Jordan died shortly thereafter. Kimble's limp, following a wild jump, was not in the script but improvised after Ford actually damaged ligaments while shooting. Almost all of the film was shot in and around Chicago, except the train crash, staged near Dillsboro, North Carolina. The whispering woman in the courtroom is played by Bernice Janssen, mother of David Janssen, who played Kimble on TV. Roy Huggins, who produced the series, served as executive producer for this film. To ready the film for its agreed-upon release date, six credited editors (and, according to some reports, several others who went uncredited) worked on post-production, which may win *The Fugitive* a spot in the Guinness Book of World Records for having more craftsmen in that category than any other Hollywood movie.

ALSO RECOMMENDED:

Davis directed the superb action-suspenser *Under Siege* (1992) with Steven Seagal. Tommy Lee Jones again plays Detective Gerard, the role that won him an Oscar as Best Supporting Actor for *The Fugitive*, in *U.S. Marshals* (1998). Ford's other best thriller is *Witness* (1985) for director Peter Weir.

27:
SHADOW OF A DOUBT (1943)

Universal Pictures

> **"The world has to be carefully watched; something goes wrong from time to time."**
> **—Detective Jack Graham**

CAST:

Joseph Cotten (*"Uncle" Charley Oakley*); Teresa Wright (*"Young" Charlie Newton*); Macdonald Carey (*Jack Graham*); Patricia Collinge (*Emma Newton*); Henry Travers (*Joseph Newton*); Hume Cronyn (*Herbie Hawkins*); Wallace Ford (*Fred Saunders*); Edna May Wonacott (*Ann Newton*); Janet Shaw, Estelle Jewell, and Emily Malyon (*townspeople*).

CREDITS:

Director, Alfred Hitchcock; screenplay, Thornton Wilder, Alma Reville, and Sally Benson, from a treatment by Gordon McDonnell; producer, Jack H. Skirball; original music, Dimitri Tiomkin; cinematographer, Joseph Valentine; editor, Milton Carruth; set design, John B. Goodman, Robert Boyle, and E.R. Robinson; running time, 108 min.

THE PLOT:

In an eastern city, Charles Oakley realizes the police are closing in, about to arrest him as The Merry Widow Murderer, an American cross between Bluebeard and Jack the Ripper. Desperate, he contacts his sister in the small California town of

Santa Rosa, announcing that beloved "Uncle Charlie" will shortly come to visit. He receives a hero's welcome from everyone, particularly his niece, Young Charlie, named after him. Shortly, Young Charlie suspects that something is amiss with the self-consciously elegant man of old-fashioned manners, who loses control while railing at the dinner table about the contemporary world turning into a cesspool.

When a handsome detective, Jack Graham, approaches Young Charlie, she reluctantly agrees to help the government put Uncle Charley away, but begs that they spare her mother's feelings by doing so as quietly as possible. Unfortunately for Young Charlie, her uncle has become aware of the girl's involvement with the law and sets out to kill her. Finally convinced by Young Charlie that he ought to leave town, Uncle Charlie attempts to murder her on the departing train, only managing to kill himself by mistake. Ironically, he receives a hero's funeral from the unsuspecting citizens of Santa Rosa.

THE FILM:

One side of Hitchcock's approach to the thriller was what he called "the domestic variety," films in which outside evil—some variaton on Jack the Ripper—enters a seemingly safe household and menaces the ordinary people living there, simple folks who thought their decent lifestyle distanced them from any evil in the world. His British films *The Lodger* (1926) and *Blackmail* (1929) were early examples of that approach. Before making *Shadow of a Doubt*, Hitchcock had been concentrat-

The universality of guilt: Joseph Cotten and Teresa Wright.

ing on international spy thrillers. About his next film, he announced, "I want to bring murder back into the home . . . where it *belongs!*"

Hitchcock's "first true American film," as he once referred to *Shadow of a Doubt*, also provided his first American version of this recurring concept. He'd already made *Rebecca* (1940) and *Suspicion* (1941) in Hollywood, but both were set in England. To compensate for his lack of understanding of the American vernacular, Hitchcock hired Thornton Wilder as his collaborator, figuring the author of *Our Town* knew how the average small-town citizen spoke more than any other writer. Hitchcock then revolutionized the style for making movies by insisting on setting the script to his location rather than the other way around. Instead of getting the words down on paper, then scouting for a place that would fit the scenario, Hitchcock and Wilder traveled the state until they came across the small, isolated village of Santa Rosa. Convinced this was their town, they took up residence and studied it carefully, then headed back to Hollywood to pen their script.

Half the film takes place during the day, half at night. The daytime scenes are typical of the "murder by daylight" concept, in which terror is highly effective when played off against brightly lit situations that seem to be absolutely safe. The nightime sequences, in which Young Charlie is forced by her charming but corrupt uncle to visit the seedier side of town, set the pace for the film noir style that other filmmakers would take up in the postwar years.

Hitchcock further developed some key themes he had already become fascinated with, in particular what French critics Eric Roehmer and Claude Chabrol refer to as his Catholic attitude: the world is not composed of the pure and the evil; rather, each person contains a mixture of the two within him- or herself. Humor mixes with horror when the father of the house and his next door neighbor, the nicest men in town, play macabre games in which they plot each other's murder, often over dinner, relating fright to food, a favorite and recurring Hitchcock technique.

TRIVIA:

The character of Emma shares her name with Hitchcock's mother, and the actress playing her, Patricia Collinge, was picked owing to her physical and vocal resemblance to Hitchcock's mom. Most locals are played by actual Santa Rosa residents, most notably little Edna May Wonacott, cast as the family's youngest child; she was the daughter of a Santa Rosa grocer. Hitchcock was not yet finished with Santa Rosa; in *The Birds* (1963), we hear that the flocks have headed there when they dessert Bodega Bay. The film was remade in 1958 as *Step Down to Terror* by director Harry Keller. Rod Taylor, who would star in *The Birds* five years later, had one of his earliest film roles, playing the MacDonald Carey part.

ALSO RECOMMENDED:

In addition to *The Lodger* (1926), *Blackmail* (1929), and *Psycho* (1960), Hitchcock's finest domestic thrillers include *The Wrong Man* (1958) with Henry Fonda, which features an even more scrupulous concentration on realism of locale.

26:

THE HAUNTING (1963)

Metro-Goldwyn-Mayer

> **"A closed mind is the worst offense against the supernatural."**
> **—Dr. John Markway**

CAST:

Julie Harris (*Eleanor Lance*); Claire Bloom (*Theodora*); Richard Johnson (*Dr. John Markway*); Russ Tamblyn (*Luke*); Fay Compton (*Mrs. Sanderson*); Rosalie Crutchley (*Mrs. Dudley*); Lois Maxwell (*Grace*); Valentine Dyall (*Mr. Dudley*); Diane Clare (*Carrie*); Ronald Adam (*Eldridge Harper*); Pamela Buckley (*The First Mrs. Crain*).

CREDITS:

Director, Robert Wise; screenplay, Nelson Gidding, from Shirley Jackson's novel, *The Haunting of Hill House*; producers, Wise and Denis Johnson; original music, Humphrey Searle; cinematographer, Davis Boulton; editor, Ernest Walter; production design, Elliot Scott; special sound effects, Tom Howard; running time, 112 min.

THE PLOT:

Hill House has been considered an evil place for most of the ninety years it has stood high and forlorn, overlooking the rural countryside, casting a dark shadow on what might otherwise be a pleasant stretch of forests and villages. Rumors ran wild, during the near-century since it was built, that the house is haunted, though logical and intelligent people consider this a silly superstition, despite the number of accidents that have occured. To determine, once and for all, whether there is such a thing as a poltergeist, Professor John Markway—who has been studying mankind's fear of the unknown—leads a team into the house with plans of remaining there until they become convinced, one way or the other, as to the existence of the supernatural.

The presence of America's greatest stage actress of the time, Julie Harris, made clear that *the Haunting* was no ordinary thriller.

He persuades Luke, a cocky, cynical young man who has recently inherited Hill House, to join him. Theodora, a lesbian, is invited, owing to her reknown as a psychic. Rounding out the quartet is Eleanor, whose own house was once attacked by ghosts; her life history bears a curious resemblance to that of a woman who died in Hill House years earlier. Importantly, Markway chose the two women in part because they knew nothing of the house's reputation; thus, if they should experience poltergeists, this cannot be written off as due to prejudicial thinking.

No sooner have they arrived than strange things begin happening. Most prominently, inexplicable noises are heard, such as a child crying in a nearby room and groans of anguish from the attic areas. While nothing is specifically seen, the old mirrors, stained with age, provide reflections that hint at something eerie—existing in another dimension—that is undeniabaly "there." Eleanor feels as if the house has picked her out as the most vulnerable, a situation which pushes her into Theodora's comforting arms, even as Eleanor plays out a pre-ordained fate in which she will share the fate of her antecedent who lived here. Theodora points out to her companions, "Haven't you noticed how nothing in this house seems to move until you look away and then you just . . . catch something out of the corner of your eye?"

THE FILM:

With a budget of $1,400,000, *The Haunting* was one of the first significant attempts to rescue the supernatural thriller from the abyss of cheapness and mediocrity it had fallen into during the 1950s. Producer-director Robert Wise's first decision was to abolish all conventions of cinematic ghost stories, so he insisted there must be no intricate patterns of spiderwebs or ghastly gargoyles of the type that were already something of a cliché when Todd Browning employed them for the interior of Bela Lugosi's castle in *Dracula*. How much more effective to make a house that, in every respect, appeared ordinary, if opulent, and then make this setting seem terrifying through the reactions of offbeat but believable characters. The realistic settings are shot from expressionistic angles; languid camera movements in and out of scenes convey the characters' fears to us without the need for any dialogue to literally tell us (thus ruining the spell) that there is terror all around. Another key decision was that the ghosts must never be shown. Essentially, Wise combined the smartness of Shirley Jackson's novel with his own experiences working for Val Lewton at RKO, where he had directed *Curse of the Cat People* (1944), the eerie and spellbinding sequel to one of the great psychological horror films of all time. The house actually becomes the most significant character, rather than a mere setting, however horrific. When members of the quartet come to believe that the house is staring at them menacingly, we feel it is doing precisely that.

TRIVIA:

Though set in New England, *The Haunting* was shot entirely in England. Robert Wise had originally hoped to use the full title of Shirley Jackson's acclaimed novel, though he ultimately decided that it ought to be changed in order to avoid confusion with William Castle's low-budget thriller, *The House on Haunted Hill* (1958). Intriguingly, both movies were remade in 1999—quite disastrously—and released within two months of one another. The main problem, for each remake, is that in the age of state-of-the-art special effects, the filmmakers believed that they had to show, beginning early-on, the creatures. What made both films such beloved exercises in suspense was that they played off our collective fear of the unknown.

ALSO RECOMMENDED:

Wise's aforementioned *Curse of the Cat People* stands as a worthy sequel to its predecessor. Other great ghost stories include Lewis Allen's *The Uninvited* (1944), which includes Victor Young's haunting theme "Stella by Starlight," and Peter Medak's *The Changeling* (1979), in which George C. Scott comes into contact with what may be a palpable ghost or a sense of darkness within himself.

25:

THE MUMMY (1932)

Universal Pictures

**"Do you have to open graves to find girls
to fall in love with?"**
—**Helen to Frank, who opened the princess's tomb**

CAST:

Boris Karloff (*Imhotep/Ardath Bey*); Zita Johann (*Helen Grosvenor/Princess Anckesen-Amon*); David Manners (*Frank Whemple*); Arthur Byron (*Sir Joseph Whemple*); Edward Van Sloan (*Doctor Muller*); Bramwell Fletcher (*Norton*); Noble Johnson (*The Nubian*); Kathryn Byron (*Frau Muller*); Leonard Mudie (*Pearson*); James Crane (*The Pharaoh*); Eddie Kane (*Doctor LeBarron*); Tony Marlow (*Police Inspector*); C. Montague Shaw (*Englishman*).

CREDITS:

Director, Karl Freund; screenplay, Nina Wilcox Putnam, Richard Schayer, John L. Balderston; producers, Carl Laemmle Jr. and Stanley Bergerman; original music, James Dietrich, with additional stock musical tracks by Michel Brusselmans, Heinz Roemheld, and (uncredited) Pyotr Ilyich Tchaikovsky (from the ballet "Swan Lake"); cinematographer, Charles Stumar; editor, Milton Carruth; art director, Willy Pogany; special makeup effects, Jack P. Pierce; special visual effects, John P. Fulton; running time, 72 min.

THE PLOT:

Death, the ancients believed, is the door to new life. With that opening line, we join an archaeological expedition as it leaves England in the mid-twenties for Egypt. The plan is to dig up Imhotep, buried alive for casting eyes on the forbidden princess. The casket in which he's found bears a cryptic statement: death will come to any who dare open this box. They do, releasing the being within, who then journeys to London in a new guise ("Ardath Bay") and becomes obsessed with a beautiful young woman, Helen, who is a precise ringer for his lost love. She finds herself in a hypnotic state, attempting to understand why she's now threatened by

Boris Karloff and Zita Johnson share a love that spans the centuries.

strange dreams and memories of some other woman from centuries ago. Only when the ancient goddess Isis appears and destroys Bay can Helen be reunited with her fiancé, Frank, and attempt to regain her old self and conventional life.

THE FILM:

Like most Universal thrillers from the early thirties, this was a tightly budgeted item, shot for just under $196,000. *The Mummy* appeared shortly after *Dracula* and *Frankenstein* rated as huge hits for the studio, then in deep financial trouble owing to the Great Depression. Producer Carl Laemmle (Sr.) had become concerned about the element of violence and the horrific impact on audiences of his silents starring Lon Chaney (Sr.), and had considered abandoning such projects. Had he gone through with this plan, Universal most likely would not have survived the difficult times. Fortunately, his son, Carl, Jr., was devoted to the thriller form, and convinced his father to put all their resources behind such films. Whereas most of the early Universal sound chillers rate as monster movies, thus not precisely right (their high quality notwithstanding) for this book, *The Mummy* plays like a predecessor to the Val Lewton thrillers, based on what J.P. Telotte calls "the presence of absence." We never actually see the Mummy, in his crumbling bandages, closely. Perhaps the most effective scene in the film (and one of the most thrilling sequences ever shot) occurs when a young man who has opened the forbidden tomb of Imhotep, sits at a desk, writing. The camera cuts back and forth from him to the Mummy, in shadows and surreal lighting, stirring. Yet when the creature approaches the Englishman, we do not see the menacing figure, only its shadow as it falls across the stunned interloper who, after a moment of shock, begins to laugh madly at the sight. The Mummy stumbles away, and the camera follows, as if attempting to catch up with this thing before it can exit. When our line of vision finally reaches the door, all we see is one long bandage as it drags out the doorway, while the Englishman's hysterical laughter continues.

TRIVIA:

Though the film conveys the authentic appearance of an Egyptian desert, it was shot in the Mojave Desert and in and around Red Rock Canyon, California. The credits suggest this is an "original screenplay," but *The Mummy* is a scene-by-scene remake of *Dracula*. One of *The Mummy*'s screenwriters, John Balderston, had penned the popular *Dracula* stage play that served as source for Universal's Bela Lugosi vehicle; here, Balderston reimagined the story with a mummy substituted for the vampire, largely because King Tut's tomb had recently been discovered and was much in the news at the time. Edward Van Sloan, who played vampire-hunter Dr. Von Helsing a year earlier, portrayed the mummy hunter Dr. Muller here; some of his dialogue is identical to the first film. The film's enormous popularity led to a long string of mummy movies at Universal, mostly starring Lon Chaney (Jr.), though they are in fact *not* sequels to this movie; in them, the Mummy—like Frankenstein's monster, Dracula, and the Wolfman—is regularly "seen," rendering them horror movies rather than suspense-thrillers. Also, he is named "Kharis," not "Imhoptep." Karl Freund had served as Todd Browning's cameraman on *Dracula*, and here made his directing debut. His last significant job was serving as cinematographer for TV's *I Love Lucy* in the 1950s.

ALSO RECOMMENDED:

Though they are more horror movies than suspense-thrillers, fans of the original will want to catch *The Mummy's Hand* (1940) with Tom Tyler and *The Mummy's Tomb* (1942) with Lon Chaney, Jr.; both contain stock footage from Freund's original, particularly for the flashback sequences. Chaney, Jr., incidentally, came up with the idea (working with Jack Pierce, Universal's makeup genius) of actually showing the Mummy moving in bandages.

24:

THE SIXTH SENSE (1999)

Hollywood Pictures

> **"I see dead people!"**
> **—Cole Sear**

CAST:

Bruce Willis (*Malcolm Crowe*); Toni Collette (*Lynn Sear*); Haley Joel Osment (*Cole Sear*); Olivia Williams (*Anna Crowe*); Donnie Wahlberg (*Vincent Grey*); Mischa Barton (*Kyra Collins*); Glenn Fitzgerald (*Sean*); Trevor Morgan (*Tommy Tammisimo*); Bruce Norris (*Cole's Teacher*); Peter Tambakis (*Darren*); Jeffrey Zubernis (*Bobby*); Greg Wood (*Collins*); Angelica Torn (*Mrs. Collins*).

CREDITS:

Director, M. Night Shyamalan; screenplay, Shyamalan; producers, Kathleen Kennedy, Frank Marshall and Barry Mendel; original music, James Newton Howard; cinematographer, Tak Fujimoto; editor, Andrew Mondshein; production design, Larry Fulton; special art effects, Stan Winston Studio; running time, 107 min.; rating, PG-13.

THE PLOT:

After receiving an award for excellent work as a child psychologist, Malcolm Crowe returns home to his upscale Philadelphia townhouse. He and his lovely wife plan to celebrate, but a distraught former patient slips inside and shoots Malcolm. Some time later, devastated, he wanders the streets, attempting to put his interrupted life back in order. Malcolm hopes to achieve this by accepting a bizarre case and

"I see dead people."

bringing a sad little boy back in touch with reality. Cole Sear suffers from the same problem as the man who shot Crowe: he claims to see dead people, walking on earth in a state of confusion, always among us though unseen by the average person. The child tells Crowe the dead don't even realize they are dead, attempting to reconnect with the living. The case soon comes to consume Crowe, much to the chagrin of his wife, who grows estranged.

Cole is drawn into a subtle emotional kinship with the child's mother, who cannot grasp what she should do about her boy's problems. Crowe finds himself growing ever more isolated from everyone in the world he once inhabited, and realizes his wife is involved with another man, who doesn't even bother to speak with Crowe when pursued by him. Attempting to rekindle his relationship with his wife, Crowe realizes, upon seeing a wedding ring that no longer fits on either spouse's hand, the child he was attempting to help has been attempting to help him. Crowe was not wounded but killed in the opening incident. Ever since, he has been one of the ghosts Cole sees.

THE FILM:

The nasty thrillers, more violent than suspenseful, had become popular: *The Texas Chain Saw Massacre* (1974), *Halloween* (1978, #56), *Night of the Living Dead* (1968), *Friday the 13th* (1980), *The Hills Have Eyes* (1977), and *A Nightmare on Elm Street* (1984), along with endless sequels and imitations. Such stuff had finally run its course by the mid-nineties. Still, audiences crave a good thriller, so the form was awaiting the right person to reinvent it. That proved to be M. Night Shyamalan, born in India and raised in an exclusive Philadelphia suburb (his parents were doctors). From childhood, he idolized Steven Spielberg even as that filmmaker had worshipped the greats of the past: Hawks, Ford, Hitchcock, and Disney. Like Spielberg, Shyamalan began as a director with projects he shot in his own backyard with a Super-8 camera. His first theatrical effort, *Wide Awake* (1998)—which he wrote, produced, and directed—led to the eerie attempt at dealing with children that would mark his masterpiece to date, *The Sixth Sense*.

Bruce Willis wears the same clothing throughout the film he had on in the opening, which makes no realistic sense. This fits in perfectly with the pay-off when we see the falling ring and realize he is himself a ghost. Likewise, we then understand why none of the living people in the film spoke with him. The movie's greatness is that most people do not notice this when watching for the first time. This qualifies *The Sixth Sense* as being a modern suspense thriller in the tradition that had been initiated by *The Cabinet of Dr. Caligari* (1919). Never does the director withold important information, for that would be "cheating." Everything that we need to know is there before us, if only we would "open our eyes."

TRIVIA:

The Sixth Sense has some amazing parallels to an earlier Bruce Willis vehicle, *Twelve Monkeys* (1995). In that film, also set in Philadelphia, there is also a character named Cole who announces, "I see dead people." As to the setting, Shyamalan set this film, as well as *Wide Awake* (1998) and *Unbreakable* (2000), in that city because he had lived and worked there for years, feeling that he knew it well enough to allow Philadelphia to emerge as a totally believable rather than arbitrary setting. However, some scenes were not shot in that city, causing a notable geographical problem for anyone who is also familiar with Philadelphia; at one point, Cole and his mother talk heatedly in an Acme parking lot, and there are mountains in the background, not possible anywhere in the Philly area.

ALSO RECOMMENDED:

Perhaps the greatest of all earlier ghost stories is Lewis Allen's *The Uninvited* (1944), in which Ray Milland and Ruth Hussey realize that the home they move into is inhabited by an "other." Also catch David Koepp's *A Stir of Echoes* (1999, from a thirty-five-year-old novel by Richard Matheson, who also wrote many *Twilight Zone* episodes) in which Kevin Bacon faces yet another "other."

23:

THE BIRDS (1963)

Universal Pictures

"Are the birds going to eat us, Mommy?"
—The Magruder Children

CAST:

Tippi Hedren (*Melanie Daniels*); Rod Taylor (*Mitch Brenner*); Jessica Tandy (*Lydia*); Suzanne Pleshette (*Annie Hayworth*); Veronica Cartwright (*Cathy*); Ethel Griffies (*Mrs. Bundy*); Charles McGraw (*Sebastian*); Ruth McDevitt (*Mrs. Magruder*); Elizabeth Wilson (*Waitress*).

CREDITS:

Director, Alfred Hitchcock; screenplay, Evan Hunter, from the short story by Daphne du Maurier; producer, Hitchcock; sound consultant, Bernard Herrmann; cinematographer, Robert Burks; editor, George Tomasini; opening credits, James S. Pollak; sets and art design, Robert Boyle and George Milo; bird trainer, Ray Berwick; running time, 120 min.

THE PLOT:

In a San Francisco pet shop, Melanie Daniels, a wealthy jet-setter, bumps into Mitch Brenner, an attractive lawyer who doesn't approve of her flighty lifestyle. Intrigued by the only man who isn't overly impressed by her, Melanie buys him a pair of lovebirds and impulsively drives up to Bodega Bay, where Mitch lives with Lydia, his mother, and Cathy, his younger sister. No sooner does Melanie arrive, however, than she is attacked by a low-flying bird. The Brenners take her into their home to tend the wound; Melanie is befriended by Annie Hayworth, a local teacher who once hoped to become romantically involved with Mitch, though Lydia—a widow afraid of being alone—ended that.

While all attend a birthday party for Cathy, birds attack. Shortly, all of Bodega Bay is under attack and Mitch and Melanie are temporarily trapped in a local diner. During a lull, they make their way home, only to learn Annie is dead. Shortly, the family is isolated in the house, Mitch nailing boards to the windows to

The image of children in danger remains the most potent image in any thriller.

keep the creatures from entering. But birds slip in through the chimney, almost killing Melanie when she searches through the house at night. The following morning, during another lull, the family slips out to their car and Cathy, still carrying the lovebirds, hops in and they drive away.

THE FILM:

Psycho (1960) was a tough act to follow, and Hitchcock wanted to top it with a one-of-a-kind film unlike anything he, or anyone else, had done before. Hitchcock worked from a story by Daphne du Maurier, whose novels served as his sources for two previous projects—*Jamaica Inn* (1939), his final English film before leaving for America, and *Rebecca* (1940), his first for David O. Selznick. Hitchcock expanded the slight literary piece into an apocalyptic epic that dared deny the audience the sort of ending he'd provided in every previous thriller, up to and including *Psycho*. There is no explanation to the long-awaited question of why the birds are attacking.

This left audiences confused and unsatisfied. They had loved watching the film yet left hating it, feeling that for the first time, Hitchcock had let them down. Today, that ambiguity is at the very heart of *The Birds*'s reputation as a classic. Donald Spoto has compared the film to a two thousand year-old play of the same name, noting that "in both Aristophanes' *The Birds* and Hitchcock's, the community is torn apart by the inversion of the expected order of nature. It is in each case an extension of the inversion of nature that already exists when people confront one another's needs cavalierly." Hitchcock has noted that "it's a film about complacency," suggesting that blasé attitudes of the main characters—and most of us— to natural surroundings will in time backfire on us as ecology goes mad from misuse and neglect.

TRIVIA:

Though many viewers at the time believed birds were a new concept for Hitchcock, he had in fact employed them as a foreshadowing of terror as early as *Blackmail* (1929), in which a seemingly average young woman who has just committed a brutal murder is awoken from her troubled sleep by the incessant screeching of a bird. Hitchcock employed bird imagery in *Psycho* (1960), Norman Bates constantly framed with stuffed birds peering over his shoulder. There is no musical score in *The Birds*, though Bernard Herrmann—who supplied the music for so many Hitchcock movies—oversaw the careful manipulation of sound effects with Remi Gassman and Oskar Sala. Three kinds of birds were used for the film: real, mechanical, and animated. The latter were designed by Ub Iwerks, a pioneer of the animation film who was once partnered with Walt Disney. Unknown TV model Tippi Hedren was chosen for the film when Hitchcock couldn't talk Grace Kelly into returning to Hollywood and Audrey Hepburn turned the role down owing to the potential danger. Hedren almost lost an eye during the full week she was forced to spend eight hours a day being mauled by real birds; Hitchcock originally planned to use mechanical ones for this sequence but felt they looked phoney. Hitchcock had long refused to make this movie, not wanting to do a film that would fall into either the science-fiction or horror genres. Only when one of his assistants provided him with newspaper clippings that chronicled actual bird attacks did he become interested, believing his thrillers must always be grounded in a possible reality—even if the term "realism" does not describe his flamboyant approach to almost all of the American movies, with only *The Wrong Man* (1957) excepted.

ALSO RECOMMENDED:

Fans of Tippi Hedren's performance will want to catch her only other work for Hitchcock, *Marnie* (1964), which has long divided viewers. People fall into two camps, some considering it his worst movie ever, others viewing the film as his most unappreciated masterpiece.

22:

DOUBLE INDEMNITY (1944)

Paramount Pictures

> **"I never knew that murder could smell like honeysuckle."**
> —Walter Neff

CAST:

Fred MacMurray (*Walter Neff*); Barbara Stanwyck (*Phyllis Dietrichson*); Edward G. Robinson (*Barton Keyes*); Porter Hall (*Mr. Jackson*); Jean Heather (*Lola Dietrichson*); Tom Powers (*Mr. Dietrichson*); Byron Barr (*Nino Zachetti*); Richard Gaines (*Norton*); Fortunio Bonanova (*Sam Garlopis*); John Philliber (*Peters*); Clarence Muse (*Man*).

CREDITS:

Director, Billy Wilder; screenplay, Wilder and Raymond Chandler, from a novel by James M. Cain; producers, Buddy G. DeSylva and Joseph Sistrom; original music, Miklós Rózsa, cinematographer, John Seitz; editor, Doane Harrison; art directors, Hans Dreier and Hal Pereira; running time, 106 min.

THE PLOT:

Disheveled, Walter Neff staggers into his insurance office one night, sits down at his desk, and begins dictating an elaborate confession. Neff relates a bizarre, convoluted story about how he arrived at the home of Dietrichson, an autombobile insurance client. The man isn't home, but Neff encounters Dietrichson's seductive wife Phyllis, who married him after nursing his ill first wife and, as we eventually learn from Dietrichson's daughter, killing the woman. Phyllis proposes a scheme in which she would secretly buy a life insurance policy for her unknowing husband, then do away with him. Though Neff suggests it might as well contain a double indemnity clause—paying twice if the husband is killed under unlikely circumstances—he turns down her offer. No sooner has he returned home, however, than he realizes he's obsessed with both the woman and the plot.

After he and Phyllis have become lovers, Neff strangles Dietrichson in his car when Phyllis drives her husband to the train station. Disguising himself with crutches and a hat, Neff rides the train himself, pretending to be Dietrichson, so when the real Dietrichson's body is discovered near the tracks, people will believe he fell from the speeding train. At the office, Neff's mentor, Keyes, immediately senses something is amiss, little realizing—at first—that Neff is the culprit. Finally, Neff—believing Phyllis plans to dump him—confronts her in her home. Each shoots the other. Neff staggers back to the office where he is confronted by Keyes, who has finally put all the pieces together.

Edward G. Robinson grows suspicious: note that the door opens from the wrong side!

THE FILM:

Double Indemnity exemplifies a script that was originally far ahead of its time, finally reaching the screen when society-at-large caught up with its dark implications. Throughout the 1930s, several producers considered filming James M. Cain's dazzlingly nasty novel, though its point of view didn't seem right for a public that loved the tragic-realism of gangster epics and escapism of Busby Berkeley musicals.

Having arrived in America with his European sophistication intact, Wilder sensed a sea change coming, and hoped to induce Cain himself to work with him on the screenplay. When this didn't work, Wilder then hired Raymond Chandler, whose novels—including *The Big Sleep*—conveyed a similar glib wise-guy attitude.

Wisely, Wilder simplified the book's complex ending, which had caused readers to go over the material several times to try and figure out what happened. The relationship between Neff and Keyes, perfunctory in the book, was given a warmer tone, allowing for a mass audience to feel some sort of honest emotion, always essential for a successful commercial film. Deciding to tell the story in flashback, with voice-over by the antihero, set the pace for many of the noirs to follow. Also influential was the tough guy's tendency to refer to his illicit lover as "baby." Perhaps most remarkable is Wilder's ability to keep us on the edge of our seats, worrying about two characters who, in fact, we morally despise. This was an innovation which, owing to the film's success, revolutionized Hollywood. In particular, the concept of the film noir woman was forever solidified when Phyllis casually remarks, "I'm rotten to the heart," and this only turns on Neff all the more. Outside of Hitchcock's films, no one has ever so beautifully portrayed the desire for the fall. As we soon see, Neff—who was successful and didn't really need the money—may actually hate rather than love Phyllis. What he wants is an escape from his overly conventional life, and is willing (indeed, eager!) to destroy himself to achieve that moment of intense passion. He and Phyllis want to commit adultery, want to kill, want to get caught, and want to be punished!

TRIVIA:

The edge-of-your-seat scene in which Neff can't get the car started after killing the husband is not in the shooting script. Wilder improvised the incident the day after he finished filming and was about to head home but his own car wouldn't start. If a mark of a great filmmaker is his ability to "cheat" on occasion, then Wilder certainly fits the bill. The intensely suspenseful scene in which Phyllis hides behind an open door while Neff stands in the doorway and Keyes is in the hallway is patently impossible, since doors in Los Angeles hotels and rooming houses always open *into* the room, not the other way around. While shooting, Fred MacMurray forgot to take off his wedding ring; this conflicts with the fact that Neff is not and has never been married. Cain based his story on an actual Queens, New York case from 1927, in which Judd Grey and Ruth Snyder murdered her husband Albert for the insurance money.

ALSO RECOMMENDED:

Among Wilder's most memorable thrillers are the legendary *Sunset Boulevard* (1950), and *Witness for the Prosecution* (1957), arguably the greatest courtroom thriller ever made.

21:
ALIEN (1979)

20th Century Fox

"In space, no one can hear you scream."
—advertising tag line

CAST:

Sigourney Weaver (*Ripley*); Tom Skerritt (*Dallas*); Veronica Cartwright (*Lambert*); Harry Dean Stanton (*Brett*); John Hurt (*Kane*); Ian Holm (*Ash*); Yaphet Kotto (*Parker*).

CREDITS:

Director, Ridley Scott; screenplay, Dan O'Bannon and Ronald Shusett and (uncredited) Walter Hill; producers, Gordon Carroll, David Giler and Walter Hill; music, Jerry Goldsmith; cinematographer, Derek Vanlint; editors, Terry Rawlings and Peter Weatherley; production design, Michael Seymour; running time, 117 min.; rating, R.

THE PLOT:

Aboard the commercial spaceship Nostromo, seven travelers rise from their plastic pods and go about the unglamorous business of piloting their cargo from one planet to another. They make the mistake of setting down on an unknown planet, where an octopus-like creature slaps against the mouth of one crew member, Ash. The thing is ripped off and, shortly, they are back in space. Then, Ash literally explodes; the "thing" implanted a seed in his mouth, which has grown inside Ash and escapes—a small but horrific alien that hides in the ventilation shaft.

The alien doesn't remain small for long. As it grows, the thing tracks down and devours each member of the crew. The closest thing to a traditional hero, Dallas, goes up against the creature in a one-to-one duel and loses. In time, Ripley and the cat are the only ones left alive. She must play a game of cat and mouse with the creature, finally tricking it: Ripley opens a hatch and sends the creature off into space. Then, Ripley and her cat go to sleep in a space pod, hoping in time to be rescued.

THE FILM:

Alien offered a unique way in which sci-fi film settings could revive one of the greatest of all suspense movie sub-genres: the haunted house film, in which diverse people are, one by one, eliminated by a vaguely glimpsed thing. Such stuff had its cinematic predecessors in James Whale's *The Old Dark House* (1932, #57) and *And Then There Were None* (1945, #51). The film from which *Alien* most directly derives is *It! The Terror from Beyond Space* (1958), a

Strong and sexy: Sigourney Weaver as the gorgeous woman who survives and defeats the alien after all the men are killed off.

less prestigious example of science fiction that terrified its audience with the claustrophobic concept of space travelers menaced by something aboard. In that film, the creature was one more tall man in a monster suit. Part of what makes *Alien* so effective is that special effects had reached a state of the art in which a totally unique creature—part insect, part lobster, part serpent—could be designed and fully realized by H.R. Giger.

Initially, Walter Hill—who worked uncredited on the script and is listed in the credits as one of the film's producers—was to have directed. Ridley Scott eventually brought his subtle, sumptuous style of shooting to the project. Scott's directorial approach is obvious from the film's first shot, opening up for us a wordless sequence in which the camera self-consciously roams the Nostromo, finding a bizarre beauty in the cold set designs. As the space travelers emerge from their technological cocoons, we experience a sense of spiritual as well as physical reawakening.

The characters are presented in a minimalist manner. There are no big speeches to reveal anyone's innermost desire, and no carefully crafted bits of action to reveal them to us. We must watch (as in every Ridley Scott film) their smallest moves in order to pick up the scant bits of information. This creates, despite the out-of-this-world setting, a sense of realism, for we feel we are glimpsing actual people, not all that different from ourselves, rather than (as in most sci-fi films films) a series of action movie archetypes.

Ripley was originally written with a male actor in mind. When any number of name stars turned down the role, it was finally assigned to Sigourney Weaver. There are no references in the film to Ripley's sexuality—despite the role being played by a beautiful woman—which, if accidentally, adds a feminist element; however attractive, Ripley is a person first, female only secondarily. Thus, she is an equal, valued by what she does, not what she looks like.

With this in mind, some critics complained about her stripping down to bikini bottom and T-shirt for her final alien encounter, arguing that this is sexist. Before the film was over, the producers had to show off Weaver's beautiful body. But however *sexy* the scene becomes, there is nothing *sexist* about it. In terms of film history in general, suspenseful sci-fi in particular, the moment plays as anti-sexist. Ordinarily in such films, when a woman's body is revealed, she is then reduced to the traditional victim figure, either devoured or saved by a male hero figure. Here, we witness the birth of the post-feminist woman on film, strong *and* beautiful. Ripley is anything but a victim, killing the creature and emerging victorious.

TRIVIA:

The cut of *Alien* released in America, both in theaters and on video, is missing a key scene present in all the other versions of the film that circulated across the globe. Near the end, Ripley discovers Dallas—half-eaten by the creature but still alive—and must accept that he's too far gone for her to save him. The brief sequence totally changes the film's mood, allowing for the film's only emotional interchange between characters.

ALSO RECOMMENDED:

The other great sci-fi action thriller is John McTiernan's *Predator* (1987) starring Arnold Schwarzenegger as a male Ripley.

20:

THE MALTESE FALCON (1941)

Warner Bros.

> **"I won't play the sap for you . . . you killed Miles, and you're going over for it!"**
> **—Sam Spade**

CAST:

Humphrey Bogart (*Sam Spade*); Mary Astor (*Brigid O'Shaughnessy*); Peter Lorre (*Joel Cairo*); Sydney Greenstreet (*Kasper Gutman*); Gladys George (*Iva*); Barton MacLane (*Lt. Dundy*); Elisha Cook, Jr. (*Wilmer*); Ward Bond (*Detective Polhaus*); Lee Patrick (*Effie*); Jerome Cowan (*Archer*); Walter Huston (*Jacobi*).

CREDITS:

Director, John Huston; screenplay, Huston, from the novel by Dashiell Hammett; producer, Hal B. Wallis; music, Adolph Deutsch; cinematographer, Arthur Edeson; editor, Thomas Richards; running time, 100 min.

THE PLOT:

Calling herself "Miss Wonderly," an attractive woman shows up at the detective agency owned by Sam Spade and Miles Archer, hiring them to protect her sister from a man named Floyd Thursby. That night, Archer goes on a stake-out and is killed by an unseen assassin. The police believe Sam may be guilty, for he's been having an affair with Archer's wife, Effie. Actually, Spade felt guilty about the affair, so he sets out to clear himself and bring his partner's killer to justice. Spade tracks down his client, whose real name is Brigid O'Shaugnessy. She admits the entire "case" was made-up, and Sam allows himself to be drawn into a romance, in part because he can't resist the lady's charms, also because he feels this may help him solve the crime.

Meanwhile, people stalk Spade, including an effeminiate little man called "Joel Cairo" and Wilmer Cook, a punk who fancies himself to be a tough guy. Both work for mysterious Casper Gutman, a.k.a. "The Fat Man." Eventually, Gutman tells Spade that the happenings stem from his desire to locate the fabulously valuable black bird of the title, an object the Knights of Malta hid away centuries ago. Brigid double-crossed them, and they believe she has taken Spade into her confidence, though he knows nothing. Captain Jacobi of the ship *Paloma* arrives in Spade's office fatally wounded, handing over the falcon before he dies. All the principles gather, and Spade suggests Wilmer ought to take the rap for the murders so the rest can split the profits they will make by selling the Falcon. But the statue turns out to be a fake, so Gutman and Cairo head off to search for the real thing. Realizing it was Brigid who killed Miles, Spade turns her in to police officers Dundy and Polhaus.

THE FILM:

First-time director Huston borrowed what had been best about the dark Depression-era films of social realism, many featuring Bogie in supporting roles as dangerous gangsters. The gumshoe hero who emerged here was, in the words of Danny Peary, "part cavalier, part crumb; part hero, part heel; part smooth, part slimy." Sam Spade is not the simple hero of earlier Hollywood suspense stories, but a morally dubious and emotionally complicated figure. The film's thriller quality dominates—despite a careful consideration of diverse characters and deeply felt personal drama laced with sly and cynical comedy—owing to crackerjack editing. Huston and Thomas Richards revolutionized the editing style that had been in place since the successful introduction of sound in 1927, creating a rapid-fire sense of getting into a scene at the last possible moment, then out of it at as quickly as

Bogart, Peter Lorre, Mary Astor, and Sydney Greenstreet investigate the "black bird."

possible, which set the pace for a brisk, hipsterish approach that's dominated ever since. Perhaps most important of all, though, is the new concept of an American leading man: not conventionally attractive but undeniably sexy in an offbeat way. Though Bogart's Spade has often been described as cynical, that's not really true. He puts on a show for the world, having previously been a sentimentalist, and having been hurt owing to his vulnerability. However glib he may appear while turning Brigid in to the police—"If they hang you, I'll always remember you"—his cool exterior crumbles the moment that she has been led away. The stoney exterior is only a show; deep down, Spade is still the sentimentalist, though he would never let anyone (except the viewer) know this about himself.

TRIVIA:

Walter Huston, father of the writer-director, makes a brief cameo performance. Though he appears to be a screen veteran in his assured performance, Sydney Greenstreet—then sixty-two years old—made his movie debut here. Audiences were so enamored with the teaming of Greenstreet and Peter Lorre that Warner Bros. featured them not only in other Bogart vehicles, notably *Casablanca* (1942), but also a series of B-movies in which they were top-billed, the best being *The Verdict* (1946). Incidentally, *The Maltese Falcon* is the only detective movie ever made in which the hero never once does any detective work!

ALSO RECOMMENDED:

Huston's films are often played for suspense, and the other greatest is *The Asphalt Jungle* (1950). The second screen version of Hammett's book, William Dieterle's *Satan Met a Lady* (1936), is an excellent adaptation, with strong suspense, and might be considered a classic except that it pales in comparison to Huston's film. Novelist Ross Macdonald took the name of Spade's doomed partner, gave him a new first name ("Lew"), and made him the hero of a suspenseful series of books. The best, *The Moving Target*, was turned into a Paul Newman vehicle, *Harper* (1966), the character's last name changed to conform with the star's series of films that begin with the letter "h": *The Hustler* (1961), *Hud* (1963), and *Hombre* (1967) completing the quartet.

I9:

ROSEMARY'S BABY (1968)

Paramount Pictures

> **"Take your child, Rosemary!"**
> **—Minnie Castevet**

CAST:

Mia Farrow (*Rosemary Woodhouse*); John Cassavetes (*Guy Woodhouse*); Ruth Gordon (*Minnie Castevet*); Sidney Blackmer (*Roman Castavet*); Maurice Evans (*Hutch*); Ralph Bellamy (*Dr. Sapirstein*); Charles Grodin (*Dr. Hill*); Angela Dorian (as Victoria Vetri) (*Terri*); Patsy Kelly (*Laura-Louise*); Elisha Cook, Jr. (*Nicklas*); William Castle (*Man on the Street*).

CREDITS:

Director, Roman Polanski; screenplay, Polanski, from the novel by Ira Levin; producer, William Castle; music, Christopher Komeda; cinematographer, William Fraker; editors, Sam O'Steen and Robert Wyman; production design, Richard Sylbert; running time, 136 min.; rating, R.

Mia Farrow as Rosemary.

THE PLOT:

A pair of newlyweds move into New York's posh, handsome Bramford hostelry, only to learn they are among the few young people living there. The old folks are charming, though, welcoming Guy Woodhouse, an aspiring actor, and his pretty, sheltered wife Rosemary, into the busy community of upscale Manhattanites. The pair quickly realize that chatty Minnie and her somber husband Roman are the titular heads of this aged elite. Though Rosemary feels vaguely uncomfortable with the new lifestyle, her husband quickly falls in with his newfound acquaintances, making Rosemary feel isolated, for she has few friends in the Big Apple.

Rosemary and Guy make love one night. During sex, her husband appears to take on aspects of the Devil, though the following morning she assumes that was only a drug-induced bad dream. Soon, she's pregnant, and at first overjoyed. Then, the attitude of her neighbors—acting as if the baby is more theirs than hers—spooks Rosemary. In time, she comes to believe Guy was possessed by the Devil that night when their unborn child was conceived. When Rosemary attempts to tell this to elderly Dr. Sapirstein or young Dr. Hill, both men try to convince her this is only a form of paranoia brought on by her pregnant state.

Rosemary tries to accept this. But when she tells her one trusted friend, Hutch, and he believes she may be right, he turns up dead. After giving birth, she realizes Guy did take on the role of Faust, selling his soul to these modern witches and warlocks to gain popularity in his profession. In return, Guy promised the child—Satan's spawn—to the coven. At first, Rosemary believes she must kill her own baby. But motherhood wins out. Whoever the father is, her will breaks down as she lovingly cares for "the child."

THE FILM:

The well-deserved critical and commercial success of *Rosemary's Baby*, a prestigious release from a major studio, serves as a perfect illustration of how the film business was changing drastically during the late 1960s. Shortly after Ira Levin's novel first appeared, schlockmeister William Castle (see *Homicidal*, 1961, #98) optioned the film rights, hoping to turn this into a low-budget film. When he brought the project to Paramount in hopes of securing financing and to direct it himself, head honcho Robert Evans agreed to back the film only if it were given to a more prestigious director, with Castle serving solely as producer. He agreed to the arrangement, and Roman Polanski was brought on board.

With its prestigious cast, *Rosemary's Baby* also marked a key change in attitude toward what had until recently been considered material worthy of only a junk-movie approach, explaining why Castle had thought the novel would provide perfect fodder for his exploitation flicks. The horror film was about to finally regain the prestige that had been lost during the forties and fifties, when major stars and directors refused to have anything to do with this genre or its cousin, the science-fiction flick. With *Rosemary's Baby*, the satanic-thriller regained its once lofty status. Also paving the way for such movies was the significant breakthrough of presenting "horror by daylight," gruesome and supernatural acts taking place in major American cities in the middle of the afternoon. The cliché of a shadow-world being necessary for a suspense film was finally dismissed as the awful events happen mostly on Park Avenue, as very realistic New Yorkers rush by, mistaking Rosemary for just another nut case.

At the time, many observers took the film as an allegory for the era's youth movement, in which the young are corrupted by the old. Certainly, the theme has much in common with Hitchcock's films, for he often employed the idea of a newlywed couple—from *Suspicion* to *Marnie*—to intellectually and artistically analyze aspects of sexual insecurity within the "safe" confines of a suspenseful entertainment. Doubtless, Hitchcock would have been far happier with the stars originally slated for the leads: Jane Fonda and Robert Redford. Farrow looks so emaciated even at the film's opening that comments about her dissipated appearance later on does not ring entirely true, while Cassavetes has such a devilish appearance that we suspect him immediately; Fonda would have looked lush and healthy in her early scenes as Rosemary, then gradually been made to look ever less so as the film wore on, while Redford's genial charms would have made audiences loathe to believe he had struck a deal with the devil.

TRIVIA:

The voice of the unseen man speaking on the phone belongs to Tony Curtis. The hotel that "plays" the Bramford in the movie is the Dakota (actually an apartment building).

ALSO RECOMMENDED:

One of the least known (other than among cineaste circles) but finest thrillers on the subject of witchcraft in the real world is Danish director Carl Dreyer's *Day of Wrath* (1943).

18:

STRANGERS ON A TRAIN (1951)

Warner Bros.

"What if we were to trade murders?"
—Bruno Anthony to Guy Haines

CAST:

Farley Granger (*Guy Haines*); Ruth Roman (*Ann Morton*); Robert Walker (*Bruno Anthony*); Leo G. Carroll (*Senator Morton*); Patricia Hitchcock

(*Barbara Morton*); Laura Elliott (*Miriam Haines*); Marion Lorne (*Mrs. Anthony*); Jonothan Hale (*Mr. Anthony*).

CREDITS:

Director, Alfred Hitchcock; screenplay, Raymond Chandler and Czenzi Ormonde, adaptation by Whitfield Cook, from the novel by Patricia Highsmith; original music, Dimitri Tiomkin; cinematographer, Robert Burks; special photographic effects, H.F. Koenekamp; editor, William H. Ziegler; running time, 101 min. (American print), 103 min. (British print).

THE PLOT:

Double cross: Farley Granger and Robert Walker.

Tennis star Guy Haines hops aboard a Washington-New York train and finds himself seated across from Bruno Anthony, a glib, cynical young man. Bruno steers the conversation toward murder. He would like his father dead and, from reading newspapers, knows that the celebrity athlete is estranged from his wife Miriam and would like to marry Ann, the daughter of a prominent senator. Guy treats all this like a bad-taste joke and returns to his normal life. So far as Bruno is concerned, however, they have cemented a pact.

Bruno stalks Miriam in an amusement park and kills her, then haunts Guy, insisting he must repay in kind. Guy, meanwhile, becomes the wrong man, as the police suspect him of having murdered Miriam. Guy becomes so distraught that he almost goes through with the murder, but cannot. Hoping to force Guy to comply with his part of the "bargain," Bruno decides to plant Guy's unique cigarette lighter—the film's MacGuffin—at the scene of the crime. The two fight on a roaring merry-go-round and Bruno is killed, at which point Guy is cleared of the crimes.

The Film:

Hitchcock's thrillers are based on the universality of guilt, and *Strangers on a Train* is no exception. Owing to his Jesuit background, Hitchcock disliked suspense films with what he called "a Protestant bent"—the protagonist a pure and heroic figure, while the villain was all bad. In his movies, the villain serves as what the Germans referred to as a doppelganger—the dark twin of a seemingly bright figure. Bruno is Guy's evil twin—evil not because he has murderous impulses (Guy would *love* to kill his wife!) but because he actually goes through with the terrible idea that the "hero" shares. What qualifies a character as a Hitchcock hero is not that he's free of dark desires, only that—in a Catholic sense—he represses them. The villain acts on his impulses.

In Patricia Highsmith's novel, Guy does go through with the murder. He and Bruno become involved in what is explicitly a homosexual relationship. This could not be filmed during Production Code days, so Hitchcock had to slyly suggest such things in the script. He and Raymond Chandler—the famed crime-novelist—didn't get along. For the author, it was necessary to first understand a character's motivations and then see where they led him. For the auteur, one set up a series of visual set-pieces—the murder of Miriam, photographed through her fallen glasses; the hysterical ride on an out of control carousel—then provided a plot that would acceptably connect them. Eventually, Hitchcock had to bring in other writers.

Throughout, Hitchcock tells the story with his camera. The idea of the male leads being doubles—matched pairs—is established in the opening sequence. Hitchcock jettisoned all of Highsmith's lengthy if effective descriptions and dialogue and concentrated his camera on each man's differing shoes, which define their unique personalities, one simple, the other natty. Hitchcock then cut back and forth between the men's legs as they walk, from opposite directions, toward the same coach on the train. This allows for a striking sense of destiny, implying at once that the two men were fated to meet—if only because, as we learn, Bruno had been after Guy for some time.

Hitchcock also continued his ongoing themes, including the idea of a dominating mother for the villain. Leo G. Carroll, who portrays the senator, was Hitchcock's favorite character actor, appearing in more of the master's suspense films than any other actor. Robert Walker was cast as Bruno because he had only played nice guys in the past, including lovable servicemen in such films as *Since You Went Away* (1944), *See Here, Private Hargrove* (1944), and *Bataan* (1943). Hitchcock loved to employ reverse-typecasting and thought it was fascinating to go against an audience's preconceptions of what any star represented onscreen.

TRIVIA:

Hitchcock had wanted William Holden for the male lead, but had to take Farley Granger, then under contract with Warner Bros. The studio also insisted that he use Ruth Roman for the female lead. This is one of two films (the other is *Psycho*, 1960, #1) that features Hitchcock's daughter Patricia in a key role. She also starred in the TV adaptation of "The Lady Vanishes," a variation on what Hitchcock often claimed was his all-time favorite story. Walker died suddenly while filming his next movie, *My Son John* (1952). To fill out that film, shots of him from *Strangers on a Train* were borrowed and edited in.

ALSO RECOMMENDED:

Fans of Hitchcock's films at this time will want to catch *I Confess* (1952), with Montgomery Clift as a priest who hears a murder while in the confessional and, owing to his vow of silence about anything learned in such a situation, cannot clear himself when accused of the crime. Farley Granger also starred for Hitchcock in *Rope* (1948).

17:

THE NIGHT OF THE HUNTER (1955)

United Artists

> **"It's a hard world for little things."**
> **—Rachel Cooper**

CAST:

Robert Mitchum (*Rev. Harry Powell*); Shelley Winters (*Willa Harper*); Lillian Gish (*Rachel Cooper*); James Gleason (*Birdie Steptoe*); Evelyn Varden (*Icey Spoon*); Peter Graves (*Ben Harper*); Don Beddoe (*Walt Spoon*); Billy Chapin (*John Harper*); Sally Jane Bruce (*Pearl Harper*); Gloria Castilo (*Ruby*); Corey Allen (*Tough Young Punk*); Paul Bryar (*The Hangman*); Gloria Pall (*Hoochie-Koochie Girl*).

CREDITS:

Director, Charles Laughton; screenplay, Laughton (uncredited) and James Agee, from the novel by Davis Grubb; producer, Paul Gregory; original music, Walter Schumann; cinematographer, Stanley Cortez; editor, Robert Golden; art director, Hilyard Brown; running time, 93 min.

THE PLOT:

Harry Powell, a demented preacher, travels the Depression-era South, sermonizing about sins of the flesh. He's also a serial killer who murders the sensuous women he isn't able to enjoy, using his switch blade knife as a substitute (and violent) phallus. Eventually, Powell is thrown into prison, where he shares a cell with young

The dead of night: Director Charles Laughton revived the style of German Expressionism for the wedding night sequence.

Ben Harper, awaiting execution for the robbery of ten-thousand dollars and inadvertant killing of a bank guard. After release, Powell shows up in Harper's sleepy river town, spellbinding inhabitants with an archly allegorical presentation of the struggle between good and evil. Powell, who has the letters L-O-V-E tatooed on his right hand and H-A-T-E on his left, provides a wrestling match in which the sinister side is defeated.

He woos the widow Willa Harper, much to the delight of the townspeople, though her son John grows suspicious of Powell's motives. Gradually, John comes to realize Powell has joined their household to find the hiding place of the money, which—unbeknownst to anyone but the children—has been stuffed inside little Pearl's rag doll. On their wedding night, Powell made clear he has no intentions of sexually embracing his new wife. Willa responds by falling into an ecstasy of repressed emotions, followed by her desire to be clean in the eyes of her Lord. But when she catches Powell abusing the children, he must kill her, pretending she has run off; her dead body—in the family car—now sits at the bottom of the river. John and Pearl must make a desperate journey downriver, past hordes of starving children and destitute farms, with Powell in pursuit.

Eventually, the children are sheltered by elderly Rachel Cooper, who lives in a shoe-like house and has so many adopted children that she doesn't know what to do. Still, she keeps them busy at work, always clean and well if simply fed, with Bible stories as entertainment in the evening. John fears the good book, owing to Powell. But when the crazed preacher arrives to take back the children, Rachel—a stalwart holdover from an earlier age of principles and values—seizes her shotgun and defends them from the monstrous man.

The Film:

When executives at United Artists took a close look at the film, they had no idea what to do with it. In desperation, they released it as a Saturday matinee movie. Thus, children and pre-teens caught the movie at a point in time when their psyches were particularly vulnerable to such a brilliant but unsettling shocker. It's not hard to understand why a film that was considered both a commercial and critical disaster at the time of release has emerged as a towering American classic, referenced in much of pop culture. Billy Joel pays homage to the man with L-O-V-E tatooed on the one hand and H-A-T-E on the other in his song "Cautious Man," while Spike Lee recounts in detail his impressions of seeing the film in one of his own best movies, *Do the Right Thing* (1989).

The Night of the Hunter contains many of the most memorable images in the history of Hollywood, beginning with the downward angle on children playing hide-and-go-seek, only to happen upon a mutilated female body; the death of innocence has never been more vividly portrayed onscreen. When Harry Powell brings his new wife into their wedding chamber, the imagery—as stark as anything in a German Expressionist film from the Weimar Republic—is framed to recall a cathedral. Nothing in the film is so nightmarish yet believable as the image of the widow Harper, in her car at the bottom of the river, her long hair dreamily moving in perfect synchronization with the weeds as they twist and turn in the current. One innovation that somehow works is the jarring juxtapositions of ultra-realistic shots of the devastated rural-South landscapes with stylized interiors recalling the grotesque alternative-world of a Francis Bacon painting. Nothing quite compares to the languidly lovely moment when the fleeing children, falling asleep in their little boat, are photographed through a spider's web.

TRIVIA:

The film was shot in and around Moundsville, West Virginia. The role of the teenager who tries to seduce "Ruby" is played by Corey Allen; that same year, he was "Buzz," the ill-fated wise guy who loses the chickie race to James Dean in *Rebel Without a Cause*. Though the script is credited to James Agee, film critic for *The Nation*, Laughton hated what Agee handed him, threw it away, and rewrote everything. Originally, Mitchum's character was to have been even more menacing, though Hollywood executives feared this would permanantly damage his leading-man status.

ALSO RECOMMENDED:

Though Laughton directed no other films, his remarkable presence adds to the thrills of numerous movies, including *Island of Lost Souls* (1933, #40) and Hitchcock's *Jamaica Inn* (1939).

16:

TAXI DRIVER (1976)

Columbia Pictures

> **"You talkin' to me?"**
> —**Travis Bickle**

CAST:

Robert De Niro (*Travis Bickle*); Jodie Foster (*Iris*); Cybill Shepherd (*Betsy*); Harvey Keitel (*Sport*); Steven Prince (*Andy*); Albert Brooks (*Tom*); Peter Boyle (*Wizard*); Leonard Harris (*Charles Palantine*); Diahnne Abbott (*Pretty Woman*); Martin Scorsese (*Man in Cab*).

CREDITS:

Director, Martin Scorsese; screenplay, Paul Schrader producers, Michael and Julia Phillips; original music, Bernard Herrmann; cinematographer, Michael Chapman; art director Charles Rosen; editors, Marcia Lucas, Tom Rolf, Melvin Shapiro; special visual consultant, David Nichols; running time, 113 min.; rating, R.

THE PLOT:

"Loneliness has followed me all my life," Travis Bickle writes in his diary, "I am God's lonely man." He drives a cab around New York, preferring the late night shift. On his circular, seemingly endless route, Travis observes what he considers the degeneracy of a Manhattan that has, in the past few years, entirely deteriorated. Sex is for sale everywhere; the city appears to be on the verge of a race war. Masochistically, Travis obsesses on this but refuses to get involved with anything, other than pathetic banter with other cabbies like Wizard. Until, that is, he meets a pair of antithetical women. Betsy is an upperclass liberal, running a campaign office for an aspiring presidential candidate; Iris is an underage street whore, under the control of her nasty pimp Sport. Ever his own worst enemy, Travis dates them both but makes the mistake of treating each woman as he should the other. The classy Betsy is dragged off to one of those very porn movies that Travis purports to hate, causing her to swiftly desert him. Meanwhile, the child-whore, Ivy, is treated as if she were a virgin, an approach that likewise backfires by offending a girl who only wants to trade sex for money. Alone again, unable to take responsibility for having blown both of these potential relationships, Travis goes over the edge.

He shaves his hair into a Mohawk, an early example of the "punk" look. He stalks the politician whom Betsy works for, planning an assassination. When federal agents thwart that, Travis turns his wrath on Sport and the other lowlives, killing them in a mass murder, walking away from the scene as a celebrity—precisely what Travis has always wanted, in that he escapes anonymity.

"You talkin' to me?"

THE FILM:

Though the movie was widely attacked on initial release as being exploitive in its violence, Martin Scorsese defended his approach by insisting it was an exploration of the violence that had come to define America in general, New York more specifically, by the mid-seventies and the alienation and anonymity that can lead to brutality. Travis, he explained, is "a guy who desperately needs to be recognized for *something*, but he has nothing he can do to gain the recognition . . . so finally, out of frustration, he turns to violence as a means of expressing himself." Violence, that is, perpetrated by those with an artistic sensibility but no corresponding talent.

Brought up with a strict Calvinist background, screenwriter Paul Schrader had enrolled in Calvin College in Grand Rapids, Michigan, before going AWOL and heading for New York, where he studied film at Columbia University. However New Yorkerish Travis Bickle and his milieu may be, Schrader has stated that his intention was "to take a hero from European fiction and film—whose essential dilemma is 'Should I exist'—and put him in an American street context." Particularly, the concept of an "underground man," based on a character in a novel by Russia's Fyodor Dostoevski. Schrader made the character a cabbie only after hearing Harry Chapin's song "Taxi" on the radio, incorporating elements of his own frustrated life as well.

Scorsese added an element of irony in his playing of Schrader's lines. At one point, Travis confides, in a voice-over, "I don't believe that one should devote one's life to morbid self-absorption." Whether Schrader actually meant that as darkly-comic is difficult to say, but Scorsese neatly played it against a visual tableau of Travis's total inability to relate, in any positive way, to the world. Ideas Travis (and perhaps Schrader) considered to be deep and profound are, in the film's context of neon lights on the wet concrete and mean streets, used to define a shallow man, isolated not because of the world but owing to something that exists within himself.

The film's first half develops as a character study of Travis and his awkward relationships. *Taxi Driver* intially appears to be shaping up as a realistic case-study of a face in the crowd. At mid-movie, Scorsese changes the tone and veers the film into a thriller mold, resulting in what Pauline Kael called "a movie in heat."

TRIVIA:

When Julia and Michael Phillips optioned Schrader's script, they originally hoped to put together a package with Jeff Bridges as Travis and Robert Mulligan (*To Kill a Mockingbird, Summer of '42*, 1962 and 1971) directing. After Scorsese was signed, the prospects of actually getting the movie made seemed so unlikely that, at one point, he seriously considered shooting it on videotape and in black and white. The film was finally shot for a mere $1.3 million. To prepare for the film, De Niro got a license and actually drove a cab. One of his passengers recognized him, and sadly said, "Wow, that's show business for you—an Oscar for *Godfather II* a year ago, and now you're reduced to driving a cab!" The famous "You talkin' to me?" scene was entirely improvised.

ALSO RECOMMENDED:

Not a thriller per se, Scorsese's early hit *Mean Streets* (1973) contains plenty of suspenseful scenes. Jean-Luc Godard's *Breathless* (1959) with Jean-Paul Belmondo was one of the films that inspired Schrader.

15:

NOTORIOUS (1946)

RKO Radio Pictures

> **"Why won't you believe me—just a little?"**
> **—Alicia to Devlin**

CAST:

Ingrid Bergman (*Alicia Huberman*); Cary Grant (*Devlin*); Claude Rains (*Alexander Sebastian*); Leopoldine Konstantin (*Mrs. Sebastian*); Louis Calhern (*Paul Prescott*); Reinhold Schunzel (*Dr. Anderson*); Fay Baker (*Girl*).

CREDITS:

Director, Alfred Hitchcock; screenplay, Ben Hecht, from an original idea by Hitchcock; producers, Hitchcock and Barbara Keon; original music, Roy Webb; cinematographer, Ted Tetzlaff; editor, Theron Warth; set design, Albert S. D'Agostino, Carroll Clark, Darrell Silvera, and Claude Carpenter; special visual effects, Vernon L. Walker; running time, 101 min.

THE PLOT:

As the war ends, a Nazi agent named Huberman is sent to prison in America. His daughter Alicia, who had never been a part of his plots, has no idea how she will be able to go on living in the U.S., as most people incorrectly associate her with her father. Alicia is given a chance to redeem herself. A government agent, Devlin, approaches her, asking Alicia to become an operative. She must go to Rio and seduce, then marry, Sebastian, an escaped Nazi, part of a ring operating in Latin America that hopes to create a Fourth Reich. To comply with Devlin, whom Alicia has fallen in love with, she agrees. Sebastian's dominating mother grows suspcious, and drugs Alicia to keep her quiet. Devlin must figure a way to get her—and the uranium the Nazis have acquired—out of the house and back to the United States.

The dominating mother induces her son to poison his wife in a typically atmospheric Hitchcock scene.

THE FILM:

Hitchcock and star Ingrid Bergman were at the time under contract to David O. Selznick, who literally sold them as part of a package to R.K.O. Films. Selznick received eighty-thousand dollars and half of the profits for a film that was budgeted at a then-hefty two million dollars but returned nine million at the box office. The movie's appeal was summed up by Bosley Crowther of the *New York Times:* "A romantic melodrama which is just about as thrilling as they come—velvet smooth in dramatic action, sharp and sure in its character and heavily charged with intensity . . . the distinction of *Notorious* is the remarkable blend of a love story with 'thriller.' "

Importantly, though, Hitchcock does not in any way tell a conventional love story. The "hero" is not named Devlin for nothing. He's something of a satanic figure, talking the heroine into becoming a virtual prostitute—which she does only because she loves him and will do anything she believes will please him—then treating her like dirt because she complied with his wishes. On the other hand, the "blocking character"—ordinarily the unpleasant husband who gets in the way of true love—is the most sincere, likable figure on view. Sebastian is a perfect gentleman absolutely adoring Alicia in a way the protagonist does not.

Devlin is unnecessarily cruel, and self-consciously insincere, right to the end. When Devlin and Alicia are trapped in the frightening mansion, Devlin insists that if Sebastian will help them to escape, he will take Sebastian (who has turned against his fellow conspirators) with him. Sebastian does everything he has been asked to do, but Devlin will not allow him to join Alicia and himself in the car, sending Sebastian back into the house to certain death. Simply, Devlin is the hero, Sebastian the villain, only because Devlin is on the American side and portrayed by charming Cary Grant, Sebastian the bad guy because he is on the wrong side (an accident of birth) and played by the less attractive Claude Rains. Hitchcock manipulates his audience's responses in unexpected ways, inducing us to root for a person who does terrible things (on a personal level) and against another who always tries his best to be nice.

The movie also contains what may be the greatest of all of Hitchcock's MacGuffins. In a central scene, Devlin must slip downstairs in the Sebastian home while a party takes place above. His mission is to find, in the wine cellar, the bottle that contains the "pumpkin"—uranium ore that the Nazis are hiding. Hitchcock then cuts back and forth between Grant, desperately searching, and the partygoers upstairs, downing great amounts of wine. This will necessitate the servers heading downstairs to get more, leaving Devlin vulnerable. The sequence is a masterful set-piece, one of the great examples of cinematic suspense, Hitchcockian or otherwise. In an early draft, written while the war was still raging, the contents of the bottle were to have been microfilm containing important secrets of the American government that are being transported, by Nazi spies, back to Germany. With the war over, Hitchcock briefly considered having the contents be diamonds, the bad guys smugglers rather than Nazis. When he learned that there were indeed "the boys in Brazil" (and elsewhere in Central and South America), Hitchcock shifted back to the Nazi theme, only this time updated the contents for the nuclear age. The point is, as he insisted, it doesn't matter what is inside that wine bottle, only that we belive it is valuable and that Devlin would risk his life to retrieve it.

TRIVIA:

The great Russian actress Leopoldine Konstantin did not care much for movies, preferring the stage. However, she agreed to do the film for the opportunity of working with Hitchcock, whom she considered a true genius.

ALSO RECOMMENDED:

Cary Grant's first appearance in a Hitchcock film was as the seemingly murderous husband in *Suspicion* (1941), also made while on loan to RKO.

14:

BELLE DE JOUR (1967)

Allied Artists

> **I cannot help myself."**
> **—Séverine**

CAST:

Catherine Deneuve (*Séverine Serizy*); Jean Sorel (*Pierre Serizy*); Michel Piccoli (*Henri Husson*); Geneviève Page (*Madame Anais*); Pierre Clémenti (*Marcel*); Françoise Fabian (*Charlotte*); Macha Méril (*Renee*); Muni (*Pallas*); Maria Latour (*Mathilde*); Michel Charrel (*Footman*); Iska Khan (*Asian Client*); Bernard Musson (*Majordomo*); Marcel Charvey (*Professor Henri*); François Maistre (*L'ensignant*); Francisco Rabal (*Hyppolite*); Georges Marchal (*Duke*); Dominique Dandrieux (*Séverine as a child*).

CREDITS:

Director, Luis Buñuel; screenplay, Buñuel and Jean-Claude Carrière, from a novel by Joseph Kessel; producers, Henri Baum, Raymond and Robert Hakim; cinematographer, Sacha Vierny; editor, Louisette Hautecoeur; production design, Robert Clavel; running time, 100 min.; rating, R.

THE PLOT:

Séverine is bored with her life as an upper-class Parisian housewife with a surgeon husband who can't satisfy her. She doesn't fancy to the idea of having an affair with one of her own "set"; that would not appear very classy if word were to get around. Yet she does have an open offer from Henri. What most attracts him to Séverine is her virtuous demeanor; though a close friend of her husband's, Henri considers the seduction of this blonde beauty to be his ultimate challenge. Perhaps that's why Séverine rejects his advances, though what she decides to do seems even less appropriate. While riding in a taxi, Séverine hears about a unique brothel, where the women are mostly non-professionals. Like Severine, they are vaguely dissatisfied with their comfortable lives and, one or two days a week, slip away from their elegant demimonde to become working girls. Each engages in anonymous sex with the various men—from wealthy business people to hideous gansters—who partake of this place and its lush, unknown women.

Madame Anais takes one look at Séverine's iceberg beauty and senses that, deep down below, a volcano is about to erupt. But why would Séverine do such a thing? Perhaps because, as a child, she was molested; then again, she may simply be a spoiled overgrown little girl who wants to have her cake and eat it too. Finally, there's the possibility that all this is merely a fantasy Séverine creates in her mind. That possibility seems less likely when a criminal client invades her home. This is only one of Séverine's problems; Henri, aware of Séverine's naughty exploits, has decided to tell her husband. Suddenly, all circumstances close in on the beautiful blonde, who realizes her ever intensifying situation can only be purged through violence.

Tie me up, tie me down! Catherine Deneuve suffers fantasies of bondage.

THE FILM:

Luis Buñuel began working in films when, in the 1920s, he left ultra-conformist Spain and landed in Paris at a time when avant-garde arts were the rage. He and a fellow surrealist, Salvador Dalí, concocted a seminal "alternative" film, *Un Chien Andalou* (1929), featuring an eyeball being cut by a razor. Bohemians loved it, but mainstream audiences were repulsed enough to condemn the film as dangerous. Over the next two decades, what had been scandalous would become a part of mainstream pop culture. In 1946, Hitchcock hired Dalí to create the dream sequence for his Hollywood extravaganza, *Spellbound*, starring Gregory Peck and Ingrid Bergman, produced by David O. Selznick. In it, paintings of eyeballs are likewise cut; no one complained.

Buñuel and Hitchcock have more in common than merely this single image and a onetime collaboration for each with Dalí. Hitchcock's films are, when considered closely, more surreal than they first seem, offering an image of the world in which nothing is what it seems; that has always been the trademark of the avant garde in general, Buñuel in particular. Always, Buñuel has offered his own variations on the Hitchcock blonde, a seemingly saintlike beauty who harbors secrets about her dark sexual past, whether it is Silvia Pinal in *Viridiana* (1961), shot in Spain, or Deneuve here. Deneuve's character is so clearly a Gallic incarnation of Grace Kelly, it's difficult to believe Hitchcock, after losing his longtime collaborator to the marriage with the Prince of Monaco, didn't choose her—seemingly impassive, though always about to explode—as his next great star.

Another Hitchcock touch is the film's MacGuffin, a small box which one of Séverine's clients brings into her bedroom. In a lengthy scene, he attempts to convince her that whatever is inside ought to be employed during the sexcapade, though she demurs. As the sequence continues, the audience longs to know what is in it. But like such boxes in Hitchcock movies—or, for that matter, Tarantino's *Pulp Fiction* (1994)—we are purposefully kept guessing. The film's sexuality, like its suspense, is subtle and muted, even as the film's "world" (a Paris that perhaps exists only in Séverine's imagination) becomes more dreamlike, sometimes pleasant, at other moments a nightmare.

TRIVIA:

In the scene featuring Séverine's rape by a crazed client, Deneuve's dress was fitted with Velcro in order to create the striking sound we hear as it's torn away from her. This and other costumes worn by Deneuve were created for her by the legendary Yves Saint-Laurent, so her elegantly icy appearance would be properly shown off.

ALSO RECOMMENDED:

Other world-class beauties are well represented in French thrillers that partake of the Hitchcock tradition. In Jean-Luc Godard's *Breathless* (1959), American expatriate Jean Seberg plays a modern femme fatale. Another New Wave writer-director, François Truffaut, cast Jean Moreau as a beauty who tracks, seduces, and kills the men who accidentally shot her husband on their wedding day in *The Bride Wore Black* (1968).

13:

HIGH NOON (1952)

United Artists

> **"There's a limit to what you can ask of a man!"**
> **—Baker**

CAST:

Gary Cooper (*Will Kane*); Grace Kelly (*Amy*); Thomas Mitchell (*Jonas Henderson*); Lloyd Bridges (*Harvey Pell*); Katy Jurado (*Helen Ramirez*); Otto Kruger (*Percy Mettrick*); Lon Chaney, Jr. (*Martin Howe*); Harry Morgan (*Fuller*); Ian MacDonald (*Frank Miller*) Lee Van Cleef (*Colby*); Sheb Wooley (*James Pierce*); Robert Wilke (*Ben Miller*); James Millican (*Baker*); Jack Elam (*Charlie*); Virginia Christine (*Mrs. Simpson*).

CREDITS:

Director, Fred Zinnemann; screenplay, Carl Foreman, from a short story by John W. Cunningham; producer, Stanley Kramer; original music, Dimitri Tiomkin, theme song by Tiomkin and Ned Washington, performed by Tex Ritter; cinematographer, Floyd Crosby; editor, Elmo Williams; art director, Rudolph Sternad; running time, 84 min.

THE PLOT:

Three killers—Pierce, Colby, and Ben Miller—ride into the small town of Hadleyville on a sleepy Sunday morning, heading directly for the train station. Word reaches the town marshal, who retired and married only moments earlier, that they are waiting for the arrival on the noon train of Miller's brother Frank, just released from prison. As Will sent Frank Miller up, there's little doubt that he's returning to murder the former marshal. Will's best friends, members of the wedding party, encourage Will to leave at once, employing the eighty minutes to escape. Though Kane attempts to leave, he finds that he cannot. He's unable to explain why, even to his loving wife—who threatens to break from him if he involves himself in violence—other than to continuously say, "I feel I've got to stay."

Deputy Harve Pell hands in his badge, not out of cowardice but owing to sexual tension; Pell's mistress, the Mexican woman Helen Ramirez, was once Kane's lover. Kane attempts to round up deputies, but old "friends" find excuses to hide. Finally, he enters the church, positive Jonas Henderson, best man at his wedding, will back him up. Instead, Jonas argues that a shooting in the street will set the town back ten years and ruin their economy; at that point, even those who were ready to back Kane up sit down and remain silent.

Promptly at noon, the train whistle signals the arrival of Frank Miller. His henchmen meet him and stalk Kane on the empty streets. One by one, Kane shoots them down, running from a barn—which they set afire—to the marshal's office. Then, his wife—who has not left after all—shoots one of the two remaining outlaws in the back. Frank Miller grabs her, forcing Kane

The ticking clock: Gary Cooper and Grace Kelly.

to emerge from hiding. They shoot it out, Miller is killed. The couple leaves town, but not before Kane bitterly stares at the gathering townsfolk and hurls his once beloved badge down in the dust.

THE FILM:

High Noon was not the first "adult western" of the 1950s, but it was certainly the best. It also rates as one of the greatest suspense movies ever made. The most significant element of most thrillers, "the ticking clock," comes from *High Noon*, for the camera constantly cuts from one timepiece to another, reminding us how few minutes Kane has left before he faces almost certain death. Heightening this element further is the fact that the film is one of only a dozen commercial movies that takes place in "real time"—that is, the amount of time that it takes to watch the film is essentially the same amount of time that elapses on screen.

From the project's inception, producer Kramer, writer Foreman, and director Zinnemann were agreed that this was to be an allegory for the blacklist mentality of the late forties and early fifties. Hadleyville is Hollywood; Miller is Senator Joseph McCarthy. When he shows up in town to destroy a respected member of the community, everyone deserts their beloved friend in order to save themselves, even as most members of the Hollywood community deserted old colleagues who were accused of being communists. The image of Kane throwing his badge in the dust was widely taken to be an anti-American statement. Writer Carl Foreman—who won an Oscar for Best Screenplay—was soon blacklisted.

High Noon would, for years thereafter, be recalled as the most liberal of all westerns. Yet when, in the early 1990s, William F. Buckley's journal *The National Review* picked the one hundred best conservative movies of all time, *High Noon* placed high on the list. The magazine pointed out that the film favors the individual over the community. *High Noon* can be interpreted as a defense of the death penalty. If Miller had been executed, none of this would have happened, and the notion of rehabilitating a criminal is proven a fallacy, which fits conservative, not liberal, thinking.

TRIVIA:

Though Gary Cooper won the Academy Award as the year's Best Actor, he never once changes his expresion or tone of voice. His "performance" is a result of the editing of his consistent reaction to varied situations around him, which cause us to believe he is offering a diverse set of reactions to them. Also, Cooper suffered from an ulcer, causing his pained expression, which audiences took to be "acting" but which, in fact, was real.

ALSO RECOMMENDED:

Another great suspense western is *The Gunfighter* (1950), with Gregory Peck as Ringo, also involved in a taut situation with a less obvious, but equally powerful, ticking clock. Zinnemann's other suspense classics include *Day of the Jackal* (1973), about a professional assassin with limited time to make a political hit.

12:

THE EXORCIST (1973)

Warner Bros.

> **"I'm afraid."**
> **—Regan MacNeil**

CAST:

Ellen Burstyn (*Chris MacNeil*); Max von Sydow (*Father Lankester Merrin*); Linda Blair (*Regan MacNeil*); Lee J. Cobb (*Lt. William Kinderman*); Kitty Winn (*Sharon Spencer*); Jack MacGowran (*Burke Dennings*); Jason Miller (*Father Damien*); Reverend William O'Malley (*Father Dyer*); Barton Heyman (*Dr. Klein*); Pete Masterson (*Dr. Barringer*); Gina Petrushka (*Willi*); Robert Symonds (*Dr. Taney*); Arthur Storch (*Psychiatrist*); Reverend Thomas Bermingham (*University President*); Vasiliki Maliaros (*Damien's Mother*); Mercedes McCambridge (*Voice of Pazuzu*).

CREDITS:

Director, William Friedkin; screenplay, William Peter Blatty from his novel of the same name; producer, Blatty, Noel Marshall, and David Salven; original music, Jack Nitzsche; non-original music, Mike Oldfield (from "Tubular Bells"), Krzysztof Penderecki; cinematographers, Owen Roizman and (Iraq sequence only) Billy Williams; editors, Norman Gay, Evan Lottman, and (Iraq sequences only) Bud Smith; production design, Bill Malley; special makeup effects, Dick Smith; sound effects, Fred Brown; special visual effects, Marcel Vercoutere; running time, 121 min.; rating, R.

THE PLOT:

In beautiful Georgetown, single mom Chris MacNeil realizes something is terribly wrong with her daughter Regan. Chris brings in a psychiatrist, but the girl attacks him. Shortly, mother and daughter find themselves isolated in their lovely home from normal activity on the street outside. Finally, Chris becomes so desperate she allows a pair of Catholic priests, young Father Damien and elderly Father Merrin, into her home to perform an exorcism.

Regan (Linda Blair) overtaken by the Devil, as a priest (Max von Sydow) attempts to salvage youth by returning to the old ways.

THE FILM:

The Exorcist is one of several films that might be considered unlikely candidates for inclusion here, since, by my own admission, the book deals with thrillers at least tangentially based on real-life situations and/or the fear of the unknown rather than a "seen" monster. Roger Ebert's description of the film justifies its inclusion, for he argues that "it's founded on characters, details, and a realistic milieu . . . it embeds the sensational material in an everyday world of misty nights, boozy parties, and housekeeping details, chats in a laundry room and the personal lives of the priests. The movie is more horrifying because it does not seem to want to be (a horror movie). The horror creeps into the lives of characters preoccupied with their everyday lives." The film introduced "modern" special effects with the believable 360 degree head-rotation effect, setting the stage for a revitalization of horror-thrillers while replacing the drive-in oriented junk movies of the fifties and sixties. The scene in which Regan masturbates with a crucifix while vomiting green bile into the faces of bystanders was attacked by some theologians who found the scene an odious exploitation of twelve-year-old child-actress Linda Blair. It was defended by many others who found this a necessary depiction of absolute evil within the context of a film that came out in favor of the church's traditional responses to the Devil.

The Exorcist may be interpreted as a parable for a mindset that developed during the early seventies, best described as a harsh reaction against the flower-power attitudes of the previous decade. The youth movement first appeared during the second half of the sixties, growing out of an intense anti-Establishment mood that incorporated anti-war and pro-civil rights attitudes. Poet William Wordsworth's romantic sensibility of the early-nineteenth century ("The child is father to the man") was restated by rock poets like Crosby, Stills, and Nash ("Teach your parents well."). Initially a self-contained counter-culture, the hippie attitudes spread to the mainstream by 1969/70. However, the beautiful dream of peace and love swiftly degenerated into a chaotic drug-culture, and America soon sensed it needed national rehab. This resulted in a backlash against the seemingly innocent youth that had turned out (in the minds of many) to be the Devil in disguise. That vision of youth was incarnated by Regan, the sweet child whose body has been overtaken by Satan; she (like the country's youth) can only be saved if the adults around her abandon modern liberal/science and return to the most conservative of approaches, the ultra-moral priests who represent that old time religion—and all its traditional values. Even the fact that Chris is divorced plays into this "reading"; God is punishing those who fail to subscribe to traditional family values by making clear their children will not turn out "right" until such people re-embrace the most conservative elements in our culture, as Chris literally does (hugging the priest who has saved her daughter) in the final shot.

Trivia:

The Exorcist predated *Jaws* (1975) in creating the contemporary sense of a "blockbuster"—that is, films that reach what has become the all-important $100 million gross target. For the 2000 special edition, digital effects were added by Jennifer Law-Stump; an additional budget of one million dollars was added to the film's original cost (twelve million) for the restoration process. The "new and improved" rerelease print, approximately eleven-and-a-half minutes longer than the original, was generally damned by critics who complained about tampering with a bona fide masterpiece in order to please a new, more technologically-oriented audience that had emerged since *The Exorcist*'s debut some twenty-five years earlier.

Also Recommended:

Fans of Friedkin's directorial style will want to catch *The French Connection* (1971), the gritty crime thriller that won Oscars for Best Picture, Best Director, and Best

Actor (Gene Hackman), among others. For devil-child movies, *The Exorcist* was preceeded by *Rosemary's Baby* (1968, #19) and followed by *The Omen* (1976). Also, catch *Village of the Damned* (1960, #91).

11:

VERTIGO (1958)

Paramount Pictures

"You should never keep souvenirs from a murder."
—Scottie to Judy/Madeleine

THE CAST:

James Stewart (*Scottie Ferguson*); Kim Novak (*Madeleine* Elster/*Judy Barton*); Barbara Bel Geddes (*Midge*); Henry Jones (*Coroner*); Tom Helmore (*Gavin Elster*); Raymond Bailey (*Doctor*); Ellen Corby (*Hotel Keeper*); Lee Patrick (*Cop*).

CREDITS:

Director, Alfred Hitchcock; screenplay, Alec Coppel and Samuel Taylor, from a novel by Pierre Boileau and Thomas Narcejac; producer, Hitchcock; original music, Bernard Herrmann; cinematographer, Robert Burks; special visual effects, John Fulton; set design, Henry Bumstead and Hal Pereira; title sequence, Saul Bass; running time, 120 min.

THE PLOT:

Former police detective Scottie Ferguson has suffered from vertigo since he almost fell to his death, along with a fellow cop who tried to rescue him, while pursuing a convict over the rooftops of San Francisco. His longtime girlfriend, Midge, attempts to help him recover, but to no avail. Then, Scottie receives a call from an old chum, Gavin Elster, who wants to hire Scottie for some private detective work. Elster explains that his wife, Madeleine, has become obsessed with a museum painting of Carlotta, a mystery woman from the old Spanish days, and—like Carlotta—

believes herself to be doomed. Elster points out Madeleine to Scottie and he begins following her, at one point saving the woman from suicide by drowning. Scottie realizes that he is falling in love with Madeleine. When she then suddenly bolts from him and is apparently killed in a fall from a high tower—Scottie's vertigo keeps him from saving her—the hero grows despondent to the point of madness.

Wandering the streets, lonely and alienated, Scottie happens to see a crude brunette, Judy Barton, whose facial structure resembles that of the elegant blonde Madeleine. Scottie stalks her and, after initially repulsing him, Judy agrees to date Scottie. He immediately proceeds to try and make her over into a precise image of the woman Scottie loved and lost. Judy resists, wanting him to love her for herself, but eventually gives in and becomes a precise double for Madeleine—too precise.

In the original ending (not used), Stewart's character strangled Kim Novak the moment that he realizes she betrayed him.

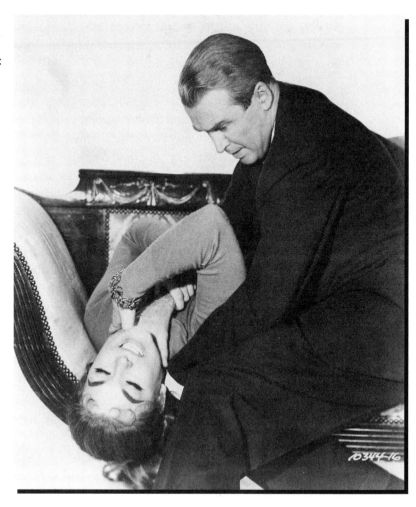

When Scottie notices that Judy wears a necklace that belonged to Madeleine, he realizes all at once that he was set up from the start. Judy and Elster conspired to murder Elster's real wife, with Scottie as their patsy. Furious, he brings her back to the scene of the crime, where Judy falls to her death—for real, this time.

The Film:

No Hitchcock movie has been more damned and praised, interpreted and discussed, than *Vertigo*. A critical and commercial failure on initial release, the edgy film gradually developed a cult following, particularly after Hitchcock had it withdrawn from circulation, both theatrical and television. Absence did make the heart grow fonder, and critics who hadn't seen *Vertigo* for years began to claim, in print, that it was the greatest suspense movie ever made. When the film was finally rereleased in the mid-eighties, it was treated as a classic and a masterpiece—for a while. In time, though, yet another reaction argued if perhaps it wasn't now as overrated as it had initially been underrated.

The main point of criticism in 1958 had been that Hitchcock ruined what might have been a marvelous mystery by giving away the ending at mid-movie. After the initial meeting between Scottie and Judy, he leaves the apartment, but we remain behind. As Judy attempts to write a confessional letter to Scottie, we see a dramatization of what "actually" occured: Madeleine and Elster, throwing Elster's wife off the roof while the vertigo-stricken Scottie remained below. But she has come to love him and can't reveal the truth. Why didn't Hitchcock save this for a final twist? The reason is simple: Hitchcock didn't care for the mystery form (he made only one, an early English talkie called *Murder!*, 1930) in which the audience is the last to know. That was the realm of Agatha Christie. Hitchcock preferred suspense—the true thriller form—and so allowed the audience to know more than the hero does. This puts each of us in state of anxiety—wanting to call out to the character onscreen but of course unable to do so—which is always the basis of a great thriller.

The film contains most all of the great Hitchcock themes: the madness of seemingly ordinary people and the deliciously duplicitous blonde as compared to the less romantic figure of the brunette, among others. Hitchcock went through several scriptwriters, each of whom read the novel that the film was to be based on and turned out a screenplay that was rejected. Finally, he realized that familiarity with the book actually hurt the attempt at adaptation, for he wanted to keep only the essence of the plot. Hitchcock then brought Alec Coppelson into his office and, for two hours, told the screenwriter (who had *not* read the book) the story as Hitchcock saw it. Coppelson quickly completed a usable screenplay.

TRIVIA:

The film was adapted from a novel by the French authors who had also penned *Diabolique* (1955, #77), which they had hoped might someday become a Hitchcock movie. With their second book, *D'Entre les Morts*, their wish finally came true. At the time, Grace Kelly had left Hollywood and Hitchcock was grooming a young actress named Vera Miles for stardom. She was his first choice for the dual female leads, but had to drop out when she became pregnant.

ALSO RECOMMENDED:

Brian De Palma has unofficially remade *Vertigo* several times; the best are *Sisters* (1973) and *Obsession* (1976).

10:

THE SILENCE OF THE LAMBS (1991)

Orion Pictures

> **"I do wish we could chat longer, but I'm having an old friend for dinner."**
> —Lector to Clarice on phone (film's final line)

CAST:

Jodie Foster (*Clarice Starling*); Anthony Hopkins (*Dr. Hannibal Lecter*); Scott Glenn (*Jack Crawford*); Anthony Heald (*Dr. Frederick Chilton*); Ted Levine (*Jame "Buffalo Bill" Gumb*); Frankie Faison (*Matthews*); Kasi Lemmons (*Ardelia*); Brooke Smith (*Catherine*); Paul Lazar (*Pilcher*); Dan Butler (*Roden*); Lawrence T. Wrentz (*Burroughs*); Don Brockett, Frank Seals Jr. (*Psychopaths*); Stuart Rudin (*Multiple Miggs*); Masha Skorobogatov (*Young Clarice*); Jeffrey Lane (*Clarice's Father*).

CREDITS:

Director, Jonathan Demme; screenplay, Ted Tally, from the novel by Thomas Harris; producers, Edward Saxon, Kenneth Utt, and Ronald M.

Bozman; original music, Howard Shore; cinematographer, Tak Fujimoto; editor, Craig McKay; production design, Kristi Zea; art direction, Tim Galvin; running time, 118 min.; rating, R.

THE PLOT:

Young FBI trainee Clarice Starling is handed an unusual mission. She must find a missing woman, then keep a serial killer who skins his victims from doing her in. Her boss, Jack Crawford, believes Clarice can best accomplish this by going to an even more fearsome killer, Hannibal Lector, now behind bars. By speaking with Lector, Clarice may grasp how such a person thinks. Lector is brilliant, a former psychiatrist who plays mind games when visited. Clarice feels mesmerized by Lector's presence and voice, always in danger of falling under his spell as she realizes they have slipped into a bizarre, deep, and significant relationship. He alone is able to grasp that she remains scarred by a childhood dream/memory of lambs slaughtered in the springtime on her family farm, and the screaming sound they made. Lector escapes, blazing a bloody trail across America, never breaking off his relationship with Clarice. At the end, she has solved her case, though perhaps an even greater evil has been loosed on the world. In the film's final shot, Clarice answers a phone call from Lector, realizing that their relationship is far from over.

THE FILM:

Author Thomas Harris became aware that the seemingly "normal" public had an insatiable thirst for information about serial killers. For the character of "Buffalo Bill," he neatly interwove three actual serial killers: Ed Gein, famed for skinning victims; Ted Bundy, who lured women with a cast on his hand that seemingly made him vulnerable; and Gary Heidnick, who hid the women he kidnapped in his basement. Harris created a fictional apotheosis of the most extreme cases. The project was offered to producer Dino De Laurentiis, because he had, in 1986, produced the film *Manhunter*, which (like the book it's based on) introduced the character of Hannibal Lector. Because that film hadn't made money, De Laurentiis passed on the new property, allowing his rights to be picked up at no cost by Orion Pictures. Once assigned, director Jonathan Demme encouraged Anthony Hopkins to improvise all he liked in creating a believable mystique, the missing ingredient in the earlier film. It was Hopkins who came up with the idea of making disgusting slurping sounds, to turn Hannibal the Cannibal into a grotesque exaggeration of any hungry person. So significant to the film's creepy quality, this aspect is nowhere to be found in the screenplay. Realizing the voice he came up with for Lector would either make or break the movie, Hopkins happily settled on "a combination of Truman Capote and Katharine Hepburn."

Most interior scenes were built and then filmed in a factory on the edge of Pittsburgh, though for authenticity's sake, the Washington, D.C. scenes were filmed in the offices of Elizabeth Dole. To visually convey the notion of Hannibal as two people inhabiting a single body, Demme reached back to Hitchcock's old notion of employing mirrors to suggest this (used throughout *Psycho*, [1960, #1] with the Anthony Perkins character) by having Hannibal, in his cell, reflected in some manner. Whenever he is not, Clarice is thusly perceived, suggesting the "good" character is more complex than we originally realize. This allows for an updating of the relationship

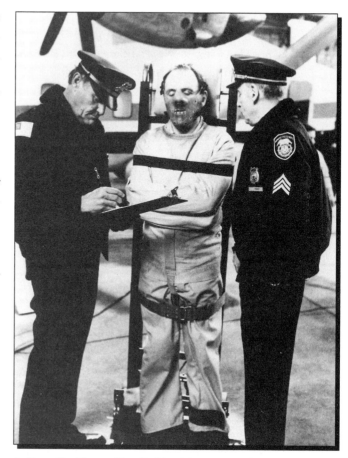

Anthony Hopkins as Hannibal Lector.

between "Uncle Charley" (Joseph Cotten) and "Young Charlie" (Teresa Wright) that Hitchcock developed in *Shadow of a Doubt* (1943, #27), in which the horrible murderer of women and his seemingly innocent niece likewise have a psychic connection, the young girl turning out to be more complex than she at first seems.

TRIVIA:

The cameo part of "Senator Ruth Martin" is played by Diane Baker; this may be intended as an homage to Hitchcock, who featured the actress in a similar (albeit younger) role in *Marnie* (1964). Another cameo, FBI agent Hayden Burke, is played by Roger Corman, the legendary producer of B-movies who gave many writer-directors their start, including Demme. Character actor Charlies Napier, who plays Lt. Boyle, is something of a good luck charm for Demme, appearing in most of his movies. An FBI agent in Memphis is played by George A. Romero, director of such suspense thrillers as *The Night of the Living Dead* (1968). This was the first film since *One Flew Over the Cuckoo's Nest* (1976) to win all five of the top Oscars, and only the fifth in Academy history to do so. Actors Frankie Faison and Dan Butler appear both in *The Silence of the Lambs* and *Manhunter*, though in different roles.

ALSO RECOMMENDED:

Michael Mann's *Manhunter*, which has gradually achieved cult status, is a must-see for anyone interested in Hannibal Lector.

9:

THE MANCHURIAN CANDIDATE (1962)

United Artists

> **"Raymond Shaw is the kindest, bravest, warmest, most wonderful human being I've ever met in my life."**
> —Captain Bennett Marco

CAST:

Frank Sinatra (*Captain Bennett Marco*); Laurence Harvey (*Raymond Shaw*); Janet Leigh (*Eugenie Rose "Rosie" Chaney*); Angela Lansbury (*Mrs. Iselin*); Henry Silva (*Chunjin*); James Gregory (*Senator John Iselin*); Leslie Parrish (*Jocelyn Jordan*); John McGiver (*Senator Thomas Jordan*); Khigh Dhiegh (*Dr. Yen Lo*); James Edwards (*Corporal Melvin*); Douglas Henderson (*Milt*); Albert Paulsen (*Zilkov*); Barry Kelley (*Secretary of Defense*); Lloyd Corrigan (*Gaines*); Madame Spivy (*Nightmare Woman*); Paul Frees (*Narrator*).

CREDITS:

Director, John Frankenheimer; screenplay, Frankenheimer and George Axelrod, from the novel by Richard Condon; producers, Axelrod, Frankenheimer, and Howard W. Koch; original music, David Amram; cinematographer, Lionel Lindon; editor, Ferris Webster; production designer, Richard Sylbert; special visual effects, Howard A. Anderson; running time, 126 min.

THE PLOT:

A squad of American soldiers, stationed in Korea, 1952, and led by then-Major Marco, are captured by the enemy and sent to a camp where each is brainwashed. The soldiers believe they are guests at a women's group meeting; they are so under the influence of their captors that Raymond Shaw casually strangles a trooper and shoots another on request. After returning home, Marco—like his fellows—recalls nothing of the event, though he suffers from terrible dreams. Also, he has only positive things to say about Shaw, whom he nominates for a Congressional Medal of Honor. Marco never particularly liked Shaw, the stepson of Senator John Iselin, who at his wife's prodding hopes to win the vice-presidential slot on a major political party's upcoming ballot.

Marco and one of his former men, Al Melvin, share the same nightmares even though they are no longer in contact. Shaw is commanded by his mother, on certain occasions, to play solitaire. When he does, and as the Queen of Diamonds comes up, Shaw finds himself without a will, awaiting his orders to kill. When Marco seeks Shaw out, he's attacked by Chunjin, Shaw's houseboy, who engages him in a martial arts battle. Shaw, meanwhile, has fallen in love with Jocie, the beautiful daughter of a liberal senator. Thomas Jordan despises the reactionary politics of Shaw's stepfather but accepts the youth as his daughter's fiancé. Then, Shaw is called upon to knowingly assassinate Jordan and, in the process, inadvertantly kills Jocie. Marco, having befriended Shaw to discover what's actually going on, gradually realizes Shaw is being set up to assassinate the Republican presidential candidate so Iselin can seize the nomination for himself.

Actually, Iselin is a pawn of the Communists, who believe that as a result of Iselin's fierce communist witch-hunting, America will—in a Marxist dialectic—react with a pendulum shift, swinging away from such conservative thinking and embracing communism. Thus, the right-wing extremist is in fact "the Manchurian candidate." Shaw takes his place at a large rally to do the shooting, even as Marco hurries to stop him. Before Marco can arrive, Shaw—seizing upon his own individual will—shoots both his stepfather and mother, then turns the gun on himself.

THE FILM:

The Manchurian Candidate is among those seminal films that set the pace for the new cinema that would emerge during the transitional decade of the 1960s, as American movies became ever more daring and less conventional. For one thing, it marked the first time that Hollywood dared parody Senator Joseph McCarthy and his witch-hunting mentality. The film also contains one of the most remark-

Frank Sinatra and Laurence Harvey as the former war buddies who find themselves involved in a political assassination plot.

able shots in the history of motion pictures, as—during the brainwashing sequence—the camera simultaneously pans and tracks a full 360 degrees. In the background, the image of middle-aged American women proudly displaying their flowers is replaced by Korean Communists; nothing that even Orson Welles or Alfred Hitchcock ever achieved surpasses this moment.

As Pauline Kael wrote at the time of initial release, "It may be the most sophisticated political satire ever made in Hollywood." Her choice of the term "satire" rather than "drama" is significant. This was written by George Axelrod, best known for his comic masterpiece *The Seven Year Itch* (1955). Only two years earlier, Hitchcock had claimed *Psycho* (1960) was best understood as a black comedy, if one that (like this film) was laced with suspense. Lansbury's mother is a variation on Hitchcock's dreaded dominating mothers, taken to its extreme, even as Shaw is Norman Bates with a university education.

TRIVIA:

During the filming of *The Manchurian Candidate*, President John Kennedy phoned the president of United Artists to insure him he had no personal objections to a film about a potential presidential assassination, particularly if it was to star his friend Frank Sinatra. When Kennedy was assassinated shortly after the film's release, Sinatra crusaded to have this and *Suddenly* (1954, #65) shelved indefinitely. As a result, *The Manchurian Candidate* could not be seen (except via bootleg prints) until 1988, when it was finally rereleased. Jilly Rizzo, a Sinatra friend, plays a bartender; that sequence was shot in Jilly's New York saloon. Each member of Marco's patrol takes his name from a soldier on Phil Silver's popular TV service-comedy, *You'll Never Get Rich*.

ALSO RECOMMENDED:

Director John Frankenheimer made a far more conventional (stylistically speaking) though extremely suspenseful political thriller, *Seven Days in May* (1964) with Burt Lancaster and Kirk Douglas, about an attempted military takeover of the United States. Rod Serling wrote the screenplay from a novel by Fletcher Knebel and Charles W. Bailey.

8:

NORTH BY NORTHWEST (1959)

Metro-Goldwyn-Mayer

> **"The matter is best disposed of at a great height—and over water."**
>
> —Vandamm, instructing Leonard to dump Eve out of the plane

CAST:

Cary Gant (*Roger Thornhill*); Eva Marie Saint (*Eve Kendall*); James Mason (*Phillip Vandamm*); Jessie Royce Landis (*Clara Thornhill*); Leo G. Carroll (*The Professor*); Philip Ober (*Lester Townsend*); Josephine Hutchinson (*Mrs. Townsend/the housekeeper*); Martin Landau (*Leonard*).

CREDITS:

Director, Alfred Hitchcock; screenplay, Ernest Lehman, from a concept by Hitchcock; producer, Hitchcock; original music, Bernard Herrmann; cinematographer, Robert Burks; editor, George Tomasini; set design, Robert Boyle; special photographic effects, A. Arnold Gillespie and Lee LeBlanc; title sequence, Saul Bass; running time, 136 min.

THE PLOT:

Roger Thornhill is a bland, ego-driven Madison Avenue executive who likes to have lunch at the Plaza Hotel with business companions. One day, after signaling to a passing waiter, he's surrounded by brutes who tell him to head outside and into a waiting car or they will kill him. Thornhill is certain that's he's being kidnapped and assures them that his mother will pay any ransom, so long as they don't hurt him. Shortly, he realizes that they believe him to be a spy named George Kaplan. They take him to an isolated mansion where their ringleader, Vandamm, tries to extricate information from the stunned Thornhill. He escapes and tells the authorities, but when they return to the house, other people are living there. Thornhill heads for the United Nations to meet with a diplomat (the actual owner of the mansion) about this, but the man is murdered with a knife, and everyone believes that Thornhill killed him. Terrified, he takes off cross country. On a train, he's hidden by Eve Kendall, later realizing she is Vandamm's mistress. They fall in love, at which point Thornhill must accept she's a double-agent, a government

Cary Grant on the run.

plant in Vandamm's operation. Thornhill also grasps that agent "George Kaplan" doesn't exist, that he was created by the CIA to throw the Russians off the trail of real agents. The enemy spies, having heard that Kaplan would take lunch at the Plaza, watched closely while someone paged Kaplan, whom they did not know by sight. When Thornhill coincidentally happened to raise his hand at that moment, they were certain that they had their man.

THE FILM:

One notable director from Hollywood's golden era dismissed the wide-screen process as "fit for nothing but filming snakes." Hitchcock proved him wrong, showing that this could be employed as a valid part of the storytelling process. He did not merely shoot in the VistaVision process, but designed all his storyboards to make the most of widescreen. Thus, such famous set-pieces as the pursuit of Grant by a low-flying plane and the Mt. Rushmore vertigo-inspiring finale do not work when *North by Northwest*'s image is reduced for a TV screen. They were conceived and created in order to positively exploit the immense landscapes which take on a unique life in the film's visual context.

Hitchcock was here working in a form that he'd pioneered in England with such early masterpieces as *The 39 Steps* (1935) and *The Lady Vanishes* (1938). The form is a picaresque, carrying its brash, charming "wrong man" hero across country as he is pursued by enemy agents and the well-intentioned but incompetent police who mistakenly think he's a bad guy. Along the way, he finds romance with a beautiful blonde, and the entire affair is played as light comedy, despite the number of corpses that pile up. He had created an American counterpart with *The Saboteur* (1942); this sub-genre of Hitchcockian thriller has been designated as a "divertissement," the pleasant escapism that takes an audiences' minds off its troubles. Hitchcock himself always admitted that the villains were all but interchangeable from one film to the next, upper-class heavies with quirky sidekicks, a concept that would be imitated in the James Bond films. Indeed, the 007 movies owe more to *North by Northwest* than to the Ian Fleming novels on which they are supposedly based.

Hitchcock was asked to direct the first Bond film, with Grant as 007, but they turned down the offer. Hitchcock felt freed and liberated by *North by Northwest*'s immense popular and critical appeal, and so set out to do different things and explore new directions. And so he embarked on such darker visions as *Psycho* (1960, #1), *The Birds* (1963, #23), and *Marnie* (1964).

TRIVIA:

While the film was in pre-production, the working title was *The Man on Lincoln's Nose*. James Stewart was originally considered for the lead, until Hitchcock realized that one key concept—Eve becoming so smitten with Thornhill at first that she risks everything to hide him from the authorities, even if he is a murderer—would work for better if the "Ah, shucks, Ma'am!" Stewart was replaced by Grant, the sexiest man on the planet. When Eva Marie Saint "shoots" Cary Grant in the Mt. Rushmore gift shop, a little boy at the far end of the screen sticks his fingers in his ears before she has even drawn the gun from hiding. Leo G. Carroll proved so memorable in his role as the head of a CIA type spy operation that he was offered virtually the same part on the mid-sixties TV series, *The Man From U.N.C.L.E.*

ALSO RECOMMENDED:

Don't miss Hitchcock's other similar films, *The 39 Steps* (1935) and *The Lady Vanishes* (1938) in particular. Arthur Hiller's *Silver Streak* (1977) nicely revives the combination of romance, comedy, and thrills.

7:

JAWS (1975)

Universal Pictures

> **"We need a bigger boat."**
> **—Police Chief Brody**

CAST:

Roy Scheider (*Chief Martin Brody*); Robert Shaw (*Quint*); Richard Dreyfuss (*Hooper*); Lorraine Gary (*Ellen Brody*); Murray Hamilton (*Mayor Vaughn*); Carl Gottlieb (*Editor Ben Meadows*); Peter Benchley (*TV Reporter*); Susan Backlinie (*Chrissie*).

CREDITS:

> Director, Steven Spielberg; screenplay, Peter Benchley and Carl Gottlieb, and (uncredited) John Milius, Howard Sackler, and Spielberg, from the novel by Benchley; producers, Richard Zanuck and David Brown; music, John Williams; cinematographer, Bill Butler; editor, Verna Fields; production design, Joseph Alves, Jr.; running time, 124 min.; rating, PG.

THE PLOT:

As a new summer season begins in Amity, pretty young Chrissie is killed by a shark while swimming at night. Police Chief Brody investigates, realizing what has happened, and he would like to issue a general warning to the public. However, Mayor Larry Vaughn and other influential locals conspire to keep the threat under wraps, for fear that hundreds of vacationers now planning to visit will cancel their trips, causing financial havoc for a community that survives on the money made during these crucial months. Reluctantly, Brody agrees to go along with their cover up, beefing up security on the beach, hoping all will go well. Then, another swimmer is killed.

The creature from the ocean floor: *Jaws* **rates as the best action-thriller ever.**

Grief-stricken, Brody determines to rid the area of the "monster." To do so, two experts are brought in to help. One is Matt Hooper, a brilliant scientist; the other, Peter Quint, an experienced shark hunter. The former is pure brain, the latter brute strength. With Brody, the common man as hero of the people, the three form a group that heads out in the *Orca* to do battle with the shark. It, however, turns out to be far more intelligent than they guessed, engaging them in a strategic battle as if the shark knows they have come to duel with him.

THE FILM:

Jaws successfully combines elements of *Moby Dick*, featuring an obsessed hero who can only come to terms with his identity by slaying a sea beast, and *The Creature From the Black Lagoon* (1954), in which a boatload of adventurers are glimpsed from the underwater monster's point of view. These suspenseful qualities were added to the mix only when Spielberg—who had previously directed only one theatrical feature, the critically well-received film *The Sugarland Express* (1974)— came aboard as director for the Zanuck/Brown production, released by Universal. Immediately, the auteur rejected the studio's idea to cast their hot young star Jan-Michael Vincent as Matt Hooper, instead showcasing Richard Dreyfuss, who had recently scored in *American Graffiti* (1973) for Spielberg's friend, George Lucas.

Vincent would have been more in line with novelist Peter Benchley's conception. In the book, he is a brash, arrogant, WASPy type who seduces Police Chief Brody's wife in a segment eliminated for the movie. Likewise, Spielberg rethought the character of Quint, who in the novel is a bald-pated phoney, a sleazebag out to trick the community into paying him a great deal of money though he fully knows he cannot get the job done. The "Quint" of Spielberg's imagination is a tragic figure, who survived the terrible WWII ordeal at sea after the USS Indianapolis was sunk and most of the men were eaten by marauding sharks. The film's Quint has suffered from guilt, for having somehow survived, ever since, and is dedicated to killing the shark to square himself. Originally, Spielberg had hoped to land either Lee Marvin or Sterling Hayden for the part.

Benchley had never wanted to do a book about a shark attack, receiving the assignment from his New York editor, who believed such a novel would sell well. Agreeing to pen such a piece, Benchley—consciously or otherwise—all but threw away the third and final act of the story, notably non-engaging, particularly so for anyone who has seen Spielberg's highly involving film. Instead, he concentrated on the very things he wanted to write about in the first place, a modern "affair" (this was, lest we forget, the decade when the sexual revolution, which had in the 1960s been the province of the youth, spread to the middle class) between an older woman and a younger man.

Also, he created an intriguing portrait of the Mafia's intrusion into what is seemingly a sacrosanct old-fashioned all-American small town. Spielberg, however, set out to fashion the kind of edge-of-your-seat popcorn-movie that he and Lucas were even then bringing back to movie screens, if in a new and improved form. Realizing that the shark, when glimpsed for too long, looked phoney, he decided to put off showing the beast (which was supposed to appear in the opening) for as long as possible, even later in the film showing it for only brief glimpses. This had the happy effect of turning what might have been a routine monster movie into one of the screen's greatest exercises in suspense.

TRIVIA:

Jaws can be credited with creating the phenomenom now known as "the summer movie." Before its release, film companies considered these months a lackluster period, but *Jaws* proved so unexpectedly popular—not only during its opening weekend but throughout the entire season—that distributors came to realize summer could be an even more lucrative time for major releases than the Christmas season. Susan Backlinie, who plays the ill-fated Chrissie, spoofs that role at the beginning of Spielberg's *1941* (1979).

ALSO RECOMMENDED:

Spielberg's other classics in the thriller genre include *Duel* (1971), *Poltergeist* (1982), and *Jurassic Park* (1993).

6.

REAR WINDOW (1954)

Paramount Pictures

> **"Let's start from the beginning. Tell me everything you saw and what you think it means."**
> —Lisa to Jeffries

CAST:

James Stewart (*L.B. Jeffries*); Grace Kelly (*Lisa Fremont*); Wendell Corey (*Tom Doyle*); Thelma Ritter (*Stella*); Raymond Burr (*Lars Thorwald*); Judith Evelyn (*Miss Lonelyhearts*); Ross Bagdasarian (*The Composer*); Georgine Darcy (*Miss Torso*); Jesslyn Fax (*Sculptress*); Irene Winston (*Mrs. Thorwald*).

CREDITS:

Director, Alfred Hitchcock; screenplay, John Michael Hayes, from a short story by Cornell Woolrich; producer, Hitchcock; music, Franz Waxman; cinematographer, Ropbert Burks; editor, George Tomasini; set design, Hal Pereira; special visual effects, John P. Fulton; running time, 112 min.

THE PLOT:

Following an accident, news photographer L.B. Jeffries finds himself wheelchair-bound in his apartment during a notably hot summer. He's attended to by a nurse, Stella, and his long-time girlfriend, the breathtaking Lisa. She is rich and famous, yet she'd happily marry the middleclass Jeffries. He's always resisted that, fearing she'll put an end to his boyish adventures and set him to work photographing weddings and the like. When he's alone, Jeffries uses his long-distance lens to spy on his neighbors. Surprisingly, he's less interested in a beautiful model (whom he nicknames "Miss Torso") than an unhappily married couple across the way. After seeing them have a terrible fight, Jeffries becomes convinced that Mr. Thorwald may have murdered his wife. He tells his police buddy, Doyle, but is dismissed as becoming paranoid. Still, Jeffries will not relent and, in time, both Stella and Lisa join him. Finally, Thorwald—who is indeed a murderer—confronts Jeff in his

Unhealthy inclinations:
Like the audience
watching the movie,
James Stewart becomes
a voyeur in *Rear
Window*.

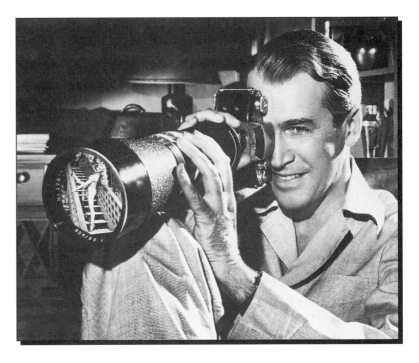

Unhealthy inclinations: Like the audience watching the movie, James Stewart becomes a voyeur in *Rear Window*.

apartment, the crippled man armed with nothing but a set of flashbulbs to repel the attack.

THE FILM:

Voyeurism is a key theme in many Hitchcock films (indeed, in most thrillers!), but *Rear Window* is the movie in which it entirely dominates all the drama. Hitchcock believed that it was as necessary to shoot this particular project on a studio set (though the story takes place in Manhattan, *Rear Window* was shot in California) as it would be, several years later, imperative to film *Vertigo* on location in San Francisco. Hitchcock didn't necessarily prefer either approach, nor did he ever make such decisions on a arbitrary basis. In his mind, *Vertigo* was actually about the city in which it takes place, with the sad little story of the lonely wanderers—lost in a world of their own mutual making—set, for ironic purposes, against authentic cityscapes that could not have been faked. *Rear Window*, on the other hand, is one of Hitchcock's subjective films. The movie takes place not in New York, or even in one corner of it, but entirely in the mind of the film's hero, Jeffries.

What we see onscreen is not meant to represent what actually happens, but the way in which he perceives it. Jeff doesn't look in the windows of all his neighbors—after a brief interest, he turns away from the most attractive woman across the way—but only enters into those apartments where marriage is an issue. What he sees is what he wants to see. As Hitchcock himself put it, "*Rear Window* is entirely a mental process, done by use of the visual." This could much more effectively be achieved inside the studio, where the created (indeed, obviously so) apartment house is so faux that it calls attention to itself—purposefully and effectively. Hitchcock had never gotten over the experience of being on the set of *The Cabinet of Dr. Caligari* (1919, #100) when he was a nineteen-year-old aspiring filmmaker visiting Germany. When he later viewed the completed film, Hitchcock realized that the moviemakers had employed their Expressionistic set design to allow the viewer a strong vision of how the hero saw the world. Hitchcock would often imitate that approach, though never so intensely as here.

The movie contains one of his striking statements on the institution of marriage which, when one considers his output closely, is at the heart of most of his movies. The ultimate Hitchcockian vision on this subject is that husbands and wives, or the members of an engaged couple, who ought to be the closest people, are actually intimate strangers. That's the case here, as Jeffries does not so much want to catch a possible killer, while hoping that Mrs. Thorwald is still alive, as he wants her to be dead so that he could then refuse to marry Lisa on the grounds that this is what a marriage eventually leads to. Lisa agrees to help him try and catch Thorwald not because she really believes that the man is guilty, but because she's under the false impression that by doing so, she will convince Jeff that she isn't some superficial socialite and that he will have to marry her once she proves her worth by risking her life.

TRIVIA:

Hitchcock had not enjoyed his working relationship with David O. Selznick, the producer who brought him to America. Selznick wanted opulent super-productions, Hitchcock hoped to make low-key thrillers. Eventually, they went their separate ways. *Rear Window* allowed Hitchcock to finally have his revenge. As the murderous Thorwald, Raymond Burr is made up to look precisely like Selznick. *Rear Window* was remade as a TV movie in 1998 with actor Christopher Reeve, actually wheelchair-bound following a riding accident.

ALSO RECOMMENDED:

Grace Kelly also shines opposite Cary Grant in Hitchcock's *To Catch a Thief* (1955), her final film, set in gorgeous Monaco.

5:

THE THIRD MAN (1949)

British Lion

"There was another man . . . a *third* man!"
—Hall Porter

CAST:

Joseph Cotten (*Holly Martins*); (Alida) Valli (*Anna Schmidt*); Orson Welles (*Harry Lime*); Trevor Howard (*Major Calloway*); Paul Hoerbiger (*Porter*); Ernst Deutsch (*"Baron" Kurtz*); Erich Ponto (*Dr. Winkel*); Siegfried Breuer (*Popescu*); Hedwig Bleibtreu (*Old Woman*); Bernard Lee (*Sergeant Paine*); Wilfrid Hyde-White (*Crabbin*).

CREDITS:

Director, Carol Reed; screenplay, Reed, Orson Welles (uncredited), Alexander Korda and Graham Greene, from the novel by Greene; producers, Reed, Korda, David O. Selznick, and Hugh Perceval; original music, Anton Karas; non-original music, Henry Love; zither performance, Anton Karras; cinematographer, Robert Krasker; editor, Oswald Hafenrichter; assistant director, Guy Hamilton; set designer, Vincent Korda; special visual (matte) effects, W. Percy Day; running time(s), 93 min. (original American release print), 104 min. (original British release print).

THE PLOT:

American pulp writer Holly Martins arrives in postwar Vienna at the bequest of old friend Harry Lime, who has been thriving in the city, now divided into four zones: Russian, British, American, and French. No sooner has Martins stepped off the train than he discovers Lime is dead; one of the mourners is mysterious Anna, a cafe and theatre performer intimately involved with Lime. Martins becomes attracted to her, partly because he believes she might help to unravel the mystery of how and why Lime died. Then, Martins is approached by a British officer, Calloway, who insists Lime was a terrible man, and that Martins ought to leave the

Orson Welles as Harry Lime.

detective work to the professionals. This only fascinates Martins all the more, particularly after being told that—in contrast to the police reports of two men at the scene of Lime's death—an eyewitness insists there was a third man.

If he can locate that elusive figure, Martins is certain he can find answers to all the questions. Though he pursues Anna, she gives him the cold-shoulder treatment. Meanwhile, people who know more than they have told—most notably that porter—die mysteriously, and some suspect Martins of the murders. As he leaves Anna's apartment late one night, he realizes he's being spied on by a man in the shadows and, pursuing him, comes face to face (briefly) with Harry Lime; the third man at Harry Lime's "death" was Lime, who helped kill another man to throw the police off his tail.

Calloway forces Martins to look at dead and dying children, victims of Lime's scheme to water down drugs. Martins is then persuaded to meet with Lime and entice him over to the English sector, where Calloway can make an arrest. But Lime bolts and is pursued through the sewers, where he is shot and killed. Martins waits for Anna, but she passes him by without a word, still dedicated to her memory of the mesmerizing Harry Lime.

THE FILM:

David O. Selznick wanted Noel Coward for the role of Lime, but Reed objected; Reed wanted James Stewart for the part of Martins, but Selznick objected.

Throughout production, Selznick constantly pushed Reed—as he had for years Reed's countryman Hitchcock—to make the film more glamorous and upbeat, less realistic and depressing. Like Hitchcock, Reed fought him all the way. The film pioneered the postwar concept of on-location shooting, rather than working on Hollywood sound stages, allowing for a grim but ultra-convincing portrait of a city where glorious buildings were now flanked by immense craters left by bombing raids, and where the culture and tradition of art, music, and performance existed within the context of a corrupt society run by black marketeers. Yet, in contrast to the realism of what was to be photographed, there was the self-conscious Expressionism of the filming style. Reed and cinematographer Robert Krasker purposefully kept their camera tilted throughout most of the movie, implying an askance point of view that mirrored postwar life, which felt as if it had been turned on end.

Lime is the proponent of a brave new world, a smug amoral man whose self-interest proves frightfully seductive. No one knows for sure how much of an impact Welles had on the film's directorial style, yet this much is certain: Welles was allowed to write Lime's most revealing speech. As he and Holly ride high on a Ferris wheel overlooking the city, Lime reminds his companion, "In Italy, for thirty years under the Borgias, they had warfare, terror, murder, and bloodshed. But they produced Michelangelo, Leonardo da Vinci, and the Renaissance. In Switzerland they had brotherly love, five hundred years of democracy, and peace. And what did that produce? The cuckoo clock."

TRIVIA:

Graham Greene, who wrote some of the great realistic spy stories of the postwar era, had occasionally served as a spy for British intelligence himself. Kim Philby, the famed double-agent and Greene's commander in Her Majesty's Secret Service, served as the author's model for Lime. Two veterans of the film world would, some fifteen years later, work together on the James Bond series; assistant director Guy Hamilton would direct several 007 films, while Bernard Lee, who plays the sympathetic sergeant, would enact the recurring role of "M." Welles starred in a radio show about the further adventures of Harry Lime, in which he was considerably less malevolent; Michael Rennie played Lime in a 1950s TV series.

ALSO RECOMMENDED:

Of Reed's other films, the finest exercise in suspense is *Odd Man Out* (1947), starring James Mason as an anti-English patriot who hides following a bungled robbery in Ireland.

4:

DR. STRANGELOVE OR: HOW I LEARNED TO STOP WORRYING AND LOVE THE BOMB (1964)

Columbia Pictures

> **"There will be no fighting in the war room!"**
> **—President Muffley**

CAST:

Peter Sellers (*President Muffley, Dr. Strangelove, Mandrake*); Sterling Hayden (*General Jack. D. Ripper*); George C. Scott (*General Buck Turgidson*); Slim Pickens ("*King*" *Kong*); Peter Bull (*Russian Ambassador*); James Earl Jones (*Flyer*); Keenan Wynn ("*Bat*" *Guano*); Tracy Reed (*Buck's Mistress*).

CREDITS:

Director, Stanley Kubrick; screenplay, Kubrick, Terry Southern, and Peter George, from the novel *Red Alert* by George; producer, Stanley Kubrick; original music, Laurie Johnson; cinematographer, Gilbert Taylor; editor, Anthony Harvey; art direction, Ken Adam; running time, 93 min.

THE PLOT:

At Burpelson Air Base, a British officer attached to the Wing Command named Mandrake becomes suspicious of his commanding officer, Jack D. Ripper. The cigar-chomping general admits he's become convinced flouridation of our water supplies is actually a Communist plot to sap the strength away from American men. For some time, Ripper has been drinking only distilled water. Now, he can no longer allow the situation to continue, so he unleashes a fleet of B-52 bombers to destroy Russia. Aware that the politicians would sooner or later get wind of his plan, he's instructed soldiers at the base that Russians have already invaded and will appear in the guise of fellow Americans, so they ought to be shot on sight.

After Ripper commits suicide, Mandrake desperately tries to warn Washington. President Muffley deals with General Turgidson and a Russian ambassador on how to minimize the problem, while remaining on the hot line with the Soviet Premiere. The planes cannot be recalled because of a fail-safe mechanism that doesn't allow them to respond to such messages, which might be from the Russians. So fighter jets are sent out to shoot down our own planes. One, however, piloted by Major

Mandrake (Peter Sellers) watches while Jack D. Ripper (Sterling Hayden) defends the purity of bodily fluids for all American men.

"King" Kong, is only disabled, and continues on, dropping the bomb with Major Kong riding it down, cowboy style. As atomic war begins, Dr. Strangelove—one-time Nazi scientist—suggests that a select few could go underground until the deadly clouds pass.

THE FILM:

Dr. Strangelove solidified what would become the 1960s sensibility, an irreverent combination of the darkest comedy and thrilling realism. Every institution, from the presidency to the Strategic Air Command to Coca Cola, is treated with the brisk, flip dismissal that would later characterize *Saturday Night Live*. This was new to mainstream viewers, though intellectual comedians like Lenny Bruce, Woody Allen, and Mort Sahl were offering such stuff in small stand-up clubs. Stanley Kubrick also pushes the envelope on the issue of sexuality, beginning with the opening sequence, in which a plane refueling in mid-air becomes a symbol for intercourse owing to ironic use of Frank Sinatra singing "Try a Little Tenderness" on the soundtrack.

Kubrick has always insisted that he originally planned to do the film as a dramatic thriller, much like the novel on which this is based. The longer he considered the material, however, the more certain he became that it had to be approached in a comic vein. As Kubrick said on reflection, "The only way to tell the story was as a nightmare comedy, where the things that make you laugh are really the heart of a paradoxical posture that make a nuclear war possible." No one has ever summed up the film's power better than William Bayer when he writes that the film "mocks the most serious things, turns a death rattle into gales of laughter, makes us titter and then makes us bleed. *Dr. Strangelove* is put together like a fine watch, charged with suspense, and, despite the claims of the U.S. Air Force, believable. [Kubrick's] film is not only daring in its subject matter, but stylistically ingenious, too. The scenes inside the B-52 are staged as they might have occured, with source lighting, giving the ultra-realistic setting a surreal sensibility."

This is the case, too, with the War Room and every other place we visit in this terrifying portrayal of an everyday situation gone out of control. As was the case with Sidney Lumet on *Fail-Safe* (1964), the government refused to allow Kubrick access to Air Force planes—he had to shoot in England—so the same stock footage of a single plane is employed again and again, though that in no way diminishes the impact. Most incredible of all is the suspense as Kong's team come ever closer to their target. Audiences are torn between a hope that they will somehow be stopped and an inexplicable desire to see them "make it."

TRIVIA:

Originally, Sellers was to have played four roles, including "King Kong." When he suffered a near-fatal heart attack, his doctors insisted he drop at least one role, at which point the part went to Pickens. Sterling Hayden, a radical who had barely escaped blacklisting during the 1950s, found himself unable to work in movies after this, owing to his early protests against the Vietnam War. *Dr. Strangelove* was released the same year and by the same studio as *Fail-Safe* (1964, #73). Purportedly, Kubrick was so upset about this that Columbia Pictures purposefully released *Fail-Safe* without fanfare so it would die at the box office and not create competition for *Dr. Strangelove*.

ALSO RECOMMENDED:

Kubrick fans will want to catch his other thrillers, *A Clockwork Orange* (1971) and *The Shining* (1980). Though not primarily thought of as a suspense movie, *Lolita* (1963) can be watched and appreciated on that level.

3:

TOUCH OF EVIL (1958)

Universal

> **"Your future is all used up."**
> —**Tanya, reading Quinlan's fortune**

CAST:

Charlton Heston (*Ramon Miguel "Mike" Vargas*); Janet Leigh (*Susan Vargas*); Orson Welles (*Capt. Hank Quinlan*); Marlene Dietrich (*Tanya*); Joseph Calleia (*Sgt. Pete Menzies*); Zsa Zsa Gabor (*Nightclub Owner*); Akim Tamiroff (*Uncle Joe Grandi*); Joanna Moore (*Marcia Linnekar*); Ray Collins (*D.A. Adair*); Dennis Weaver (*Motel Night Manager*); Joi Lansing (*The Blonde*); Joseph Cotten (*Police Surgeon*); Valentin de Vargas (*Pancho*); Mercedes McCambridge (*Female Gang Leader*); Mort Mills (*Al Schwartz*); Victor Millan (*Sanchez*); Lalo Rios (*Risto*); Michael Sargent (*The Boy*); Phil Harvey (*Blaine*); Harry Shannon (*Gould*); Keenan Wynn (*Man*).

CREDITS:

Director, Orson Welles; screenplay, Welles and (uncredited) Paul Monash, from the novel *Badge of Evil* by Whit Masterson; producer, Albert Zugsmith and (1998 restoration) Rick Schmidlin; original music, Henry Mancini; cinematographer, Russell Metty; editors, Aaron Stell, Virgil Vogel, and (uncredited) Edward Curtiss, and Walter Murch (director's cut); running time, 108 min. (original release), 111 min. (restoration print).

THE PLOT:

In Los Robles, a border town between Mexico and the United States, a man places a bomb in the trunk of a car about to cross over. In an adjoining automobile are Mike Vargas, a Mexican drug-enforcement officer, and his wife (they are newly-weds), Susan, who find themselves in the wrong place at the wrong time. The bomb explodes just behind them. They rush to the disaster area to see if they can be of help, and Mike shortly finds himself drawn into an investigation run by the swaggering sheriff, Hank Quinlan. This is a massively obese, egomaniacal man, who insists the explosion had to be caused by dynamite (it wasn't). When Mike dares confront the sheriff with an alternative view, Quinlan sets about attempting to frame Mike and his wife for the crime that he himself was actually involved in.

Mike must struggle to defend himself and his bride from an odd, eccentric assortment of adversaries. In addition to Quinlan, there is Menzies, a deputy who will unquestioningly kill to protect the boss that he admires—even loves—beyond comprehension; Grandi, the ruling crime lord in this sleazy corner of the world, who maintains a begrudging cease-fire with Quinlan, the local law, each respecting while coveting the other's power; Madame Tanya, a brothel owner who has slipped into a desultory relationship with Quinlan, to survive in their seedy demimonde; a nameless lesbian street criminal who has an eye for Susan; and a perverted hotel clerk whose obsessions threaten to break loose at any moment. But Quinlan's time is up; eventually, he falls down dead in the dirt and mud, a fitting end to a corrupt man.

Dennis Weaver (in a role that may have inspired Norman Bates) and Charlton Heston in *Touch of Evil*.

THE FILM:

Touch of Evil was written off as a somewhat superior B-movie on its initial American release, most reviewers approaching the film from a prejudicial position, comparing what seemed to be nothing more than a humble genre piece to Welles's great early and highly ambitious work like *Citizen Kane* (1941) and *The Magnificent Ambersons* (1942). Meanwhile, a youthful generation of French film critics, writing for *Cahiers du Cinema*, argued that Americans were the worst judges of their own country's films, overpraising pretentious message-movies at the expense of "pure cinema"—those movies (thrillers, westerns, comedies, etc.) that express their key ideas through the director's employment of camera, editing, and creative sound scoring. François Truffaut and Jean-Luc Godard, who would soon create the French New Wave, were instrumental in having *Touch of Evil* named as Best Film of the Year.

The opening crane shot, in which Welles sweeps us from a close-up of the bomb being planted through the unpleasant little town, then down again to the male and female leads as they obliviously embark on their journey, is now recognized as one of the great movie moments. Lasting nearly three-and-a-half minutes, the continuous movement—once criticized as mere flamboyance by a show-off director who dared call attention to his style—is completely functional, visually setting up the territorial proximities and fatalistic philosophy which will motor the entire movie. For the 1998 rerelease print, the credits (which had been superimposed over the grand opening sequence) were moved to the end, so viewers could concentrate on the remarkable camerawork without distraction. Henry Mancini's theme music had played as the camera moved; supervising producer Rick Schmidlin, aware that Welles had wanted only incidental music (from radios, etc.) and realistic sounds here, eliminated the Mancini score from this sequence and replaced it with what Welles had hoped for but been denied by Universal.

TRIVIA:

The entire film was shot in and around Venice, California. Stars Joseph Cotten, Mercedes McCambridge, and Keenan Wynn all appeared unbilled, playing cameo roles as a favor to Welles and the opportunity to work with one of the great directors. Though associated with this lofty project, producer Al Zugsmith would shortly step down to exploitation flicks, including *Sex Kittens Go to College* (1960) with Mamie Van Doren. Several film historians have advanced the theory that the nervous, ticky hotel clerk played by Dennis Weaver may have provided Hitchcock (a huge fan of Welles's films—he would certainly have caught *Touch of Evil*) with the concept of Norman Bates.

ALSO RECOMMENDED:

Welles's other great thriller is *The Lady From Shanghai* (1948), also based on a pulp novel which he transformed into a genre masterpiece. The film stars his then-wife Rita Hayworth as a film noir femme fatale. Most memorable is the final shoot-out in a carnival hall of mirrors.

2:

M (1931)

A Nero Film

> **"I have no control over this, this evil thing inside of me, the fire, the voices, the torment!"**
> —**Hans Beckert**

CAST:

Peter Lorre (*Hans Beckert*); Ellen Widmann (*Madame Beckmann*); Inge Landgut (*Elsie Beckmann*); Otto Wernicke (*Inspector Karl Lohmann*); Theodor Loos (*Police Commissioner Groeber*); Gustaf Gründgens (*Schraenker*); Friedrich Gnaß (*Franz the Burglar*); Fritz Odemar (*Dynamiter*); Paul Kemp (*Pickpocket*); Theo Lingen (*Bauernfaenger*); Georg John (*Blind Beggar*); Franz Stein (*The Minister*); Ernst Stahl-Nachbaur (*Police Chief*).

CREDITS:

Director, Fritz Lang; screenplay, Lang, Thea von Harbou, Paul Falkenberg, Egon Jacobson Article, Adolf Jansen, and Karl Vash; producer, Seymour Nebenzal; non-original music, Edvard Grieg (from "Peer Gynt"); cinematographer, Fritz Arno Wagner; editor, Paul Falkenberg; art directors, Emil Hasler and Karl Vollbrecht; special art/design effects, Edgar G. Ulmer (uncredited); special sound effects, Adolf Jansen; running times, 99 min. (original release print), 117 min. (director's cut).

THE PLOT:

In a German city, an unknown man molests and murders eight children. Hans Beckert now buys balloons from a blind man, gives them to a little girl, then leads her away. An already tense mood grows even more desperate; a mob forms and almost kills an innocent man for merely speaking politely with a child he bumped into on the street. Great pressure is put upon the police, who sense their reputation is on the line. Desperate, they randomly arrest anyone who looks suspicious, also raiding underworld dens which they previously left untouched. Concerned that

The killer is cornered: Peter Lorre in *M*.

this will cut into their profits, the gangsters decide to do what they police are clearly incapable of achieving: find the killer and bring him to justice.

Street beggars are instructed to keep their eyes open, though ironically it's the blind beggar who recalls that the murderer whistled a particular tune. Even as Beckert closes in on another child, the beggars circle him. He hurries away but is cornered in a building. Methodically, the gangsters take the bulding apart, piece by piece, until his hiding place is revealed. Then, they drag him off to their head-quarters and put Beckert on trial. The prosecuting "lawyer" insists that because Becher is a compulsive killer, he must be destroyed or such crimes will continue; the defense "barrister" insists a man who cannot help himself shouldn't be held accountable. Beckert hysterically turns on the "judge" and "jury," screaming that they are the true villains, choosing to be criminals, whereas he, in a bizarre way, is innocent. Beckert is a criminal owing to forces beyond his control. Before they can execute him, the police arrive and take Beckert into custody.

THE FILM:

Originally, Lang and his co-scenarist wife Thea von Harbou had settled on the title *The Murderers Among Us*, though the ever more influential Nazi party blocked production, certain such a movie would contain a masked criticism of their escalating activities, precisely what Lang—Jewish and fervently anti-Nazi—intended. Lang was doing in Germany precisely what Hitchcock was then achieving, under less pressing circumstances, in England: the "redemption" of the thriller, at its most routine a superficial exercise in genre formulas. By undermining genre expectations and forms to subtly comment on a real social situation, simultaneously employing innovative techniques, the filmmaker turns out a film that's important as well as entertaining.

M offers a vivid study of the paranoia that was at first quietly, then explosively rising to the surface of everyday German life. The film was also light-years ahead of its time in terms of moviemaking technique, proving that the recently developed concept of sound—at first considered a detriment to creative camerawork—could be an integral and organic part of the filmmaking process. The whistle that identifies M is the forerunner of Hitchcock's "musical MacGuffin," a song that seems a realistic part of the scene until eventually revealed as the key to the mystery, perhaps most effectively used in *The Lady Vanishes* (1938). Also, Lang understood early on that sound did not restrict the camera but in fact freed it. By focusing on the image of a vulnerable child, while featuring the killer's whistle—offscreen—he created, through non-synchronous sound, a thriller element impossible during the silent era.

While the Germans were never considered as effective at editing as their Russian counterparts, Lang does effectively employ montage to convey his message. He cross-cuts from the police in their headquartes to the gangsters in theirs so rapidly, we reach a point where we can't tell the two groups apart. This is precisely what Lang hoped for; he wordlessly conveys that in the age of the Gestapo, no one could grasp where the authorities left off and the criminal element began.

TRIVIA:

The story was inspired by an actual child-murderer in the town of Düsseldorf. Peter Lorre could not whistle, so the sound was dubbed in by director Lang. It was while watching this film that Hitchcock discovered Lorre, offering him a villainous role soon thereafter in the original English version of *The Man Who Knew Too Much* (1934). Lang's wife Thea became mesmerized by Hitler, even as her husband felt more threatened. Shortly, Lang deserted his native land for England, then America, while she remained behind, becoming a part of the Third Reich's filmmaking team.

ALSO RECOMMENDED:

Fritz Lang's classic thrillers include *The Testament of Dr. Mabuse* (1933), shot in Germany, and—after coming to America—a wide assortment of edge-of-your-seat masterpieces including *Fury* (1936), *You Only Live Once* (1937), *The Woman in the Window* (1945), *Scarlet Street* (1945), and *The Big Heat* (1953).

I.

PSYCHO (1960)

Paramount Pictures

"Sometimes we all go a little bit crazy . . . don't we?"
—Norman Bates

CAST:

Anthony Perkins (*Norman Bates*); Janet Leigh (*Marion Crane*); John Gavin (*Sam Loomis*); Vera Miles (*Lila Crane*); Martin Balsam (*Milt Arbogast*); John McIntire (*Sheriff Chambers*); Simon Oakland (*Dr. Richmond*); Frank Albertson (*Millionaire*); Patricia Hitchcock (*Caroline*); Mort Mills (*Cop*).

CREDITS:

Director, Alfred Hitchcock; screenplay, Joseph Stefano, from the novel by Robert Bloch; producer, Alfred Hitchcock; original music, Bernard Herrmann; cinematographer, John L. Russell; editor, George Tomasini; set design, Joseph Hurley; special photographic effects, Clarence Champagne; running time, 109 min.

THE PLOT:

Marion Crane can't stand her life in Phoenix, Arizona. Though a beautiful blonde, she's caught in a low-paying job and desperately in love with a married man. Returning to the office after a lunch-hour tryst with Sam Loomis in a seedy hotel, Marion impulsively steals money from the office and drives off, headed she knows not where. Eventually, Marion drives through a rainstorm and finds herself on a nearly abandoned highway, in front of the Bates motel. She checks in and shares some time with Norman, the motel clerk, who seems nice enough, if a tad odd, always running off to deal with his bedridden mother.

Once in her room, Marion decides to take the money back and give herself up. She's taking a cathartic shower when someone—seemingly Norman's mother—rips open the curtains and kills the young woman. When Norman arrives on the scene and finds the body, he's horrified, but cleans up the bloody mess, then disposes of Marion and her car in the swamp. Marion's sister, Lila, and Sam Loomis investigate her disappearance. Lila enters the Bates home and slips down to the fruit cellar, where she's attacked by what she realizes is Norman in his mother's clothing. He had murdered his mother years earlier, and mummified her, though her dominating personality gradually overtook him entirely.

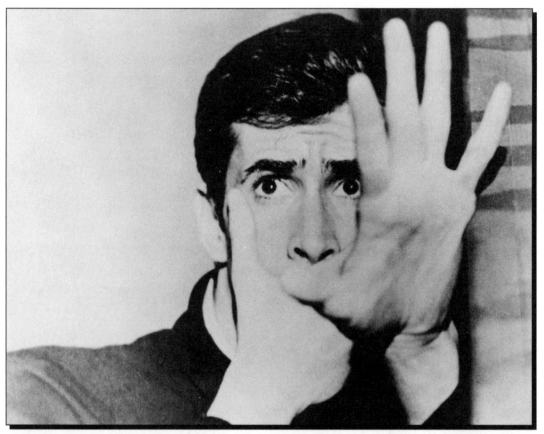

Anthony Perkins was chosen for Norman Bates in part because his previous roles had mainly been nice, normal teenagers.

THE FILM:

Following *North by Northwest* (1959, #8), Hitchcock wanted to experiment rather than grow stale. *Psycho* was his first attempt to retain what was essential to a Hitchcock thriller while admitting that, in the early sixties, life was about to change drastically—and, with it, the movies. He initially considered telling the story on his TV show, which had just been expanded form a half-hour format to a full sixty minutes, as a two-parter. But the intense sex and violence, particularly in the famed shower sequence, were too much for TV at the time. Undaunted, he decided to do it as a movie but using his TV crew. The film was shot for a mere $800,000, not much more than it would have cost to shoot two TV hour-long installments back to back.

In the past, his villains had mostly been spies, first from Germany (during World War II) and later from Russia (during the Cold War). Hitchcock was aware, though, that in the sixties, the great threat of violence came from the seemingly normal people just down the street. Treatises would be written about the escalating element of violence in America, and the fact that more often than not, it derived from failings of our society. Norman Bates stands as an early symbol of all that, and the film initiated a decade-long discussion about violence, both in life and on film.

In the case of *Psycho*, discussion centered on the controversial shower sequence. This took a full week to shoot. Both Janet Leigh and a stand-in were used for the victim. Anthony Perkins was not around, and an extra played Norman/mother. However much he may have been influenced by German Expressionism in terms of mis-en-scène, Hitchcock was equally impressed by the Russian theories of montage, which held that the manner in which a film was edited could actually determine its meaning. He found fascinating their theory that things shouldn't be shown but suggested, the actual image created in each viewer's mind. With this in mind, Hitchcock insisted the blade never once make contact with Marion's body. Instead, through a series of quick cuts—her desperate hands, her terrified face, the water splattering down, the dimly-perceived intruder, the blood (actually, chocolate syrup) running down the drain—the audience would see something in their mind's eye that did not exist on the screen.

When the movie was completed, Hitchcock was concerned that the advertising campaign, including theatrical trailers, might give away too much of the plot. Instead, he insisted on a campaign in which he—the director as superstar—would be featured, only revealing the slightest hints of what the movie was actually about. He was right in believing that he was to suspense-thrillers what Walt Disney was to family entertainment: so well known as the filmmaker who would satisfy in that particular department that moviegoers would be willing to trust in his name alone.

TRIVIA:

The film returned an enormous—and then amazing—sixteen million dollars on its original roadshow engagement. Hitchcock chose Phoenix, Arizona, because its name refers to a bird; the phoenix of legend could rise from its own ashes, which happens twice in the film—first, when Norman assumes his dead mother's personality, allowing her to live again; second, when Marion Crane is replaced by look-alike Lila. In addition to acting ability, Anthony Perkins was chosen for Norman because his previous films—notably as Gary Cooper's son in *Friendly Persuasion* (1957)—cast him as a gentle boy next door; thus, no one would suspect him of being the killer.

ALSO RECOMMENDED:

The best take-off on *Psycho* is William Castle's *Homicidal* (1961, #98).

APPENDIX # 1

THE BIG HITCH: RATING THE MASTER

As mentioned in the opening note on selection, the greatest difficulty in selecting the one hundred best thrillers of all time is determining how many Alfred Hitchcock films ought to be included. It would be easy to fill the top twenty-five entries with his best, though that would necessitate eliminating numerous films and filmmakers that account for the genre's richness. Here, then, is a necessary addendum: all of Hitchcock's thrillers with a commentary and rating (low of one star to a high of five). Hitchcock's non-suspense movies are not included.

The master at work: Hitch directs William Devane and Karen Black in *the Family Plot*.

The Lodger (1927)   Ivor Novello, Marie Ault. 83 min. A Jack the Ripper type killer who focuses on beautiful girls is on the loose in London; could the handsome lodger living upstairs be the culprit? Hitchcock's first "wrong man" thriller offers a virtuoso display of silent filmmaking technique at its best, with one potential victim as the first Hitchcock blonde. From the play by Mrs. Belloc-Lowndes. ★★★★★

Blackmail (1929)   Anny Ondra, Sara Allgood. 86 min. Members of a respectable working-class family wonder who killed a playboy living down the street, never guessing it might be their own "flapper" daughter. Then her detective boyfriend is assigned to crack the case. The first British sound film is an expert variation on the domestic thriller form, with then-innovative use of Expressionistic sound. ★★★★

Murder! (1930)   Herbert Marshall, Nora Baring. 104 min. An actor sends his attractive young protégée to the provinces so as to end their May–December romance. When she's then accused of a crime, he turns sleuth to prove she's actually the wrong woman. Memorable drama dares deal with then-forbidden theme of interracial love. Hitchcock's only exercise in the murder-mystery style reveals him in top form. ★★★★

Number Seventeen (1932)   Leon M. Lion, Anne Grey, Barry Jones. 63 min. Easy-going drifter Lion finds himself face-to-face with a pack of robbers, catapulting him into danger as well as romance with very pretty Grey. Appealing if ultimately forgettable exercise in the lighthearted thriller vein, occasionally bolstered by Hitchcock's tongue in cheek directorial approach toward serious material. ★★★

The Man Who Knew too Much (1934)   Peter Lorre, Edna Best. 75 min. A normal upper-middleclass British family heads to Switzerland for a ski vacation, finding themselves plunged into intrigue when their young daughter is kidnapped by enemy agents. Hitchcock's first spy-thriller is uneven but ultimately a winner, with cryptic Lorre a knockout as the first truly memorable Hitchcock super-villain. ★★★★

The 39 Steps (1935)   Robert Donat, Madeleine Carroll. 87 min. From a novel by John Buchan comes Hitchcock's first indisputable sound masterpiece. A likable Canadian living in London picks up a pretty girl at a show, then finds himself plunged into the world of agents and counter-spies. Smart, funny, brash, exciting, and surprisingly frank about sexuality in general, and bondage in particular. ★★★★★

Secret Agent (1936) Madeleine Caroll, Robert Young. 86 min. Mismatched man and woman are persuaded to pretend they are married to uncover an enemy spy. Long considered a lesser British film, this brilliant black comedy definitely shines when perceived as it was meant to be seen: grim, edgy humor rather than serious drama. John Gielgud and Peter Lorre steal the show from nominal star Young. ★★★★

Sabotage (1936) Sylvia Sidney, Oscar Homolka. 79 min. Joseph Conrad's novel *The Secret Agent* inspired this, *not* Hitchcock's film of that name. Beautiful woman marries gruff fellow, certain he'll care for her retarded brother, with ironic results. Hitchcock shifts family's profession to theatre owners and comes up with an early example of reflexive cinema. Several great moments in a less-than-great film. ★★★

Young and Innocent (1937) Nova Pilbeam, Derrick De Marney. 83 min. One more wrong man on the run meets one more beautiful blonde willing to help him, whether he's the killer or not, owing to her romantic obsession with the mysterious fellow. Not a single false moment in this appealing if conventional genre piece, and the twitching drummer at the jazz club will leave you dazzled. ★★★★

The Lady Vanishes (1938) Michael Redgrave, Margaret Lockwood. 97 min. Two Englishwomen, one young and one old, happen to board a train together. The girl falls asleep and when she awakens, her new companion is gone; everyone insists the elderly lady did not exist. Comes pretty close to perfection in blending romance, suspense, and oddball humor. Dame May Whitty is the dotty old gal. ★★★★★

Jamaica Inn (1939) Charles Laughton, Maureen O'Hara. 98 min. Hitchcock's first adaptation of a Daphne Du Maurier story concerns piracy on the Cornish coast, with Laughton mincingly marvelous as the villain, O'Hara a ravishing heroine. Nonetheless, a near-disaster, with unlikely occurances sabotaging the plot at every turn. Occasionally atmospheric, never convincing enough to succeed. ★★

Rebecca (1940) Joan Fontaine, Laurence Olivier. 130 min. Du Maurier again, only this time terrific! Plain young woman is swept off her feet by tall, dark, handsome stranger, though the romantic dream quickly turns into a nightmare. Oscar-winning Best Picture is a prime example of old-fashioned Hollywood gloss, though producer David O. Selznick ran the show, not Hitchcock, and it shows. ★★★★

Foreign Correspondent (1940) Joel McCrea, Laraine Day. 119 min. American reporter abroad gradually becomes aware of the Nazi threat, attempts to get word home in time. Least appreciated of all Hitchcock films, neatly combines anti-Nazi polemics with all the expected Hitchcock elements for a perfect time capsule. Most memorable shot of all: endless umbrellas massed together in a sudden rainstorm. ★★★★★

Suspicion (1941) Cary Grant, Joan Fontaine. 99 min. Youngish spinster impulsively marries a reckless and charming man, gradually comes to believe he's planning to poison her for an inheritance. Exquisite atmosphere, low-key suspense, with Grant in a brilliant is-he-or-isn't-he-a-killer? performance, Fontaine Oscar-winning Best Actress. Best moment: the milk! Marred by a rushed ending. ★★★★

The Saboteur (1942) Robert Cummings, Priscilla Lane. 108 min. Hitchcock's "wrong man" theme shifted to America. A munitions worker, accused of setting a fire, rushes off to find the actual criminal, pursued by authorities *and* the Nazis. Traveling circus sequence is a delight, Statue of Liberty finale exciting, but suffers seriously from lightweight Cummings in role intended for Gary Cooper. ★★★

Shadow of a Doubt (see #27) ★★★★★

Lifeboat (1944) Tallulah Bankhead, John Hodiak. 96 min. Motley group find themselves stranded on title object when a ship is torpedoed by Nazis. Most didactic of all Hitchcock films (thanks to John Steinbeck's socially-oriented script) proves you really can, in Hitchcock's own words, "shoot a film in a goldfish bowl." Lots of wartime propaganda doesn't diminish ever-heightening and intimate suspense. ★★★★

Spellbound (1945) Gregory Peck, Ingrid Bergman. 111 min. Head of an institution for the insane is revealed as crazier than patients in Hitchcock's unofficial remake of *The Cabinet of Dr. Caligari* (#100). The film that initiated Hollywood's postwar trend for psychological thrillers. Back-projection in ski sequence, use of overly Freudian symbolism cannot diminish the considerable impact. ★★★★

Notorious (see #15) ★★★★★

The Paradine Case (1947) Gregory Peck, Alida Valli. 119 min. Solid, married British barrister defends femme fatale, becomes obsessed with getting her off though she's obviously guilty. Hitchcock's dark meditation on one man's desire for the fall, sadly undercut by producer Selznick's tarting it up with unnecessary trappings of "class." Charles Laughton's hamming makes it worthwhile. ★★★

Rope (1948) John Dall, Farley Granger. 80 min. A fictionalization of infamous Leopold-Loeb case, with James Stewart miscast as intellectual academic who realizes his top students have committed a cold-blooded murder. Shot in one room, but in long takes, without the creative editing that might have redeemed it from being a recorded stage play. The film has its followers; see for yourself. ★★

Under Capricorn (1949) Ingrid Bergman, Joseph Cotten. 117 min. Tepid, uninvolving mish-mash set down under, with stars utterly unbelievable as Aussie husband and wife, experiencing existential ennui long before anyone ever heard of Michelangelo Antonioni. Little suspense in a creaky, soap-operish plot that goes absolutely nowhere and, worse still, takes forever getting there. Blah! ★

Stage Fright (1950) Marlene Dietrich, Jane Wyman. 110 min. A young woman learns that her fiancé has been unfaithful with a beautiful older actress, yet sets out to prove he didn't kill the actress's husband. Marred by a dishonest ending that's more an unfair trick than an acceptable twist. Alastair Sim brightens every scene he's in. Better than its reputation; still, second-tier. ★★★

Strangers on a Train: (see #18) ★★★★★

I Confess (1953) Montgomery Clift, Anne Baxter. 95 min. Priest takes killer's confession, only to realize he himself is the main suspect. Yet he's unable to reveal what he knows owing to religious vow. Canadian-lensed thriller with Karl Malden particularly effective as one of Hitchcock's well-intentioned but wrongheaded detectives. Intriguing production marred by phoney Production Code ending. ★★★

Dial M for Murder (1954) Grace Kelly, Ray Milland. 105 min. Husband plans the murder of his cheating wife, though nothing goes quite according to scenario. Milland acceptable in a role Cary Grant was born to play, Kelly charismatic as ever. From a stage play by Frederick Knott, though this is truly cinematic despite essentially a single setting. John Williams wonderful as the perturbed police officer. ★★★★

Rear Window: (see #6) ★★★★★

To Catch a Thief (1955) Cary Grant, Grace Kelly. 106 min. Against lush, lavish Monaco backdrops portrayed in rich color, retired (perhaps) cat burglar Grant may be out to seduce nouveau-riche American princess Kelly, or steal her jewels, or both. Enchanting, from the first moment to last, with spectacularly sensuous fireworks display as mid-movie eye-popper. Sophisticated and diverting all the way. ★★★★

The Trouble with Harry (1955) Edmund Gwenn, Shirley MacLaine. 99 min. Residents of small New England village (though it looks more like Wales) appear notably unperturbed by the discovery of a dead body, as investigator John Forsythe discovers every one of the nice neighbors had strong motivation to do the deed. Offbeat dark humor piece about the universality of guilt. ★★★★

The Man Who Knew too Much (1956) James Stewart, Doris Day. 120 min. Day sings "Que Sera, Sera" so many times you'll want to scream; Stewart runs around in circles trying to save their missing child. Big-scale production values can't keep this overlong and overly melodramatic remake of Hitchcock's early classic from disappointing fans. Utterly Devoid of a strong pace. Acceptable, but nothing more. ★★

The Wrong Man (1957) Henry Fonda, Vera Miles. 105 min. Hitchcock's only attempt at docudrama accurately chronicles the true story of an innocent man arrested, tried, convicted, even imprisoned for a bank robbery done by his lookalike. Main liability: Fonda does not look all that much like the actor playing his doppelganger. Otherwise, taut, convincing, realistic, and emotionally disturbing. ★★★★

Vertigo: (see #11); ★★★★★

North by Northwest: (see #8); ★★★★★

Psycho: (see #1); ★★★★★

The Birds: (see #23); ★★★★★

Marnie (1964) Tippi Hedren, Sean Connery. 129 min. Wealthy man realizes his secretary—a compulsive thief and frigid virgin—plans to rob him. He marries her and agrees to a platonic relationship, all the while obsessively waiting for her to

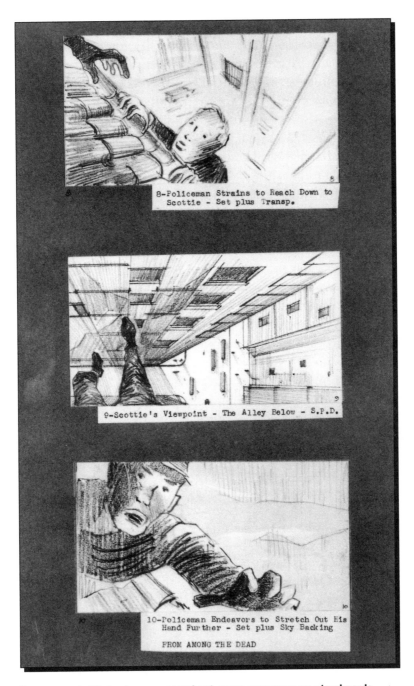

8-Policeman Strains to Reach Down to
Scottie - Set plus Transp.

9-Scottie's Viewpoint - The Alley Below - S.P.D.

10-Policeman Endeavors to Stretch Out His
Hand Further - Set plus Sky Backing

FROM AMONG THE DEAD

**Be prepared: Hitch always mapped-out every sequence on storyboards,
including this—the original—for the opening shot of *Vertigo***
(courtesy of the Alfred Hitchcock Estate).

steal so he can rape her on the spot. What should have been Hitchcock's finest foray into the dark side of sexuality is dull and plodding, if never uninteresting. ★★

Torn Curtain (1966) Julie Andrews, Paul Newman. 128 min. Unwise return to *39 Steps/North by Northwest* picaresque gambit involves two top stars (there's absolutely no charisma between them) in notably non-thrilling chase. Utterly devoid of beloved Hitchcock flourishes, save only for one effective black-comedy sequence in which Newman and Andrews kill an enemy agent by baking him in an oven! ★★

Topaz (1969) Karin Dor, John Forsythe. 127 min. Spies and counter-spies, plots and counter-plots, double and triple crosses abound in Hichcock's worst film. Like watching a below-par episode of the *Mission: Impossible* TV series that threatens to go on forever. Only striking moment: murder of Dor from a bird's-eye-view shot. ★

Frenzy: (see #39) ★★★★★

Family Plot (1976) Barbara Harris, Bruce Dern. 120 min. Complicated, mostly engrossing comedy-thriller involves a fake psychic who allows her "gifts" to be used by a seedy social climber (William Devane) hoping to inherit a fortune. Then, strange things happen. Though a notable step down from the considerable heights of *Frenzy*, this minor, unmemorable film is still consistently appealing. ★★★

The ultimate Hitch moment: Janet Leigh in the shower sequence of Psycho.

APPENDIX # 2

THE FRENCH CONNECTION: THE GREAT GALLIC THRILLERS

Though *Rebecca* won the Oscar for Best Picture of the Year in 1941 (it went to producer Selznick), Hitchcock—now widely considered the greatest director of all time—didn't receive a statuette, then or ever. Hollywood likes to hand out prizes to people who make "serious" films with social messages, many of them proving unwatchable only a few years later. Fortunately, the French sensed that Hitchcock's thrillers exemplified pure cinema, owing to a genius-level employment of camera, editing, and musical score to carry story and theme. Throughout the 1950s, critics for *Cahiers du Cinema* forced the world to realize that beneath the unpretentious exterior of Hitchcock's films, there existed a profound vision of life.

By 1960, many of those aficionados were making their own thrillers, intended as homages to the master. The best, *Diabolique* (#77) and (though directed by a Spanish filmmaker) *Belle de Jour* (#14), are included in this volume; others, such as *The Wages of Fear* (1952), are also recommended in the text. Here are twelve more masterpieces worth seeking out, each by a key director:

12. **The Bride Wore Black** (1968) Jeanne Moreau, Michel Lonsdale. 107 min. When her fiancé is accidentally killed moments before their wedding, a beautiful woman turns femme fatale—seeking out the identities of the men responsible for the accident, seducing and then killing them one by one. François Truffaut enlisted Bernard Herrmann, Hitchcock's favorite composer, to create the proper musical score.

11. **The Tall Blond Man With One Black Shoe** (1972) Pierre Richard, Mireille Darc. 90 min. Easygoing thriller-farce about harmless, appealing fellow who

Diana the Huntress:
Jeanne Moreau in *The
Bride Wore Black*.

departs a plane and is immediately mistaken for a superspy. Sweet-spirited in tone thanks to director Yves Robert's pleasantly offhand style, Richard's irresistible eccentricity. And Mme. Darc's black backless dress is the ninth man-made wonder of the world.

10. **Purple Noon** (1960)   Alain Delon, Marie Laforêt. 118 min. Social climbing misfit befriends wealthy playboy, covets his life and girlfriend, and plots a murder. The first film version of Patricia Highsmith's *The Talented Mr. Ripley* outclasses the affected 1999 version. Here, René Clément creates a sumptuous yet surreal world of continental complacency in a French-Italian co-production.

9. **Topkapi** (1964)   Melina Mercouri, Maximilian Schell. 119 min. Lovely lady engages a variety of professional thieves and plans what ought to be the perfect crime. Arguably the greatest caper movie ever, though Joseph Dassin had already reached an apex earlier with *Rififi* (1954). Peter Ustinov's gleefully irreverent performance will have you in stitches. Adapted from Eric Ambler's novel.

8. Monsieur Hire (1989)   Michel Blanc, Sandrine Bonnaire. 81 min. A closet voyeur develops an obsession for the woman across the way on whom he regularly spies. Catching her participation in a murder, he must decide whether to become involved in helping her escape. Patrice Leconte neatly updates Georges Simenon's novel, previously filmed as *Panique!* (1946) by Julien Duvivier— also terrific!

7. The Sleeping Car Murder (1965)   Yves Montand, Simone Signoret. 90 min. A killing occurs on a speeding train, causing husband and wife star team to ferret out the murderer before other passengers die. Sébastien Japrisot's cult novel neatly adapted by Costa-Gavras, here making his directorial debut; he'd later focus on political thrillers, including the Oscar-winning Best Foreign Film *Z* (1970).

6. Diva (1981)   Wilhelmenia Wiggins Fernandez, Thuy An Luu. 123 min. A gorgeous opera singer chooses not to do recordings of her performances, so one diehard fan secretly tapes her in concert. Shortly, his prized possession becomes a Hitchcockian MacGuffin, as this tape is confused with another containing deadly underworld secrets. Unrelentingly stylish early work by the ever flamboyant auteur Jean-Jacques Beineix.

5. That Man From Rio (1964)   Jean-Paul Belmondo, Françoise Dorléac. 114 min. Non-stop chase, played for comedy and thrills, turns Belmondo into a cross between Cary Grant in *North by Northwest* (#8) and Harold Lloyd in *Safety Last* (#53) as he pursues spies around the globe. Delicious, delightful, doomed Dorléac is his redheaded companion. A triumph of audience-pleasing fun from Philippe de Broca.

4. Cat and Mouse (1975)   Serge Reggiani, Michèle Morgan. 107 min. Romance and suspense balance neatly as top cop Reggiani attempts to discover who did away with the husband of gorgeous Morgan, becoming ever more fascinated with the lady—who probably did the deed herself. Recalls Hitchcock's lighter films, particularly *To Catch a Thief* (1955) as Claude Lelouch captures dazzling vistas and delightful stars.

3. The Vanishing (1988)   Gene Bervoets, Johanna Ter Steege, Bernard-Pierre Donnadieu. 101 min. Couple on vacation drive into a rest-stop; she disappears without a trace. Unrelenting pursuit follows in George Sluizer's near-perfect French-Dutch co-production. Anxiety-inducing thriller relies on the old Hitchcock style: suggest rather than show violence. In 1992, the same director mounted an unconvincing American remake.

2. **Les Biches** (1968)   Stéphane Audran, Jacqueline Sassard. 93 min. Two women—one mature and wealthy, the other young and streetwise—drift into a lesbian relationship. All goes well until a man (Jean-Louis Trintignant) appears; both fall in love with him and deceptions soon begin. Perhaps Claude Chabrol's most effective vehicle for wife Audran, though *Le Boucher* (1969) and *La Femme Infidèle* (1970) come close.

1. **Breathless** (1959)   Jean Seberg, Jean-Paul Belmondo. 89 min. A cheap hoodlum, fancying himself a Gallic Bogart, shoots a cop and takes up with a former girlfriend, an American expatriate with intellectual pretensions and shallow values. Cinema verite exploded on the screen with Jean-Luc Godard's rapid-fire experiment that transcends the thriller form. It is a modern parable about love and betrayal.

INDEX

ABOUT THE AUTHOR

Photo credit: Eric Severance.

DOUGLAS BRODE is the author of twenty-five books on the visual and performing arts, most often focusing on film. These include volumes on actors Denzel Washington and Robert De Niro, directors Steven Spielberg and Woody Allen, and such significant eras as the 1950s and 1980s. The translation of Brode's various works into numerous languages for world-wide publication ranks him alongside Leonard Maltin and Roger Ebert as one of the most internationally read film historians, as well as earning him a cult following and comparison to such legendary iconoclastic critics as Raymond Durgnat, Manny Farber, and Parker Tyler. An educator, Professor Brode teaches Cinema Studies at Syracuse University's Newhouse School of Public Communications in the fall semester and Film History at Onondaga College, Syracuse. His most universally acclaimed volume, *Shakespeare in the Movies*, originally published in hardcover by Oxford University Press, has been released in an updated paperback format by Berkley/Penguin. Several releases from KINO Video International include Brode's commentaries as liner notes for the *Silent Shakespeare* DVD series. Brode has lectured on aspects of cinema in places as diverse as the Hudson Valley Film Festival near Lake George, New York, and the International Literary Festival in Aspen, Colorado. Leading newspapers including the *New York Times* and *Washington Post* regularly cite his opinions on the relationship of media to society. His comments are also included in many installments of the BRAVO channel's "Profiles" series and A&E's "Biography." Popular magazines that have published his work include *Rolling Stone* and *TV Guide*; Brode's analyses have also appeared in more academic journals such as *Cineaste* and *Television Quarterly*. Two of his original plays, *Heartbreaker* and

Somewhere in the Night, have been professionally produced in regional theatre. His screenplay, *Midnight Blue* (filmed by The Motion Picture Corporation of America and released on home video by Orion) was hailed by one reviewer as "the best of the low-budget erotic thrillers." Upcoming projects include two books on Walt Disney for the University of Texas Press, Austin, as well as a volume on westerns for that publisher. Also, he will edit a commemorative anthology of essays on *Annie Hall* for Cambridge University Press. His recent contributions to the Kensington/Citadel film series include *Sinema: Erotic Adventures in Film* and *Boys and Toys: Ultimate Action Films*. As we go to press, Brode is completing work on *Elvis Cinema*, the first serious study of Presley's musicals, for McFarland (Fall 2004).